Qualitative Research in Business & Management

42-19 Macpherson Av.
Kingston, ON   K7M6W4

For Paper:

* Talk about measures, items

* Preliminary result

* make tables of correlations !

Qualitative Research in Business & Management

Michael D. Myers

Los Angeles | London | New Delhi
Singapore | Washington DC

First published 2009

Reprinted 2009

SAGE Publications Ltd
1 Oliver's Yard
55 City Road
London EC1Y 1SP

SAGE Publications Inc.
2455 Teller Road
Thousand Oaks, California 91320

SAGE Publications India Pvt Ltd
B 1/I 1 Mohan Cooperative Industrial Area
Mathura Road
New Delhi 110 044

SAGE Publications Asia-Pacific Pte Ltd
33 Pekin Street #02-01
Far East Square
Singapore 048763

Library of Congress Control Number: 2008926223

British Library Cataloguing in Publication data

A catalogue record for this book is available from
the British Library

ISBN 978-1-4129-2165-7 (hbk)
ISBN 978-1-4129-2166-4 (pbk)

Typeset by C&M Digitals (P) Ltd, Chennai, India
Printed and bound in Great Britain by Athenaeum Press Ltd., Gateshead, Tyne & Wear
Printed on paper from sustainable resources

CONTENTS

PREFACE

This book is aimed primarily at graduate and postgraduate students in business and management. It is especially appropriate for research Masters and PhD students who are intending to conduct their first qualitative research project. Additionally, the book might be helpful for faculty members who have been trained in quantitative research methods, but want to learn more about the potential of qualitative research. For instructors and lecturers, a companion website for the book is available at www.sagepub.co.uk/myers.

This book is relevant for students in almost all of the business disciplines, including accounting, employment relations, finance, human resource management, information systems, international business, management, marketing, operations management, organization development, and strategic management.

The content of the book is derived from approximately 20 years of teaching qualitative research to postgraduate students in information systems at the University of Auckland, New Zealand. I have also taught qualitative research workshops for PhD students and faculty members in many other countries, including Australia, China, Finland, and the United States. These workshops have varied from half a day to three days in length. Additionally, I have published many qualitative research articles in academic journals and books, and have served as a senior editor of the two top research journals in information systems (*Information Systems Research* and *MIS Quarterly*). For both these journals I have handled qualitative manuscripts only.

In addition to this experience within the field of information systems, in 2003 I was appointed as the Associate Dean (Postgraduate and Research) at the University of Auckland. My five years of experience in this role enabled me to familiarize myself with the research being conducted in all of the business disciplines. I began to realize that many of the issues that qualitative researchers face in information systems were remarkably similar to those being faced in every other business discipline. Although some business disciplines are further ahead than others in their acceptance and use of qualitative research, all have followed a fairly similar path. Whereas most business disciplines favoured quantitative research in the 1980s, from the 1990s there was an increased interest in qualitative research. Today many articles using qualitative research are now being published in the top peer-reviewed journals of virtually every business discipline. It is now generally recognized that both qualitative and quantitative research have their strengths and weaknesses, and both are needed to study business and management.

However, I think it is also fair to say that the research training and materials available to students of qualitative research in business and management are not still as good as they could be. I hope this book goes some way towards filling that gap.

Perhaps I should point out that the structure of this book, as a general rule, follows the one I developed for my website entitled 'Qualitative Research in Information Systems' at http://www.qual.auckland.ac.nz. This particular work was accepted for publication by *MISQ Discovery* in 1997 and AISWorld Net (an entry point of resources for information systems academics and practitioners). This website also received the Value-Added Site Award for 1996–7 sponsored by the Academy of Management's Organizational Communication and Information Systems Division and AISWorld. More recently, this work received an AISWorld Challenge Award from the Association for Information Systems in 2004. A similar structure was also used for an edited book providing a collection of qualitative research readings in the information systems field (Myers & Avison, 2002).

Of course, this particular book is substantially different from those two earlier works in that this one is concerned with qualitative research in all of the business and management disciplines (as contrasted with the earlier one which focuses solely on the field of information systems). Also, this book is a sole-authored work representing an expanded treatment of my own views about qualitative research, rather than a collection of readings.

I hope you find the book interesting and helpful.

ACKNOWLEDGEMENTS

I would like to thank all the qualitative researchers who have encouraged and inspired me over the years. I am especially grateful to Heinz Klein, with whom I enjoyed a very productive and collaborative relationship from 1994 until recently. Sadly, Heinz passed away in 2008. As a relatively young researcher when we first met in 1992, Heinz taught me what it takes to get published in a top research journal. I have also enjoyed working with many other scholars, such as David Avison, Richard Baskerville, Kevin Crowston, Lynda Harvey, Mike Newman, and Cathy Urquhart. I consider it a privilege to have worked and become friends with so many talented people around the world.

I would also like to thank: Mariyam Adam, who helped me prepare many of the examples of qualitative research from various business disciplines and also helped in compiling an EndNote library for the book; Margo Buchanan-Oliver, who made many suggestions for improvement, particularly to the chapter on semiotics; and Delia Alfonso and Anne Summers at Sage Publications, for their encouragement and patience in waiting for me to finish writing the book.

I am also grateful to my wife, Kathleen, for supporting me in my research work all these years. She commented on and proof-read every chapter (it's very handy having an English teacher as a wife).

MICHAEL D. MYERS

Auckland
April 2008

PART ONE

INTRODUCTION

Part I provides a general introduction to qualitative research in business and management. Chapter 1 suggests how you can use this book to best advantage. Chapter 2 provides an overview of qualitative research. It discusses the motivation for doing qualitative research, the differences between qualitative and quantitative research, triangulation, and how qualitative research can contribute to the rigour and relevance of research in business and management.

1

HOW TO USE THIS BOOK

I decided to write this book for several reasons. First, there are few textbooks that deal specifically with qualitative research in business and management. Often, professors and teachers of qualitative research in business schools use books that are written for a much wider audience, such as the social sciences more generally.

Second, of the few books that are available for students of business and management, most tend to be somewhat narrow in their treatment. They focus on just one or two research methods (such as action research and/or case study research) and often fail to appreciate the potential of different underlying research philosophies (e.g. interpretive research), or of different ways of analysing qualitative data.

Third, I have noticed a tendency for writers of qualitative books in business and management to be somewhat defensive about the use of qualitative research. The tone is one of lamenting the current lack of acceptance of qualitative research in business. Often there are complaints about how difficult it is to get qualitative research articles in the top journals.

The purposes of this book, therefore, are as follows:

- to provide a qualitative textbook that focuses specifically on business and management;
- to provide a broad, reasonably comprehensive discussion of the various qualitative research methods (and their philosophical underpinnings) that researchers can use;
- to provide a qualitative textbook that is enthusiastic and positive about the use of qualitative research in business and management.

With regard to the last point, this book provides examples of qualitative studies drawn from many business and management disciplines. Almost all of the examples have been drawn from the top journals in the disciplines concerned, e.g. *Accounting, Organizations and Society* in accounting, *MIS Quarterly* in the field of information systems, or *Journal of Consumer*

Research in marketing. This selection of examples from some of the top research journals shows that qualitative researchers in business no longer need to be apologetic or defensive about their research. It seems obvious to me that both qualitative and quantitative research are needed to study business phenomena.

In the remainder of this short chapter I will outline the structure of the book and highlight some of its significant features.

Part I provides an introduction to the book and an overview of qualitative research. A key theme is the contribution that qualitative research can make to research in business and management.

Part II provides an overview of some fundamental concepts in qualitative research. It looks at various approaches to research philosophy, research design, and research ethics. I believe it is important for research students to be aware of the different underlying assumptions and research designs that can inform qualitative research. All qualitative researchers should make their research designs and underlying philosophical assumptions explicit.

Part III deals with the most common research methods that are used in business and management today. I define a research method as a strategy of enquiry or a way of finding empirical data about the (social) world. Chapter 6 deals with action research, Chapter 7 case study research, Chapter 8 ethnographic research, and Chapter 9 grounded theory. A key feature of this part of the book is that it outlines the advantages and disadvantages of the various research methods.

In Part IV, I discuss the use of qualitative techniques for data collection. In business and management, the most important qualitative technique is the use of interviews (Chapter 10). However, participant observation and field-work are discussed in Chapter 11 and the use of documents in Chapter 12.

Part V focuses on analysing and interpreting qualitative data. The tremendous variety in approaches is reviewed in Chapter 13, whereas the following three chapters discuss three specific approaches in more detail. These are hermeneutics (Chapter 14), semiotics (Chapter 15), and narrative and metaphor (Chapter 16).

In Part VI, I look at writing up and publishing qualitative research. Chapter 17 focuses solely on the process of writing up (mostly for a thesis or dissertation), whereas Chapter 18 focuses on getting published. As journal articles tend to count much more than books in all the business and management disciplines, I provide some practical guidance with respect to getting qualitative research work published in peer-reviewed conferences and academic journals. This is one of the distinguishing features of the book.

Part VII is the concluding section. Chapter 19 looks at qualitative research in perspective. This is followed by a glossary of some of the most commonly used terms in qualitative research.

2

OVERVIEW OF QUALITATIVE RESEARCH

Objectives

By the end of this chapter, you will be able to:

- Understand the purpose of qualitative research
- Appreciate the benefits of qualitative research
- Recognize what counts as research and what does not
- Distinguish between quantitative and qualitative research
- Decide whether or not to use triangulation
- See how qualitative research can contribute to the rigour and relevance of research

WHY DO QUALITATIVE RESEARCH?

Qualitative research methods are designed to help researchers understand people and what they say and do. They are designed to help researchers understand the social and cultural contexts within which people live.

One of the key benefits of qualitative research is that it allows a researcher to see and understand the *context* within which decisions and actions take place. It is often the case that human decisions and actions can only be understood in context – it is the context that helps to 'explain' why someone acted as they did. And this context (or multiple contexts) is best understood by talking to people.

Qualitative researchers contend that it is virtually impossible to understand why someone did something or why something happened in an organization without talking to people about it. Imagine if the police tried to solve a serious crime without being able to talk to the suspects or witnesses. If the police were restricted to using only quantitative data, almost no crimes would be solved. Imagine if lawyers and judges were not allowed to question or cross-examine witnesses in court. The validity and reliability of any court decision would be thrown into serious doubt. So, likewise, qualitative researchers argue that if you want to understand people's motivations, their reasons, their actions, and the context for their beliefs and actions in an in-depth way, qualitative research is best. Kaplan and Maxwell (1994) say that the goal of understanding a phenomenon from the point of view of the participants and its particular social and institutional context is largely lost when textual data are quantified.

One of the primary motivations for doing qualitative research, as opposed to quantitative research, comes from the observation that, if there is one thing which distinguishes humans from the natural world, it is their ability to talk. It is only by talking to people, or reading what they have written, that we can find out what they are thinking, and understanding their thoughts goes a long way towards explaining their actions.

TYPES OF QUESTIONS USING QUALITATIVE RESEARCH

The questions that a qualitative researcher might typically ask are what, why, how, and when questions:

- **What** is happening here?
- **Why** is it happening?
- **How** has it come to happen this way?
- **When** did it happen?

WHAT IS RESEARCH?

In a university setting, research is defined as an *original investigation* undertaken in order to contribute to knowledge and understanding in a particular field. Research is a creative activity leading to the production of *new* knowledge. The knowledge produced is new in the sense that the facts, the interpretation of those facts, or the theories used to explain them might not have been used in a particular way before in that specific discipline.

Research typically involves enquiry of an empirical or conceptual nature and is conducted by people with specialist knowledge about the subject matter, theories, and methods in a specific field. Research may involve contributing to the intellectual infrastructure of a subject or discipline (e.g. by publishing a dictionary). In some fields, such as engineering, computer science, or information systems, research can also include the experimental design of new artefacts. Engineers often try to develop new or substantially improved materials, devices, products, or processes.

Of course, as more research is published, the subject matter, theories, and methods used in a particular field may change over time. For this reason, scholars in many disciplines will write a literature review of previous relevant research to show that they understand and are up-to-date with the latest thinking.

But how do we know that the research results are new? How do we know that the findings are original? How do we know that the research was conducted in a rigorous manner?

The only way to tell if the research findings are both sound and original is if those findings are open to scrutiny and formal evaluation by experts in a particular field. That is, the findings must be evaluated by those who are experienced and 'qualified' to do so. If these experts, in evaluating the research, find that the results are sound, and that the findings are new *to them*, then we can say that the research project represents an original contribution to knowledge.

This way of evaluating the quality of research in science is called the peer review system. The peer review system exists in all scientific disciplines and is in effect a system of quality assurance. Of course, the peer review system is a social system, and as such it has its drawbacks, but it does ensure that only research of a certain standard is published. I discuss the peer review system and the publication process in more detail in Part VI.

It should be clear from the above discussion that some activities do not count as research in a university setting (Tertiary Education Commission, 2005). Some of these activities are as follows:

- The preparation of teaching materials. Teaching materials are excluded since they are not normally formally evaluated by experts in the field as a whole. For example, case study books written for teaching purposes are written primarily for students, not researchers. As Yin describes, 'For teaching purposes, a case study need not contain a complete or accurate rendition of actual events; rather, its purpose is to establish a framework for discussion and debate among students'(2003: 2). The distinction between producing case studies for teaching and research is discussed more fully in Chapter 7.
- The provision of advice or opinion, e.g. consulting work.
- Feasibility studies (where the output is a recommendation to a client).
- Routine data collection (where there is no attempt to contribute to new knowledge in the field as a whole).
- Routine information systems development (where the output is a new or improved product for a client, not the experimental design of a new product or service).
- Any other routine professional practice.

QUANTITATIVE AND QUALITATIVE RESEARCH COMPARED

There are many different ways to classify and characterize different types of research. However, one of the most common distinctions is between qualitative and quantitative research methods (Table 2.1).

Table 2.1   Examples of qualitative and quantitative research

Qualitative research A focus on text	Quantitative research A focus on numbers
Action research	Surveys
Case study research	Laboratory experiments
Ethnography	Simulation
Grounded theory	Mathematical modelling
Semiotics	Structured equation modelling
Discourse analysis	Statistical analysis
Hermeneutics	Econometrics
Narrative and metaphor	

Quantitative research methods were originally developed in the natural sciences to study natural phenomena. Examples of quantitative methods now well accepted in the social sciences include survey methods, laboratory experiments, formal methods (e.g. econometrics), and numerical methods such as mathematical modelling. All quantitative researchers emphasize numbers more than anything else. That is, the numbers 'come to represent values and levels of theoretical constructs and concepts and the interpretation of the numbers is viewed as strong scientific evidence of how a phenomenon works' (Straub, Gefen, & Boudreau, 2004). Most quantitative researchers use statistical tools and packages to analyse their data.

Qualitative research methods were developed in the social sciences to enable researchers to study social and cultural phenomena. Examples of qualitative methods are action research, case study research, and grounded theory. Qualitative data sources include observation and participant observation (fieldwork), interviews and questionnaires, documents and texts, and the researcher's impressions and reactions. Qualitative data are mostly a record of what people have said. For example, interviews (the most common technique for collecting qualitative data) record what one of your informants said about a particular topic; field notes record what the researcher experienced or thought about a particular topic or event; and documents record what the author of the document wrote at the time. In all cases, these qualitative data can help us to understand people, their motivations and actions, and the broader context within which they work and live.

In the 1980s most business disciplines favoured quantitative research. In the 1990s, however, there was an increased interest in qualitative research in almost every business discipline. The quality of this research improved over time such that many articles using qualitative research have now been published in the top peer-reviewed journals of virtually every business discipline.

My view is that both quantitative and qualitative research approaches are useful and needed in researching business organizations. Both kinds of research are important, and both kinds of research can be rigorous. Most of the resources and readings cited in this book have been peer reviewed by leading experts and published in the top journals in the various business disciplines. However, there are advantages and disadvantages in each approach.

Generally speaking, quantitative research is best if you want to have a large sample size and you want to generalize to a large population. In this case the objective is to study a particular topic across many people or many organizations. You want to find out trends or patterns that apply in many different situations. Various statistical techniques can be used to analyse your data.

A major disadvantage of quantitative research is that, as a general rule, many of the social and cultural aspects of organizations are lost or are treated in a superficial manner. The 'context' is usually treated as 'noise' or as something that gets in the way. The quantitative researcher trades context for the ability to generalize across a population.

Qualitative research is best if you want to study a particular subject in depth (e.g. in one or a few organizations). It is good for exploratory research, when the particular topic is new and there is not much previously published research on that topic. It is also ideal for studying the social, cultural, and political aspects of people and organizations.

A major disadvantage of qualitative research, however, is that it is often difficult to generalize to a larger population. You can generalize from qualitative research, but not by using sampling logic. For instance, if you conduct three in-depth case studies of three organizations, a sample size of three does not count for much in statistical terms. Three cases are no better than one. Therefore it is normally impossible for qualitative researchers to make generalizations from a sample to a population.

However, you can generalize from qualitative research to theory, and you can generalize from just one case study or one ethnography (Klein & Myers, 1999; Lee & Baskerville, 2003; Yin, 2003). How you can use qualitative research to make generalizations and how the contributions and quality of qualitative research studies can be evaluated is discussed in each of the chapters in Part III.

Although the qualitative/quantitative distinction in research methods is by far the most common, there are other distinctions which can be made. Research methods have variously been classified as objective versus subjective (Burrell & Morgan, 1979), as being concerned with the discovery of general laws (nomothetic) versus being concerned with the uniqueness of each particular situation (idiographic), as aimed at prediction and control versus aimed at explanation and understanding, as taking an outsider (etic) versus taking an insider (emic) perspective, and so on. Considerable controversy continues to surround the use of these terms (Myers & Avison, 2002). However, a discussion of these distinctions is beyond the scope of this book. For a fuller discussion see Luthans and Davis (1982) and Morey and Luthans (1984). See also Chapter 3 which discusses the various philosophical perspectives that can inform research.

TRIANGULATION

Triangulation is the idea that you should do more than just one thing in a study. That is, you should use more than one research method, use two or more techniques to gather data, or combine qualitative and quantitative research methods in the one study. Triangulation is an excellent idea if you want to look at the same topic from different angles. It allows you to gain a 'fuller' picture of what is happening. It allows you to triangulate data from interviews with data from documents, or data from two different research methods (e.g. a qualitative case study with quantitative data from a survey).

TRIANGULATING CASE STUDY DATA

Doing marketing research, Fournier (1998) conducted three in-depth case studies looking at the relationships consumers form with brands. She triangulated data within her case studies. She used multiple stories from the same person, interviews conducted with the same persons at multiple points in time, and information from other data sources such as grocery lists, shelf contents, stories of other household members, and so forth. In addition, researchers who had multiple encounters with informants in previous stages were employed. Thus interpretations were triangulated across researchers and authors as well.

It is relatively common for qualitative researchers to triangulate data within a study using just one research method. For example, a researcher conducting a case study of one organization might triangulate interview data with data from published or unpublished documents; or an ethnographer might triangulate data from interviews with data from observation. Many qualitative research methods require the triangulation of data in some way or other.

Much less common, however, and much more difficult, is when researchers try to combine two or more research methods in the one study. The idea is to triangulate data and findings on the same topic, but to use different methods. Triangulation is especially challenging if the research methods are substantially different in their underlying philosophy or approach, e.g. when researchers try to combine qualitative and quantitative research methods.

TRIANGULATING QUALITATIVE AND QUANTITATIVE DATA

An excellent example of triangulating data obtained from the use of qualitative and quantitative research methods is Markus' (1994a) study of how and why managers use email. Her study questioned the assumptions of media richness theory (that 'richness is better') and demonstrated how a 'lean' medium such as email could be used for complex communication.

To answer her research question, 'how and why do managers use email?', Markus used two research methods. First, she used a quantitative method, a statistically analysed survey. The survey was sent to a large sample of managers. Second, she used a qualitative method called analytic induction. The data were purely textual – mostly she used email messages that were sent by managers. She also obtained data from interviews.

Using both quantitative and qualitative research methods meant that Markus had quantitative data (e.g. frequency of email use) and qualitative data (transcripts of email message exchanges). Her findings and conclusions are rigorous and convincing.

I believe it can be difficult for most people to do this kind of triangulation well. This is because you need to be well trained and become an expert in multiple research methods, not just one. Also, each method has its own underlying perspective and involves the use of certain techniques. It can take months, if not years, for someone to become proficient in the use of just one particular method, e.g. ethnography. However, if you have the inclination, enthusiasm, and time, this is certainly a worthwhile and viable option. It is something that can be done (Mingers, 2001).

A slightly easier way to achieve the triangulation of research methods is for a single study to include multiple researchers. In this case, each researcher brings to the table his or her own method of expertise and experience. Having multiple researchers and multiple perspectives on any research topic can be positive. A key requirement for the project to be successful, however, is for the researchers concerned to respect each other's expertise and method. There must be mutual respect for any real dialogue to take place. In such cases, the research findings can be truly outstanding.

RESEARCH IN BUSINESS AND MANAGEMENT

All research in business and management focuses on a topic that is of relevance to one or more of the business and management disciplines. This disciplinary area is actually very broad and depending upon your background and institution may include the following: accounting and finance; commercial law; economics; human resource management; logistics and supply chain management; organizational behaviour and organizational development; information systems; management strategy and international business; marketing; and operations management. Of course, these business and management disciplines often build on research from other disciplines, such as statistics, psychology, or sociology. The list of potentially relevant disciplines is very large.

A key feature of a qualitative or quantitative study, as opposed to a purely conceptual study, is that it is an empirical investigation, i.e. it relies on empirical data from the natural or social world. The empirical investigation seeks to contribute to the body of knowledge in a particular field. A simple model of the process of empirical research in business and management is represented in Figure 2.1.

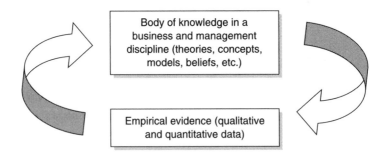

Figure 2.1 A model of research in business and management

As can be seen in the figure, a researcher finds a topic or a research problem that is relevant to the body of knowledge in a particular discipline. Normally the research questions are derived from the research literature, but they could come from current business practice or your own intuitive hunches (Marshall & Rossman, 1989). In order to answer the questions raised by the problem, the researcher subsequently uses a research method to find some empirical evidence. These findings are hopefully significant enough such that they are published and hence add to the body of knowledge. A new researcher then comes along and starts the process once more.

RIGOUR AND RELEVANCE IN RESEARCH

A perennial issue for researchers in business and management is the apparent trade-off between rigour and relevance (Table 2.2). It has become a common complaint over the past decade that research in business schools has become more rigorous at the expense of relevance.

Table 2.2 Rigour and relevance

Rigorous research	Relevant research
'Scientific research'	Relevant to business practitioners
Emphasis on meeting scientific standards such as validity and reliability	Emphasis on being immediately relevant to practice
Subject to academic peer review	Published in consulting reports or industry magazines
Published in academic journals	
Theoretical contribution	Practical contribution

Rigorous research is usually defined as research that meets the standards of 'scientific' research; it is research that has been conducted according to the scientific model of research, subject to peer review, and published in an academic journal. Unfortunately, much of the research that is published in academic business journals is often seen as being too theoretical and of little practical relevance to business professionals.

Relevant research is usually defined as research that is of immediate relevance to business professionals. The research results can be used right away. This kind of research is usually seen as more akin to consulting. Unfortunately, much of this kind of research is difficult if not impossible to get published in academic journals in business and management. The lack of a theoretical contribution almost guarantees rejection.

In my own field of information systems, the issue of rigour versus relevance seems to be discussed at almost every conference. Most academics tend to agree with the notion that research in information systems and business schools more generally should be more relevant to business professionals. In practice, however, they are faced with the need to gain tenure and promotion. In order to gain tenure, most business schools in research universities require faculty members to have a record of publication in reputable academic journals. This job requirement means that most faculty members end up postponing indefinitely their desire (if they have one) to conduct 'relevant' research.

As an example of this debate in the management literature more generally, Bennis and O'Toole (2005) argue that business schools focus far too much on what they call 'scientific' research. Writing in the *Harvard Business Review*, they claim that business management is not a scientific discipline, but a profession. They lament the fact that business schools have followed a scientific model of research rather than a professional model (as found, for example, in medicine and law). They say that graduating business students are ill equipped to wrangle with the complex, unquantifiable issues that are the reality of business. As most decisions in business are made on the basis of messy and incomplete data, they are particularly critical of statistical and quantitative research which they believe can blind rather than illuminate (Bennis & O'Toole, 2005).

I must admit that I do not entirely agree with Bennis and O'Toole's argument. In my view, the focus on research in business schools has transformed them from having a mostly vocational focus to being proper scholarly institutions. Faculty members have become scholars rather than consultants. Also, while most academic research may not be immediately relevant to business professionals, it may become relevant over the longer term. In fact, I would argue that one of the failings of contemporary management is the predilection to seek 'silver bullets', i.e. quick fixes, or magic solutions to more deep-seated problems. Few silver bullets turn out to be of any long-lasting value.

However, I do agree with them that research in business and management could be much more relevant than it is right now, and that it should be able to deal with 'complex, unquantifiable issues that are the reality of business'. And this is where the value of qualitative research lies.

It is my view that qualitative research is perhaps the best way for research in business and management to become both rigorous and relevant at the same time. It allows scholarship and practice to come together. Qualitative researchers study real situations, not artificial ones (as, for example, in a laboratory experiment). To do a good qualitative study, qualitative researchers need to engage actively with people in real organizations. An in-depth field study, in particular, needs to look at the complexity of organizations including the 'complex, unquantifiable issues' that are the reality of business. A case study researcher or an ethnographer may well study the social, cultural, and political aspects of a company.

Hence, if you are trying to decide whether to do qualitative or quantitative research in a business discipline, the choice should not be made on the basis of whether one approach is more rigorous than the other. This would have been a valid question in the 1980s and early 1990s, but it is no longer a valid question today. Rather, the choice should be more on the topic, on the research question you want to ask, on the basis of your own interest and experience, and how relevant you want to be to practice. It is also important to consider the expertise of your supervisor or faculty members in your institution. If you want to use qualitative research but there is no one with the qualifications, interest, or experience to supervise you at your university, then it is probably best to choose a different topic and method, or change university.

Exercises

1   Conduct a brief literature search using Google Scholar or some other bibliographic database and see if you can find both qualitative and quantitative articles in your chosen field. What kinds of topics appear?
2   Looking at some of the articles you found in more detail, can you describe the research problem and the research questions? Can you describe the research method(s) that the author(s) used? Did any of them use triangulation?
3   Looking at these same articles, would you describe some of them as more rigorous or relevant than the others? Why?

Further Reading

📖 Books

There are two books which I recommend for anyone wanting to do qualitative research at PhD level; both these books are required or recommended texts in many doctoral-level courses in business.

First, *The Sage Handbook for Qualitative Research* (Denzin & Lincoln, 2005) provides a collection of readings with authors selected from many disciplines. It examines the various paradigms for doing qualitative work, the strategies developed for studying people in their natural setting, and a variety of techniques for collecting, analysing, interpreting, and reporting findings.

Second, *Qualitative Data Analysis: An Expanded Sourcebook* (2nd edn) (Miles & Huberman, 1994) is also very useful.

A third book that is an excellent primer for novice researchers is *Doing Qualitative Research* (Silverman, 2005).

Websites on the Internet

There are quite a few useful websites on qualitative research:

- The ISWorld Section on Qualitative Research is at http://www.qual. auckland.ac.nz/
- The Qualitative Report is an online journal dedicated to qualitative research and critical enquiry at http://www.nova.edu/ssss/QR/index.html
- Sage Publications is arguably the leading publisher of qualitative methodology texts at http://www.sagepublications.com
- Narrative Psychology is an excellent resource on narrative and related areas at http://narrativepsych.com
- The Association for Qualitative Research has useful information at http://www.latrobe.edu.au/www/aqr/
- QualPage includes calls for papers, conferences, discussion forums, and publishers at http://www.qualitativeresearch.uga.edu/QuaiPage
- The International Journal of Social Research Methodology is a new cross-disciplinary journal designed to foster discussion and debate in social research methodology at http://tandf.co.uk/journals
- Forum: Qualitative Social Research is a bilingual (English/German) online journal for qualitative research edited by Katja Mruck. The main aim of the forum is to promote discussion and cooperation between qualitative researchers from different nations and social science disciplines at http:// qualitative-research.net/fqs/fqs-eng.htm
- Evaluation and Social Research Methods has links to books, manuals, and articles on how to do evaluation and social research at http://gsociology.icaap. org/methods

PART TWO

FUNDAMENTAL CONCEPTS OF RESEARCH

Part II provides an overview of some fundamental concepts relating to qualitative research. Chapter 3 discusses research design and provides a model of qualitative research. This model is used as the structure for the entire book. Some advice is also given about writing a research proposal. Chapter 4 looks at the various philosophical perspectives that can inform qualitative research, namely positivist research, interpretive research, and critical research. Chapter 5 reviews some of the most important ethical principles relating to qualitative research in business and management.

RESEARCH DESIGN

Objectives

By the end of this chapter, you will be able to:

- Appreciate why you need a research design
- Work out how to choose a topic
- Understand the essential features of every qualitative research design
- Be more confident in writing a research proposal
- See how various research designs have been used in business and management

INTRODUCTION

A research design is the plan for an entire qualitative research project. This plan should be written in a research proposal that says what you are going to do. Research design involves deciding upon all the various components of a research project: your philosophical assumptions, your research method, which data collection techniques you will use, your approach to qualitative data analysis, your approach to writing up, and, if applicable, how you plan to publish your findings.

The main purpose of research design is to provide a road map of the whole research project. It should include clear guidelines and procedures with regard to what you intend to do and when. However, as most qualitative research is iterative, you should never regard your research design as final. Your research proposal should not become a chain around your neck. Rather, you should be flexible and willing to change your plan as the research project progresses. However, even though things might change, it is still worthwhile writing a research proposal and spending time on research design. You should not be changing your research design every five minutes. You still need to have some plan of what you want to do.

Another (but equally important) purpose of a research design is to convince your potential supervisor(s), advisory committee, department, school, and/or research funding committee that you are capable of doing the research and that your research project is viable. A proposal is essentially an argument 'intended to convince the reader that the proposed research is significant, relevant, and interesting, that the design of the study is sound, and that the researcher is capable of successfully conducting the study' (Marshall & Rossman, 1989: 12). A well-written proposal can make all the difference between being accepted and rejected as a student. If the literature review in your research proposal is inadequate, your potential supervisors are unlikely to be impressed. Likewise, if your proposal is poorly structured and not well written, you may have difficulty in finding supervisors and may be seen as a potentially 'high-maintenance' student. On the other hand, a well-written proposal that is convincing and compelling is bound to be more favourably received.

Therefore, it is always a good idea to spend the extra time and effort designing your research project. You might also be able to use parts of your research proposal later (such as some sections of the literature review in your thesis).

CHOOSING A TOPIC

One of the first things you need to do, before you even start designing a qualitative research project, is to decide upon a topic. You should be able to describe your topic in just a few sentences. For example, if you are a student studying human resource management (HRM), your topic might be related to HRM practices and organizational performance; if you are a student in information systems, your topic might have something to do with the business use of social networking systems; if you are a student in marketing, your topic might be related to consumers' perceptions of brand value. Obviously, the topic will depend upon your previous experience and training in a particular subject. It will also depend upon your familiarity with the literature in that subject.

There are three important requirements in deciding upon a topic:

1   *You are interested in the topic.* I consider it to be absolutely essential for you to be interested in the topic. If you are bored by a potential topic, I suggest you should choose something else. As most qualitative research projects take time and effort, realistically you will only do a good job if you are interested in it.
2   *A faculty member is prepared to supervise you.* If your research project will be completed as part of the requirements for a degree, then it is also essential to have a faculty member at your institution who is prepared to supervise you. Hopefully this person will have some expertise in qualitative research and the topic, and at a minimum be supportive of your proposed research project.

3   *You can obtain relevant qualitative data on the topic.* The third requirement means that you are able to obtain data on the topic. There is little point in choosing a topic related to, let us say, software start-up companies in Latin America, if you have no possibility of funding to obtain any qualitative data from Latin America. On the other hand, if you can travel easily to Latin America and you speak Spanish or Portuguese, then a topic related to Latin America might be ideal (as long as requirements 1 and 2 can be met as well).

Once you have decided upon a topic, the next task is to develop one or more research questions. These questions should be framed in such a way that they are answerable empirically, i.e. by obtaining qualitative data. The questions should also be relevant to a particular issue that is (or potentially is) of concern in your chosen field of study. The questions should be designed to answer a research problem.

Although it is possible to develop research questions from business practice, I find that most of my students develop their research questions from the research literature. From the literature you might be able to identify 'gaps' and these gaps might be a fruitful avenue for further research. When you are writing an essay or a literature review on a particular topic, you will find that most articles have a section near the end in which they make suggestions for further research. In other words, their particular research project has answered some research questions, but raised a few new ones. Their suggested future research questions might well be viable research questions for your own research project.

Collis and Hussey (2003) suggest a useful procedure for starting the process of research design. This is summarized in Figure 3.1.

As you can see, the first step is to read the research literature on a particular topic in a business discipline. After going through the other steps, such as generating a list of potential research questions, you are then ready to move on to the next stage of research design.

THEORETICAL FRAMEWORK

After you have chosen a topic and generated a list of potential research questions, the next stage of research design is to choose a theoretical framework. Of course, this is the next stage from a logical point of view, but in practice many qualitative researchers change their theoretical framework or choose their theoretical framework much later on. This is especially the case with research methods that emphasize the iterative nature of qualitative research, such as grounded theory.

There are many different theoretical frameworks that can be used, from grand sociological theories such as structuration theory or actor network

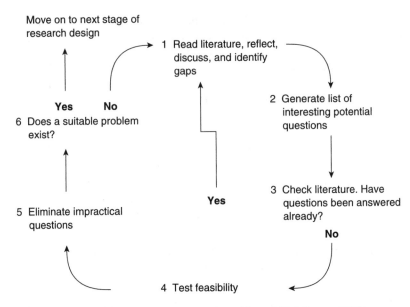

Figure 3.1 How to identify a research problem (adapted from Collis & Hussey, 2003)

theory, through to mid-range or lower level theories such as transaction cost theory or the theory of planned behaviour. I will not discuss these various theories here, since most theories deal with substantive matters rather than research methods. Suffice to say, however, that all qualitative research projects need to have some kind of theoretical framework, which may be more of less developed before you begin the empirical research.

A MODEL OF QUALITATIVE RESEARCH DESIGN

Assuming that you have decided to do qualitative research to answer your research questions (or at least conduct some qualitative research), and that you have some idea of your theoretical framework, every completed qualitative research project consists of the following essential building blocks or steps:

- A set of philosophical assumptions about the social world
- A research method
- One or more data collection techniques
- One or more approaches to qualitative data analysis
- A written record of the findings.

This model of a qualitative research project is represented in Figure 3.2.

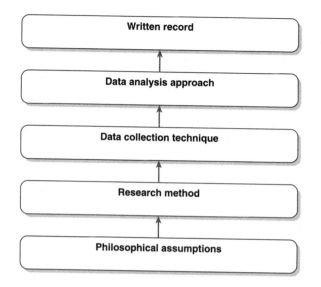

Figure 3.2 A model of a qualitative research design

Philosophical Assumptions

Every research project is based on some philosophical assumptions about the nature of the world and how knowledge about the world can be obtained. Often these assumptions are taken for granted and are implicit in a researcher's mind; however, I believe every qualitative researcher should make their philosophical assumptions explicit. These assumptions provide the foundation for everything that follows. Three philosophical perspectives or 'paradigms' are discussed in Chapter 4: these are the positivist, interpretive, and critical perspectives.

For example, if you are intending to conduct a positivist study, then most likely you will think of your research design as one involving the testing of one or more hypotheses. If you are intending to conduct an interpretive study, however, then most likely you will think of your research design as involving the exploration of a research topic or theory, rather than being a test of it.

Along with one's chosen philosophical perspective, all researchers need to think about their own ethical stance in relation to their own research project. Ethical principles relating to qualitative research are discussed in Chapter 5.

Research Method

All qualitative researchers need to decide how they are going to investigate the social world. How are you going to answer your research questions? For example, do you need to study organizations in the public sector, consumers, or managers? Do you want to study one case or many?

Although there are various definitions in the literature, I define a research method as a *strategy of enquiry*. A research method is a way of finding empirical data about the world. Each research method builds on a set of underlying philosophical assumptions, and the choice of research method influences the way in which the researcher collects data. Specific research methods also imply different skills and research practices.

The four research methods that are discussed in Chapters 5–9 are action research, case study research, ethnography, and grounded theory. There are other research methods; however, the four methods discussed in this book are the ones that are most commonly used in business and management.

Each research method can be used with any of the philosophical perspectives discussed in Chapter 4. For example, an action research study can be positivist, interpretive, or critical, just as a case study can be positivist, interpretive, or critical.

Royer and Zarlowski (1999) suggest a few useful guidelines for choosing a research method:

- Is the method appropriate to my research question?
- Will the method enable me to arrive at the desired *type* of result?
- What are the conditions of use of this method?
- What are the limitations or the weaknesses of the method?
- What other methods could be appropriate to my research question?
- Is the method better than other methods? If so, why?
- What skills does this method require?
- Do I possess these skills or can I acquire them?
- Would the use of an additional method improve the analysis?
- If yes, is this second method compatible with the first? (p. 120)

It is also important to decide upon the unit of analysis. Of course, this will depend upon the research problem and research questions, but you should be able to decide whether or not the unit of analysis is an individual, an event, an object (e.g. a service), a relationship (e.g. buyers and sellers), or an aggregate such as a group, organization, or industry (Collis & Hussey, 2003).

Another important decision relates to site selection. Your research questions should be the primary guide to site selection (Marshall & Rossman, 1989). Site selection is discussed in more detail in Chapter 11.

Data Collection Technique

Once you have decided upon a research method, the next step is to decide upon which qualitative data collection technique (or collection of techniques) you are going to use. The ones that are discussed in this book are interviews, fieldwork (participant observation), and using documents.

All three data collection techniques can be used singly or in combination in any qualitative research project, although some research methods tend to rely on some more than others. For example, case study researchers in business and management tend to rely mostly on interviews, whereas ethnographic researchers make extensive use of participant observation and fieldwork. However, an ethnographer might use all three techniques for gathering data, just as a grounded theorist might do the same. The choice of one or more data collection techniques will depend upon your choice of a research topic, your research method, and the availability of data. The availability of data is crucial to the successful outcome of any research project (Collis & Hussey, 2003). Your data collection methods should enable you to collect all the information needed to answer your research questions (Royer & Zarlowski, 1999).

Data Analysis Approach

Once you have collected your data, the next step is to analyse your data. As most qualitative research projects generate lots of data, you need to have a plan with regard to how you are going to deal with them.

There are literally dozens of ways to analyse qualitative data, and some of these are mentioned briefly in Chapter 13. Three of the most commonly used qualitative data analysis approaches in business and management are discussed in Chapters 14–16: these are hermeneutics, semiotics, and narrative analysis.

Although data collection and data analysis are logically different steps, in an actual qualitative research project they often go hand in hand. The data collection and analysis often proceed in an iterative manner (especially if you are using an iterative approach such as grounded theory).

Written Record

The last step in a qualitative research project is to write it up. Your findings can be written up in the form of a thesis, a book, a conference paper or a journal article, and so forth. There are also various writing styles or genres that can be used.

In qualitative research the process of writing up your research is just as important as doing the research itself. When you write up your findings, you are deciding what story you are going to tell. Chapters 17 and 18 discuss the issues surrounding the writing up and publishing of qualitative research.

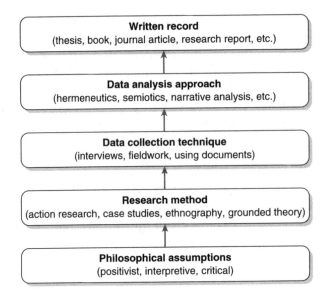

┌───┐
│ **Written record** │
│ (thesis, book, journal article, research report, etc.) │
└───┘
                    ↑
┌───┐
│ **Data analysis approach** │
│ (hermeneutics, semiotics, narrative analysis, etc.) │
└───┘
                    ↑
┌───┐
│ **Data collection technique** │
│ (interviews, fieldwork, using documents) │
└───┘
                    ↑
┌───┐
│ **Research method** │
│ (action research, case studies, ethnography, grounded theory) │
└───┘
                    ↑
┌───┐
│ **Philosophical assumptions** │
│ (positivist, interpretive, critical) │
└───┘

Figure 3.3   Possibilities for qualitative research design

The Model in Perspective

Although I have presented the five steps of the model in a logical order, in any qualitative research project there is usually much iterative activity between them. For example, while the data analysis phase logically follows the data gathering stage, in practice your analysis of the data might prompt you to gather more data later. You might suddenly realize that you need to interview another person or re-interview someone once again. Likewise, when you are writing up your findings, you might suddenly realize that you need to change the title and abstract of your thesis, or even your theoretical framework. The iterative nature of qualitative research means that you can never plan everything perfectly from day 1. However, it is still better to have some plan – even if it changes later – than none at all.

Various possibilities for designing a qualitative research project are summarized in Figure 3.3.

What you will notice from Figure 3.3 is the tremendous variety of possible research designs. Here are some examples:

- A positivist case study might use interviews and documents as the main source of data. The data analysis approach might be analytic induction. The findings are written up for a paper published in a refereed conference and also in a journal article.
- An interpretive action research study might use mostly interviews and participant observation (fieldwork). The data analysis approach might be

semiotics and the findings written up in a thesis and subsequently published in a book.

- A critical ethnography might use interviews, fieldwork, and documents. The data analysis approach might be a combination of narrative analysis and hermeneutics. The findings could be published in a book chapter and a journal article.

The choice of which design to use is not one that can be made on purely 'rational' grounds. Rather, the choice often has more to do with your experience and the experience of your supervisor/advisory committee and what is considered to be acceptable within your own institution and discipline. However, what counts as a legitimate design may change over time. Hence, it is not necessary simply to go along with what everyone has done beforehand. It may be possible to try something new, depending upon how much support you are able to muster.

WRITING A RESEARCH PROPOSAL

Now that you understand the building blocks that comprise a qualitative research design, it is time to start thinking about writing a research proposal. I suggest every qualitative research proposal in business and management should include at least ten items. The items are summarized in Table 3.1. Note that these ten items do not need to be in ten separate sections of the proposal, as some could be combined into fewer sections; also, the ten items do not need to be in exactly the same order as the table. However, all ten items should appear somewhere in the proposal.

Table 3.1 Items of a research proposal

Item
1   A title
2   An abstract
3   An introduction
4   A literature review
5   A topic
6   A theoretical framework
7   A research method
8   A qualitative data analysis approach
9   A timeline to completion
10   A list of references

1   A Title

Every research proposal should include a provisional title for the research project, the author name(s), and contact details. I suggest you should try to come up with a short, interesting title, one that captures the focus or topic of the study.

2   An Abstract

The abstract should succinctly summarize the main point of your research project, how you plan to conduct the research, and the expected findings.

3   An Introduction

The introduction should clearly state the purpose and motivation of the research project. Why is this project important? What new knowledge will be gained? Who is the intended audience? It is probably a good idea to indicate here who your supervisor or potential supervisor is likely to be (if appropriate). The introduction sets the scene for what follows.

4   A Literature Review

The literature review should demonstrate your knowledge of the literature relevant to the subject and the topic area. A literature review should be more than just a summary of the relevant literature; it should also include your own critical and analytical judgement of it. The literature review provides the context for your research topic and builds on prior research. You should be aware that, in most business and management disciplines, research published in highly ranked academic journals tends to be much more influential than research published in conferences and books. Hence, 'You should quote from the experts, the leading commentators who write in key academic journals' (Collis & Hussey, 2003: 132).

If you are planning to use grounded theory, some grounded theorists advocate that you should leave your literature review until later (after you have collected and analysed your data). However, the injunction not to conduct a literature review early on is mostly to ensure that a researcher keeps an open mind when analysing his or her data. When you are analysing your data using grounded theory, the idea is that the codes, categories, and themes should emerge from your analysis of the data, not from your earlier reading of the literature (which almost defeats the point of doing grounded theory). Hence, if you will be using grounded theory, it is up to you and your supervisor to decide how comprehensive your literature review needs to be. However, my personal view is that there should be some review of the literature, so that the topic and research questions are clearly defined, even if this review is not as comprehensive as it might be later on.

5 A Topic

Your research proposal should have a clearly defined topic or research problem along with one or more suggested research questions. This topic should be described in just one or two sentences.

If you are planning to use some other research method besides grounded theory, you might want to indicate your proposed theoretical framework for the research project. A theoretical framework might include a set of concepts, constructs, hypotheses, propositions, or models. In positivistic studies, this usually involves expressing a relationship between variables. In interpretive and critical studies, the theories tend to be larger meta-theories that are used more as a sensitizing device. Theories are seldom tested in interpretive and critical research projects but tend to be used in an exploratory fashion.

6 A Theoretical Framework

Your research proposal should include a description of your proposed theoretical framework. Depending upon the research method you plan to use, this framework may be more or less developed (in grounded theory studies, for example, one might expect the framework to be developed in an iterative fashion later on).

7 A Research Method

Your research proposal should include a description of the research method along with the underlying philosophical approach you plan to take. The most common qualitative research methods used in business and management are action research, case study research, ethnography, and grounded theory. You should specify how you plan to gather your qualitative data. As I mentioned earlier, the three data collection techniques that are most commonly used in qualitative research are interviews, fieldwork, and using documents.

8 A Qualitative Data Analysis Approach

You should also specify how you propose to analyse your data. Various data analysis approaches are mentioned in Chapters 13–16, such as analytic induction, hermeneutics, semiotics, and narrative analysis.

9 A Timeline to Completion

Your research proposal should include a timeline indicating the due date for the final version of the written report. Once you know the deadline (e.g. the due date for submission of your thesis), then I suggest you work backwards. For example, can you suggest dates for the first drafts for each of the chapters? Can you set a date by which the data gathering phase needs to be completed? As a general rule, you should allow at least 25 per cent of the total time for the writing-up phase of a thesis or book.

In working out a reasonable timeline I think it is a good idea to draft an outline of the thesis along with an extended table of contents. For some people a thesis or a book can seem so daunting that it is hard to see how it can possibly be done. They procrastinate getting started simply because they have not broken the project down into manageable segments. On the other hand, some people seem to think that a thesis or a book is relatively easy to complete and that it will not take them long to finish it once they get started. The danger of overconfidence is that, when you finally get started writing, the project suddenly seems a lot bigger than it appeared from a distance. It can end up taking so much longer than anticipated. Hence, for both these reasons I recommend writing a draft outline of the thesis in your research proposal, so that you have a clearer understanding of what lies ahead.

10 A List of References

Lastly, every research proposal should include a list of references at the end. This list shows your advisory committee which academic sources you have used in developing your ideas. Make sure that the spelling and details of your references are 100 per cent correct.

Optional Items

As well as the ten items that I consider to be essential, some institutions may require additional items to be present in your research proposal. For example, some may require you to include a budget and a description of possible funding sources (e.g. scholarships or research grants). The budget may include the anticipated costs of various expenses such as travel, accommodation, and transcription costs. Other institutions may require proof of an ethics committee approval, a statement of resources required to complete the project, or a statement of support from a referee, and so forth.

DEFENDING A RESEARCH PROPOSAL

If you are defending a research proposal, make sure that you have good answers to any likely questions or objections. Quantitative researchers will often ask about sample size, the reliability and validity of the findings, and so forth. Over the years, I have found that a two-pronged approach to defending a qualitative proposal works best.

First, make sure that you refer to influential qualitative works in the first-tier journals in your field (from your literature review). I have found that all scholars, no matter what type of research they do, respect work that is published in their own top journals (whether this work is qualitative or quantitative). If the scholars in the audience believe that your proposal builds on this earlier work, you will find that their objections tend to melt away.

Second, point out why qualitative research is needed to address your chosen topic or answer your research questions. Proponents of qualitative research designs 'do best by emphasizing the promise of quality, depth, and richness in the research findings' (Marshall & Rossman, 1989: 19).

If possible, however, I strongly recommend presenting your proposal to a sympathetic audience first, particularly if you are new to qualitative research. There is nothing worse for a young researcher than having a proposal shot down by academics who do not properly understand the method or the planned approach. You want constructive critical feedback, not destructive feedback which questions the validity of your chosen qualitative research method and approach. Of course, if you are a faculty member or a doctoral student nearing the end of your studies, you should be able to explain and defend your qualitative research project to anyone. But at the start, try to make sure that you have a reasonably sympathetic audience (i.e. sympathetic to qualitative research, not necessarily to your particular project).

At my own university (the University of Auckland), we started a 'Qualitative Research Group' precisely for this reason. Although the group was started from within the business school, we have seen it grow in membership to include scholars from non-business disciplines such as anthropology, sociology, and nursing. This group holds regular seminars for both senior and junior scholars. Our postgraduate students, in particular, appreciate the nurturing aspect of the seminars. If you think this kind of activity might be useful, and you have sufficient numbers of people, I suggest starting something of a similar nature within your own institution.

Another alternative is to try to present your research proposal to a sympathetic audience at a conference. Although many conferences tend to be dominated by peer-reviewed papers, sometimes there are informal workshops before or after the conference. For example, in information systems the International

Federation of Information Processing (IFIP) Working Group 8.2, concerning the relationship between information systems and organizations, tends to have a workshop immediately before the International Conference on Information Systems (ICIS) every year. This informal workshop is especially designed for PhD students or junior faculty to present their work in its early stages and get feedback from more senior researchers in a friendly environment.

Yet another alternative is to present your proposal to a doctoral consortium. Although most doctoral consortia tend only to accept students later on, when they are reasonably close to completion, sometimes it is possible to go earlier.

EXAMPLES OF VARIOUS RESEARCH DESIGNS

A Positivist Grounded Theory Study in International Business

Danis and Parkhe's (2002) topic concerns international cooperative ventures (ICVs) between Hungarian and Western partners.The authors used grounded theory in which the underlying philosophical perspective was positivism. The authors developed a set of propositions about ICVs and subsequently proposed a theoretical model to explain their findings. They suggest that this model provides testable questions for future research projects. They used a number of analysis techniques (e.g. pattern matching) to ensure construct validity, internal and external validity, and reliability of the results. The data were obtained mostly from semi-structured interviews with managers. The data were analysed using a qualitative data analysis software package (NUD*IST) in which they looked for common patterns across the various ICVs.

An Interpretive Grounded Theory Study in Marketing

Flint, Woodruff, and Gardial's (2002) topic is concerned with how customers perceive value from suppliers. The authors used grounded theory as their research method. They used interviews, participant observation, and documents as their data sources, although they relied mostly on interview data. To analyse their data, they used standard grounded theory coding techniques (open, selective, and axial coding). Their analysis was facilitated by NUD*IST, a qualitative data analysis software package (Flint et al., 2002).

A Critical Ethnography in Information Systems

Myers and Young (1997) revealed the hidden agendas of management in the development of an information system in the health sector. Their research method was critical ethnography. They say their data were obtained via participant observation, structured and unstructured interviews, unpublished documents (such as minutes of meetings), and newspaper and magazine reports. The authors provide a narrative analysis of their data using Habermas's theory of societal development as a guide.

Exercises

1 Conduct a literature search using Google Scholar and some other bibliographic database such as Emerald Insight or ProQuest and see if you can find articles relating to a topic in which you are interested. I suggest you try a few different databases and search terms.
2 If you are having difficulty locating relevant articles, ask a librarian for help or a faculty member who does work in your chosen subject.
3 Read a few of the research articles that you find. Analyse them using Figure 3.3 as a guide. Can you identify all five building blocks?
4 Looking at the same research articles, are there any suggestions for future research towards the end?
5 Write a more comprehensive literature review on this same topic. Can you find any gaps in the literature?
6 If you have identified a gap in the literature, does a suitable research problem exist? If so, can you draft one or more research questions related to the problem?
7 Evaluate the feasibility of your topic and research questions. Can you obtain the necessary data? Do you have access to the required resources? Is there someone with the appropriate interests and expertise able to supervise you?
8 Write a research proposal, making sure you include all ten items listed in Table 3.1.
9 Think of all the possible objections to your research proposal. What might a quantitative researcher say about it? Write out your answers to these objections.
10 Present your proposal to a class or group of fellow students. Use the feedback to improve your proposal.

Further Reading

📖 Books

The book by Marshall and Rossman (1989) provides a very useful summary of all the various issues that need to be considered in research design. The book by Punch (2000) is a comprehensive guide to writing a research proposal.

Websites on the Internet

There are quite a few useful websites on writing a research proposal:

- The Writing Center at Saint Mary's University of Minnesota has a useful site on writing a research proposal at the following web address: http://www2.smumn. edu/deptpages/~tcwritingcenter/Forms_of_Writing/Research Proposal.htm
- The Proposal Writer's Guide by Don Thackrey is hosted at the University of Michigan. See http://www.research.umich.edu/proposals/PWG/pwgcontents. html
- The Learner Development Unit at Birmingham University has a guide on writing a research proposal at http://www.ssdd.bcu.ac.uk/learner/writing guides/1.07.htm
- The University of Queensland has a useful site for PhD students, including a section on writing a research proposal. See http://www.uq.edu.au/student-services/linkto/phdwriting/index.html

4 PHILOSOPHICAL PERSPECTIVES

Objectives

By the end of this chapter, you will be able to:

- Understand the underlying assumptions in research
- Identify the differences between positivist, interpretive, and critical research

UNDERLYING ASSUMPTIONS IN RESEARCH

As I mentioned in Chapter 2, one of the most common ways to classify research methods is to make a distinction between quantitative and qualitative research. However, another useful way to classify research methods is to distinguish between the underlying philosophical assumptions guiding the research. All research, whether quantitative or qualitative, is based on some underlying assumptions about what constitutes 'valid' research and which research methods are appropriate. Hence, in order to conduct and/or evaluate qualitative research, I believe it is important to know what these (sometimes hidden) assumptions are (Myers, 1997c).

For our purposes, the most pertinent philosophical assumptions are those that relate to the underlying epistemology which guides the research. Epistemology comes from the Greek word *epistēmē*, which means 'knowledge'. It refers to the assumptions about knowledge and how it can be obtained (Hirschheim, 1992). Epistemology is defined in the *Concise Oxford English Dictionary* as 'the theory of knowledge, especially with regard to its methods, validity, and scope' (Soanes & Stevenson, 2004). Clearly, it is important for all those who are intending to use qualitative research methods that they should understand the grounds of their knowledge, especially with

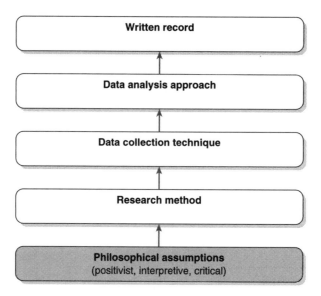

```
┌─────────────────────────────────────────┐
│             Written record                │
└─────────────────────────────────────────┘
                    ↑
┌─────────────────────────────────────────┐
│          Data analysis approach           │
└─────────────────────────────────────────┘
                    ↑
┌─────────────────────────────────────────┐
│         Data collection technique          │
└─────────────────────────────────────────┘
                    ↑
┌─────────────────────────────────────────┐
│             Research method                │
└─────────────────────────────────────────┘
                    ↑
┌─────────────────────────────────────────┐
│        Philosophical assumptions           │
│      (positivist, interpretive, critical)  │
└─────────────────────────────────────────┘
```

Figure 4.1   Qualitative research design

reference to the validity and scope of the knowledge that they obtain. They also need to understand the limits of that knowledge.

Guba and Lincoln (1994) suggest four underlying 'paradigms' for qualitative research: positivism, post-positivism, critical theory, and constructivism. Orlikowski and Baroudi (1991), following Chua (1986), suggest three categories, based on the underlying research epistemology: positivist, interpretive, and critical. This three-fold classification is the one that is adopted here, as illustrated in Figure 4.1. However, it needs to be said that, while these research epistemologies are philosophically distinct (as ideal types), in the practice of social research these distinctions are not always so clear cut (e.g. see Lee, 1989). There is considerable disagreement as to whether these research 'paradigms' are necessarily opposed or can be accommodated within the one study (Myers, 1997c).

It should be clear from the above that the word 'qualitative' is not a synonym for 'interpretive'. Qualitative research may or may not be interpretive, depending upon the underlying philosophical assumptions of the researcher. Qualitative research can be positivist, interpretive, or critical (see Figure 4.2). It follows from this that the choice of a specific qualitative research method (such as the case study method or ethnographic research) is independent of the underlying philosophical position adopted. For example, case study research can be positivist (Yin, 2003), interpretive (Walsham, 1993), or critical (Myers, 1995), just as action research can be positivist (Clark, 1972), interpretive (Elden & Chisholm, 1993), or critical (Carr & Kemmis, 1986). These three philosophical perspectives are discussed below.

Figure 4.2 Underlying philosophical assumptions

POSITIVIST RESEARCH

Positivism is the dominant form of research in most business and management disciplines. It is the style of research with which most business and management scholars are familiar.

Positivist researchers generally assume that reality is objectively given and can be described by measurable properties, which are independent of the observer (researcher) and his or her instruments. Positivist studies generally attempt to test theory, in an attempt to increase the predictive understanding of phenomena. In practice it is often assumed that the units of analysis which make up reality can be classified objectively into subjects and predicates (subjects are also often referred to as entities or objects).

Positivism has been described as the natural science model of social research (Lee, 1994). The research methods and tools of the natural sciences are seen as appropriate for studying social and organizational phenomena. Positivist researchers typically formulate propositions that portray the subject matter in terms of independent variables, dependent variables, and the relationships between them.

Hence, in their analysis of the research literature in information systems, Orlikowski and Baroudi (1991) classified IS research as positivist if there was evidence of formal propositions, quantifiable measures of variables, hypothesis testing, and the drawing of inferences about a phenomenon from the sample to a stated population.

The article by Benbasat, Goldstein, and Mead (1987) is a good example of a positivist approach to doing case study research in information systems. The article by London and Hart (2004) is a good example of a positivist approach to theory building in international business. The authors develop a number of propositions relating to how multinational corporations can successfully enter emerging markets.

INTERPRETIVE RESEARCH

Interpretive (or 'interpretivist') research is not as common as positivist research in business and management, but has gained ground over the past 20 years. Interpretive research articles are now generally accepted in the top journals of virtually every business discipline.

Interpretive researchers assume that access to reality (given or socially constructed) is only through social constructions such as language, consciousness, shared meanings, and instruments. Interpretive researchers do not predefine dependent and independent variables, but focus instead on the complexity of human sense-making as the situation emerges (Kaplan & Maxwell, 1994); they attempt to understand phenomena through the meanings that people assign to them (Boland, 1991; Orlikowski & Baroudi, 1991).

Generally speaking, the research methods and tools of the natural sciences are seen as being inappropriate for the study of social and organizational phenomena. The reason for this is the human phenomenon of subjective understanding, something that has no counterpart in the subject matter of the natural sciences (Lee, 1994). Many social scientists claim that the social scientist does not stand, as it were, outside of the subject matter looking in; rather the only way he or she can understand a particular social or cultural phenomenon is to look at it from the 'inside'. In other words, a social researcher must already speak the same language as the people being studied (or, at the very least, be able to understand an interpretation or translation of what has been said) if he or she is to understand any data at all. The 'raw data' for a social scientist include words that have already been meaningfully pre-structured by a group of fellow human beings.

This feature of social science is sometimes described as the 'double hermeneutic'. Giddens (1976) describes the double hermeneutic as follows:

> Sociology, unlike natural science, stands in a subject-subject relation to its 'field of study', not a subject-object relation; it deals with a pre-interpreted world; the construction of social theory thus involves a double hermeneutic that has no parallel elsewhere. (p. 146)

What the double hermeneutic recognizes is that social researchers are 'subjects' and are just as much interpreters of social situations as the people being studied.

Hence, interpretive researchers tend to focus on meaning in context. They aim to understand the context of a phenomenon, since the context is what defines the situation and makes it what it is.

Let me illustrate the importance of context. What does the following question mean: 'Did you watch the football last night?' If you have lived in various countries, you will know that the answer is not immediately obvious. To understand the question correctly, you need to understand what the speaker meant by the word 'football'. How do we know what the speaker meant by that word? The only way to decipher the riddle is to understand the context within which the speaker asked the question. If I were to tell you that the speaker was English and an ardent fan of Manchester United, then by the context it would become immediately obvious that the speaker was asking about soccer. However, if I told you that the speaker lives in Chicago and is an ardent fan of the Chicago Bears, then by the context it becomes obvious that the speaker was asking about American football.

The key point here is that the meaning of a particular word depends upon its context within a sentence, paragraph, or culture. Without an understanding of this broader context it is impossible to understand the correct meaning of a single piece of data (in this case, the meaning of the single word 'football'). Similarly, then, the meaning of a social phenomenon depends upon its context, the context being the socially constructed reality of the people being studied.

The differences in epistemological assumptions between positivist and interpretive research are summarized in Table 4.1. This table is mostly adapted from Bernstein (1983), who summarizes Hesse. In the original context, Bernstein reviews the commonly assumed differences between the natural and social sciences, and argues that all of the epistemological assumptions which supposedly distinguish the human sciences apply equally well to the natural sciences. Bernstein points out that there is a necessary hermeneutical dimension to all science. Kuhn's historical analysis of the nature of paradigm shifts in science supports this view (Kuhn, 1996).

As can be seen from the table, the first row is concerned with the nature of objectivity and empirical reality. In positivism, empirical data ('the facts') are

Table 4.1 Differences between positivist and interpretive epistemology (adapted from Bernstein, 1983)

Epistemological assumptions of positivism	Epistemological assumptions of interpretivism
Experience is taken to be objective, testable, and independent of theoretical explanation	Data are not detachable from theory, for what counts as data is determined in the light of some theoretical interpretation, and facts themselves have to be reconstructed in the light of interpretation
Theories are held to be artificial constructions or models, yielding explanation in the sense of a logic of hypothetico-deduction (if T is true, phenomenon X follows)	In the human sciences, theories are mimetic reconstructions of the facts themselves, and the criterion of a good theory is an understanding of meanings and intentions rather than deductive explanation
Generalizations (law-like relations) are derived from experience and are independent of the investigator, his or her methods and the object of study	The generalizations derived from experience are dependent upon the researcher, his or her methods, and the interactions with the subject of study. The validity of the generalizations does not depend upon statistical inference 'but on the plausibility and cogency of the logical reasoning used in describing the results from the cases, and in drawing conclusions from them' (Walsham, 1993: 15)
The language of science can be exact, formalizable, and literal	The languages of the human sciences are irreducibly equivocal (because of multiple, emergent meanings) and continually adapt themselves to changing circumstances
Meanings are separate from facts	Meanings in the human sciences are what constitute the facts, for data consist of documents, intentional behaviour, social rules, human artefacts, etc., and these are inseparable from their meanings for agents

assumed to be objective; the data are used to test a theory. In interpretivism, however, the correct meaning of data is determined by the context (the theory).

The second row in the table is concerned with the nature of theory. In positivism, theory takes the form of hypothetico-deductive logic; a good theory is one where the hypotheses are tested and found to be supported by the data. In interpretivism, a good theory is one that helps the researcher to understand the meanings and intentions of the people being studied.

The third row is concerned with the nature of scientific generalization. A positivist researcher looks to develop law-like generalizations, ones that apply regardless of the context. An interpretive researcher, by contrast, looks to develop generalizations that are more context bound, ones that are more closely related to the researcher and his or her research methods (for a more detailed discussion of generalizability, see Lee & Baskerville, 2003).

The fourth row is concerned with the language of science. Positivist researchers try to develop exact, formal, and literal definitions of a phenomenon (e.g. a variable or construct); it is important for such definitions to be as precise as possible. Interpretive researchers, on the other hand, tend not to be so concerned about precise definitions. Rather, they assume that meanings are emergent and depend on the context – it is these emergent meanings that they seek to elucidate.

The fifth row of the table is concerned with the nature of data. In positivism, 'facts are facts'; it is assumed that the facts are neutral and that they speak for themselves. In interpretivism, it is assumed that the facts already inscribe certain meanings. The facts are what a particular social community says they are.

Examples of an interpretive approach to qualitative research include Walsham's work in information systems (1993) and Kozinets's work in marketing (2001). Klein and Myers (1999) suggest a set of principles for the conduct and evaluation of interpretive research.

INTERPRETIVE RESEARCH IN INFORMATION SYSTEMS

A good example of an interpretive approach to ethnographic research is the article by Orlikowski (1991).

Orlikowski examined the extent to which information technology deployed in work processes facilitates changes in forms of control and forms of organizing. She conducted an ethnographic field study in a large, multinational software consulting firm.

Her findings indicate that information technology reinforced established forms of organizing and facilitated an intensification and fusion of existing mechanisms of control. Her paper shows that when information technology mediates work processes, it creates an information environment which, while it may facilitate integrated and flexible operations, may also enable a disciplinary matrix of knowledge and power (Orlikowski, 1991).

CRITICAL RESEARCH

While both positivist and interpretive forms of research are fairly well known in most business and management disciplines, the same cannot be said of critical research. Critical research is much less common. However, there are signs that critical research may be on the increase. For example, the Critical Management Studies Conferences in the United Kingdom have become fairly well established in the field of management. In information systems, three special issues of journals have been devoted to critical research since 2001 (Brooke, 2002; Kvasny & Richardson, 2006; Truex & Howcroft, 2001).

I believe that critical research has much to offer the business and management disciplines, but its full potential has yet to be realized.

Interpretive research and critical research are similar in many ways. For example, both kinds of research explicitly recognize the double hermeneutic in social research (i.e. that social research stands in a subject–subject relation to its field of study). To a large extent, the epistemological assumptions of interpretivism as described in Table 3.1 apply equally well to critical research. However, critical research is a distinct paradigm from interpretive research, as I will now explain.

Critical researchers assume that social reality is historically constituted and that it is produced and reproduced by people. Although people can consciously act to change their social and economic circumstances, critical researchers believe that their ability to do so is constrained by various forms of social, cultural, and political domination. Hence, not all interpretations are given equal weight in any given social situation. Some interpretations are preferred over others (and are sometimes imposed by one person or group of people upon another).

The main task of critical research is thus seen as being one of social critique, whereby the supposedly restrictive and alienating conditions of the status quo are brought to light. It is assumed that the current social conditions are preventing the achievement of enlightenment, justice, and freedom. Rather than simply describing current knowledge and beliefs (as an interpretive researcher might do), the idea is to challenge those prevailing beliefs, values, and assumptions that might be taken for granted by the subjects themselves.

HABERMAS'S MODEL OF SOCIETAL DEVELOPMENT

Myers and Young (1997) applied Habermas's model of societal development to information systems development.

Using ethnographic research, they looked at how hidden agendas, power, and other 'taken for granted' aspects of social reality can be deeply embedded within information systems development projects. The authors examined the introduction of market principles into health care and saw the introduction of a new information system as an attempt by management to colonize the lifeworld of the clinicians in a hospital (Myers & Young, 1997).

Connerton (1976) defines this kind of social critique as follows:

Critique (in this sense) 'denotes a reflection on a system of *constraints* which are humanly produced: distorting pressures to which individuals, or a group of individuals, or the human race as a whole, succumb in their process of self-formation'. (p. 18)

Of course, if one is going to critique the current social situation, a critical researcher needs to have some basis for doing so. Hence, almost all critical researchers have an explicit ethical basis that motivates their research work. Critical researchers advocate ethical values such as open democracy, equal opportunity, or environmental sustainability.

As well as performing a critique of the current social situation, critical researchers might also suggest improvements. The extent to which critical researchers suggest social improvements varies considerably, but the concept of emancipation has been developed the most by a group of scholars from the Frankfurt school. The verb 'to emancipate' is defined by the *Concise Oxford English Dictionary* as to 'set free, especially from legal, social, or political restrictions'. To be 'free from slavery' is the first example given of the meaning of the word in the dictionary (Soanes & Stevenson, 2004). As developed by the critical researchers of the Frankfurt school, the concept of emancipation refers to the emancipation of people from false or unwarranted beliefs, assumptions, and constraints (Ngwenyama & Lee, 1997). Emancipation

> describes the process through which individuals and groups become freed from repressive social and ideological conditions, in particular those that place socially unnecessary restrictions upon the development and articulation of human consciousness. (Alvesson & Willmott, 1992: 432)

The most well-known member of the Frankfurt school is Jurgen Habermas. Habermas developed a theory of communicative action that he argues is the basis of modern societies (Habermas, 1984).

Another critical theorist is Pierre Bourdieu. Bourdieu was a French sociologist who focused on the power of symbolic systems and their domination over the construction of reality. Bourdieu pioneered concepts such as social, cultural, and symbolic capital. Symbolic capital, for example, refers to the resources available to an individual on the basis of honour, prestige, or recognition (Bourdieu, 1977; 1990).

Michel Foucault is another well-known critical theorist. His work looked at the relationships between power, knowledge, and discourse (Foucault, 1970; 1972). He described himself as a 'specialist in the history of systems of thought' (Macey, 2000: 133).

A good overview of the critical approach to research in business and management is Alvesson and Deetz's book (Alvesson & Deetz, 2000). Barratt (2002) provides an overview of the contribution that scholars using the ideas of Foucault have made to human resource management. Cooper (2002) draws upon the work of Bourdieu to look at the role of critical accounting academics in Scotland. Examples of a Habermasian approach to critical research in information systems are the articles by Myers and Young (1997) and Ngwenyama and Lee (1997).

Exercises

1 Conduct a brief literature search using Google Scholar or some other bibliographic database and see if you can find two or three qualitative positivist articles in your chosen field. What kinds of topics appear? What hypotheses or propositions are tested?
2 Conduct another brief literature search, but in this instance look for interpretive and critical articles in your chosen field. What kinds of topics appear? What theories are used?

Further Reading

Books

A good book explaining the interpretive perspective as it relates to information systems is the book by Walsham (1993). A good overview of the critical approach to research in business and management is Alvesson and Deetz's book (Alvesson & Deetz, 2000).

Websites on the Internet

There are a few useful websites:

- The ISWorld Section on Qualitative Research at http://www.qual.auckland.ac.nz/ provides many references on positivist, interpretive, and critical research articles in information systems
- The Qualitative Report website lists many resources for qualitative researchers including some related to philosophical perspectives: http://www.nova.edu/ssss/QR/qualres.html

5

ETHICS

Objectives

By the end of this chapter, you will be able to:

- Appreciate the importance of ethics
- Understand important ethical principles related to research
- Recognize ethical dilemmas that can arise in the practice of research

THE IMPORTANCE OF ETHICS

Ethics is defined by the *Concise Oxford English Dictionary* as 'the moral principles governing or influencing conduct' or 'the branch of knowledge concerned with moral principles' (Soanes & Stevenson, 2004). The first meaning is the one that is most relevant for us. Hence, research ethics can be defined as the application of moral principles 'in planning, conducting, and reporting the results of research studies. The fundamental moral standards involved focus on what is right and what is wrong' (McNabb, 2002: 36). This chapter focuses on moral principles as they apply to qualitative researchers in business and management.

For qualitative researchers, ethical practice is usually defined as a moral stance that involves 'respect and protection for the people actively consenting to be studied' (Payne & Payne, 2004: 66). However, while we might be able to agree on some general principles, in practice there can be many ethical dilemmas. For example, sometimes there might be a conflict between protecting the rights of the people you studied and the wishes of your sponsors or funders. At other times there might be a conflict between your responsibilities to your university and the wider public.

Most qualitative researchers would probably say that, where there is an ethical conflict, the researcher's primary responsibility is to the people being studied. The American Anthropological Association says that an anthropologist's paramount responsibility is to those he or she studies. If there is a conflict of interest, these people must come first (Spradley, 1980).

However, Westmarland (2005) raises the question of how to balance one's responsibility to the people being studied versus one's responsibility to the wider public. In her case, she came across unnecessary force being used by the police during her study of police behaviour. The alternatives were (a) colluding through inaction when unnecessary force was used or (b) 'blowing the whistle' (Westmarland, 2005). She says it is difficult to propose a set of ethical guidelines and rules for such cases.

McNabb (2002) says that four practical ethical principles are most relevant to research in public administration. These four principles are truthfulness, thoroughness, objectivity, and relevance. *Truthfulness* means that it is unethical for researchers purposefully to lie, deceive, or in any way employ fraud. *Thoroughness* demands that researchers should be methodologically thorough and not cut corners. *Objectivity* means that researchers, especially in positivist studies, should not allow their own values or biases to affect the study. *Relevance* means that research should never be done for frivolous, wasteful, or irrelevant purposes (McNabb, 2002).

IMPORTANT ETHICAL PRINCIPLES RELATED TO RESEARCH

There are many important ethical principles related to research. Some of these will now be discussed in more detail.

The Golden Rule

The golden rule is perhaps the most fundamental ethical principle of all. The golden rule states that you should do unto others as you would have them do unto you. Applied to research, this means that if you are unsure about the ethics of a particular action on your part, then it is a good idea to put yourself into the other person's shoes (Jackson, 1987). How would you feel if someone was taking notes about your activities? How would you feel if they published something about you without having the opportunity to review it beforehand?

Maylor and Blackmon (2005) translate the golden rule for researchers in business and management as follows:

> Treat others as you yourself want to be treated and provide benefit to the organization and individuals involved in your work. (p. 281)

Most of the following rules build on this fundamental ethical principle.

Honesty

Honesty is fundamental to all research. Without honesty, the entire edifice and stock of knowledge on which a particular discipline is built would come crumbling down.

Imagine if a researcher was able to publish a paper that contained fictitious data and lies about the research methods. What would this do to the reputation of the journal in which the paper appeared? As soon as it became public knowledge, the reputation of the journal in question would be in tatters. It is also very likely that the field itself would be brought into disrepute. The fact that such a paper was able to be peer reviewed and yet still be accepted would cast doubt on the expertise of the editorial board of the journal. More far-reaching questions would probably be asked about the reliability of the knowledge in that particular discipline – can the stock of knowledge in this field be trusted?

Hence, honesty is absolutely essential. All researchers should be honest about their data, their findings, and their research methods. Without honesty, all our claims to creating original knowledge or discovering important insights go out of the window. However, this does not mean that we cannot disagree about the meaning of our data and our findings. As Payne and Payne (2004) point out:

> The requirement for proper conduct in the production of knowledge does *not* mean that what is published should be regarded as absolute 'truth.' … 'Findings' are not self-evident: it is entirely legitimate to debate the strength of evidence (Reliability and Validity), or its interpretation. (p. 67)

Plagiarism

Plagiarism is considered to be one of the worst possible sins in academia. Plagiarism is the deliberate copying of someone else's work and presenting it as one's own. The whole peer review system of conference and journals, and the awarding of diplomas and degrees at universities, is based on the principle that scholars only claim credit for what they themselves have done. If material has been copied or referenced from somewhere else, then these sources must be properly acknowledged.

Unfortunately, the Internet has made it easy to plagiarize material from someone else. While we tend to think of this happening only with student essays, there are instances where the qualitative data for theses, conference papers, and even journal articles have subsequently been shown to have been plagiarized.

Informed Consent

Informed consent is an important ethical principle in qualitative research. Informed consent means that potential informants should, as far as possible, 'be enabled freely to give their *informed consent* to participate, and advised that they can *terminate their involvement for any reason*, at any time (Payne & Payne, 2004: 68). Of course, if you are doing fieldwork, it is unrealistic to expect that you can obtain the consent of everyone you might meet. However, if you are studying a company, you should obviously obtain permission from an appropriate manager to conduct the research. Also, if you are intending to conduct interviews, then your interviewees should be asked for their informed consent beforehand.

Some qualitative researchers argue, however, that informed consent prevents researchers from uncovering corrupt, illegitimate, or covert practices of government or business. For example, 'prisoners' rights are rarely a matter of concern to the authorities until someone wants to do research on prisons. In effect, authorities can protect themselves under the guise of protecting the subjects' (Punch, 1986: 38). Punch argues, therefore, that some deception might be acceptable in some circumstances if it enables you to obtain data not obtainable by other means (Punch, 1986).

Hence, I think there can be a trade-off in certain situations between informed consent and finding out inconvenient truths for the public good. Such trade-offs are perhaps best evaluated on a case-by-case basis and in discussion with a supervisor or colleague.

Permission to Publish

Often some of the data you collect will be owned by the people or company. In this case it is essential to ask permission from the appropriate person to use the material in your own work. In the case of the data that you have collected yourself, this is not so straightforward. If you are planning to use real names for the people and the organization, then I believe it is a common courtesy to let them know and let an appropriate person from the organization read and comment on your work before it is published. I realize that journalists will often refuse to provide a copy of an article before publication, but I believe we, as qualitative researchers, should aim for a higher standard. If you prefer not to seek any comments from the people or organization concerned (perhaps because your article or thesis might be seen by them as too critical), then another solution is to use pseudonyms and change some of the other details to disguise their identities. I think it is important to maintain confidentiality if that was assumed or requested by the people being studied.

The identity of the organization should be disguised, perhaps by hiding or changing any identifying information (Payne & Payne, 2004).

On the other hand, you might find that a government department or company wants to withhold consent to the publication of your article simply because the results are politically unwelcome. In this case you have an ethical dilemma – do you agree with the request not to publish, or do you publish your findings for what you consider to be the greater public good? I would think that in some situations the rights of the public to know can sometimes override the rights of the people and organization where you conducted your research. However, deciding the rights and wrongs in any particular case is tricky and has to be carefully thought through.

The Research Report

Maylor and Blackmon (2005) suggest three ethical issues should be considered in relation to the write-up of a research project. These are:

- **Maintaining privacy – make sure that confidentiality is preserved.**
- **Representation of data – make sure that you report and analyse your data honestly.**
- **Taking responsibility for your findings – make sure that you are prepared to stand behind your results, particularly if your findings are unfavourable (Maylor & Blackmon, 2005).**

Action Research

Action research raises a number of ethical concerns (Clark, 1972; Rapoport, 1970). One of the key issues relates to whose interests are being served in an action research project. If the goals of the researcher and client differ significantly, there could be difficulties. Hult and Lennung (1980) suggest that a minimal ethical requirement is for an action researcher to state clearly the value premises of his or her work.

Another key issue relates to the issue of payment. If a researcher is paid by the sponsoring organization, to what extent does this influence the researcher to favour the client? At a minimum I would suggest that an action researcher should disclose any financial support from the sponsoring organization.

Interviews and Fieldwork

If you decide to conduct interviews, participant observation, or fieldwork, you always need to tell people at the start what you are doing, why you are doing it, and what you will do with the findings. Obviously it would be unethical to say one thing, but do another. For example, if you promise informants that you will keep any information they share with you confidential, then publishing any information from them later would constitute a breaking of your promise. If you misrepresent the purpose of your research, this too is an ethical breach. Deception and misrepresentation should really have no place in research in business and management.

One contentious issue in the literature on qualitative methods is covert participant observation. Some researchers believe that covert observation is wrong on principle given that it appears to violate ethical principles related to informed consent, invasion of privacy, and the obligation to avoid bringing harm to subjects (Miller, 2006). Other researchers, however, argue that it can be used if it is the only way to obtain the data. The only way to study crime or corruption, for example, is by covert means. Miller argues in favour of covert observation in some circumstances, saying that to ban it entirely 'places artificial boundaries on science and prevents study of what potentially may be very important and consequential activities in society' (Miller, 2006: 17). My own view is that covert observation is unlikely to be needed in most qualitative studies in business and management. However, if there is a good scientific argument for its use, then I tend to agree with Miller that the ethical considerations should be evaluated on a case-by-case basis (Miller, 2006). I would not ban it outright, but instead use it with caution; make sure that you discuss your project with your supervisor or a trusted colleague.

Online Ethics

As it is becoming more common for researchers to gather qualitative data via the Internet, it is important to consider the ethical principles that might be relevant to the online world. Consider the following examples:

- You send out a large number of unsolicited emails, but the emails might be considered to be spam.
- You copy a website from the Internet for a legitimate research purpose; however, failing to get permission to do so might be considered a breach of copyright by the owner.
- You surreptitiously enter an online community in order to gather data on community activities; however, some might accuse you of spying.

Ethical Codes

Many academic and professional associations have ethical codes that define what is or is not ethical behaviour in a certain field. For example, the

Academy of Management's (AOM) Code of Ethics sets forth principles that underlie the professional responsibilities and conduct of the AOM's membership: 'The principles are guidelines for everyday professional activities. They constitute normative statements for academicians, researchers, and managers and provide guidance on issues that AOM members may encounter in their professional work' (Academy of Management, 2008). The AOM code also includes 'enforced ethical standards'. Enforced standards are those that individuals must adhere to when participating in and carrying out the work of the AOM.

Most universities or research institutions also have their own ethical guidelines, which their own employees or research contractors are expected to follow. It is common practice for all researchers to be required to obtain permission from their institutional review board or human subjects' ethics committee before the research project begins.

Lincoln (2005), however, argues that institutional review boards can exercise unwarranted constraints on qualitative research. For example, such boards can limit the kinds of research that qualitative researchers are allowed to do, in some circumstances can pose a threat to institutional autonomy, and can sometimes make inappropriate decisions. There is a danger that such review boards may silence critical research projects that are oriented towards opposing oppression and supporting social justice (Lincoln, 2005).

Rubin and Rubin (2005) take a slightly more pragmatic stance. They suggest that qualitative researchers should attempt to deal with the checklist requirements of institutional review boards as best they can. However, qualitative researchers 'ought to keep in mind that mindlessly following the rules of the IRB can lead to conducting poor and inadequate research without increasing any protection to those being studied' (Rubin & Rubin, 2005: 106). Where there are conflicting ethical principles, they recommend determining whether the aggregate good to be achieved will exceed the harm done (Rubin & Rubin, 2005).

The Law

In many countries there are laws that impinge on the uses of qualitative data. For example, based on the privacy principles of the European Union, the New Zealand Privacy Act makes it illegal to collect data on people for one purpose, only to use it for another. It is a legal requirement for all New Zealand universities and their researchers to protect sensitive personal data.

Exercises

1. Discuss and debate the ethical principles related to covert participant observation. Is covert observation always unethical, or can it be justified in certain situations?

2. Imagine that, while you are in the middle of conducting an interview, your informant confides in you about bribery and corruption practices within the organization. What should you do? Discuss the relevant ethical principles that apply in this case.

3. Imagine that your research findings are unfavourable to the organization you studied. You know that your findings will make some people in the organization angry. What should you do?

4. Download the form for ethics approval from your own institution. Which ethical principles seem to be emphasized more than others?

5. Examine the ethical guidelines published by an academic association in your chosen field (see the list of websites below). Do you think any of the guidelines could place an unwarranted restraint on your research?

Further Reading

 ### Journals

There are a few academic journals devoted to business ethics, and occasionally they publish articles about ethics in relation to doing qualitative research in business and management. Some of these journals are:

- *Journal of Business Ethics*
- *Business Ethics: A European Review*
- *Business Ethics Quarterly*
- *Electronic Journal of Business Ethics and Organization Studies.*

Websites on the Internet

There are quite a few useful websites relating to ethics and qualitative research.

- The Academy of Management's Code of Ethics is available online at http://www.aomonline.org
- The American Marketing Association's Statement of Ethics can be found at http://www.marketingpower.com
- The Association for Information Systems' (AIS) Code of Research Conduct is available at http://home.aisnet.org/

PART THREE

QUALITATIVE RESEARCH METHODS

Part III discusses four qualitative research methods, as illustrate d in Figure III.1. I define a research method as a strategy of enquiry, a way of finding empirical data about the world. Chapter 6 looks at action research; Chapter 7 looks at case study research; Chapter 8 focuses on ethnographic research; and Chapter 9 discusses grounded theory. All four chapters discuss various approaches to each of the methods, and examples are provided of the use of these methods in business and management.

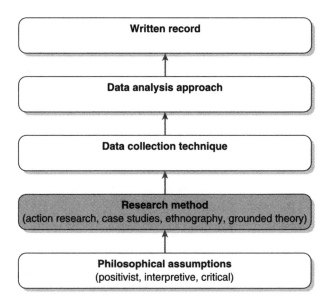

Figure III.1   Qualitative research design

ACTION RESEARCH

Objectives

By the end of this chapter, you will be able to:

- Understand the purpose of action research
- Appreciate the distinctive features of action research
- Identify the advantages and disadvantages of action research
- Evaluate action research studies
- See how action research has been used in business and management

INTRODUCTION

Action research aims to solve current practical problems while expanding scientific knowledge. Unlike other research methods, where the researcher seeks to study organizational phenomena but not to change them, the action researcher is concerned to create organizational change and simultaneously to study the process (Baburoglu & Ravn, 1992). It is strongly oriented towards collaboration and change involving both researchers and subjects. Typically it is an iterative research process that capitalizes on learning by both researchers and subjects within the context of the subjects' social system. Action research is thus an excellent way to improve the practical relevance of business research.

There are numerous definitions of action research; however, one of the most widely cited is that of Rapoport (1970), who defines action research in the following way:

> Action research aims to contribute both to the practical concerns of people in an immediate problematic situation and to the goals of social science by joint collaboration within a mutually acceptable ethical framework. (p. 499)

This definition draws attention to the collaborative aspect of action research and to possible ethical dilemmas which can arise from its use. It also makes clear, as Clark (1972) emphasizes, that action research is concerned to enlarge the stock of knowledge. It is this aspect of action research that distinguishes it from applied social science or applied business research, where the goal is simply to apply scientific knowledge but not to add to the body of knowledge (Avison, Baskerville, & Myers, 2001).

ACTION RESEARCH HELPS TO DEVELOP ACTIVITY-BASED COSTING AND THE BALANCED SCORECARD

Kaplan (1998) and his colleagues used action research to develop two new management accounting approaches – activity-based costing and the balanced scorecard.

They initially documented a major limitation in contemporary management accounting practice, and then identified a new concept to overcome this limitation. They continued to apply and improve the concept through publication, teaching, and active participation with companies. By using one kind of action research called 'innovation action research', the researcher enhances the underlying theory and, in the process, also becomes a skilled implementer of the new concept.

Kaplan (1998) says there are four basic steps in the innovation action research cycle:

Step 1 Observe and document innovation practice. The innovation action research cycle starts by identifying plausible solutions to the documented shortcomings in existing practice.

Step 2 Teach and speak about the innovation. Kaplan (1998) and his colleagues began to teach the new cases about early activity-based costing activities in their MBA courses and executive programmes. To teach the cases they prepared teaching strategies and teaching notes. The preparation and teaching process motivated them to understand the underlying phenomenon in a deeper, more systematic, and more conceptual way.

Step 3 Write journal articles and books. After new cases have been taught several times to diverse audiences and speeches about the phenomena have been delivered on multiple occasions, the innovation action research cycle continues by exposing the ideas to an even wider audience. Kaplan (1998) and his colleagues did this for activity-based costing through papers aimed primarily at a practitioner audience. These articles appeared in many different journals.

Step 4 Implement the concept in new organizations. The active involvement of the researcher with new implementations serves several critical functions:

1   Validates that the new concept can be implemented beyond the initial set of companies with which the concept was initially developed. Also, tests whether the concept can create value for these new organizations.

2   Provides learning opportunities to advance knowledge about the concept.

3   Creates knowledge about the implementation process for the new concepts (Kaplan, 1998).

The distinctive feature of action research is that the researcher deliberately intervenes while at the same time studies the effect of that intervention. It involves collaboration with business people in real organizations. This is quite different from most other research methods. Researchers using other research methods usually try not to intervene or to interfere with their subject matter. Any kind of interference, particularly in positivist research projects, is seen as a source of bias and can invalidate the research findings. Of course, researchers using other qualitative research methods do in fact affect the people and the organization they are studying in some way. Qualitative researchers are not invisible; they are not like ghosts. However, any intervention in the research setting is not done deliberately. Qualitative researchers using other methods such as case study research or ethnography tend to be interested observers, rather than active participants.

As a research method, action research emerged soon after the end of the Second World War. Kurt Lewin developed the method at the Research Center for Group Dynamics at the University of Michigan. He wanted to apply the theories of social psychology to practical social problems. Independently, the Tavistock Clinic (later the Tavistock Institute) developed a similar method in the United Kingdom in the 1950s and 1960s. The Institute worked with former soldiers and others who had served in the Second World War and were suffering from psychological and social disorders. In both cases the idea was to apply existing theory to solve a practical problem, learn from the experience, and then add to the body of knowledge by modifying the theory or suggesting new theory. Their findings were published in the academic literature.

We can see, then, that action research is not applied research, but neither is it consultancy. Applied research, such as applied marketing, simply applies already existing research findings in marketing to business but does not add to the body of knowledge. A consultant, likewise, simply takes existing knowledge or an existing methodology that is recommended by his or her consulting firm, and uses this in his or her own consulting practice. Consultants usually do not change the methodology or add to it in any way; neither do they publish their findings.

An action researcher, by contrast, is concerned to add to the body of knowledge. The whole idea of action research is to learn from the intervention in an organization and then use that learning to benefit others.

The Action Research Process

Baskerville and Myers (2004) say that the essence of action research is a simple two-stage process. First, the diagnostic stage involves a collaborative analysis of the social situation by the researcher and the subjects of the research. Theories are formulated concerning the nature of the research

Figure 6.1 The cyclical process of action research. Reprinted from 'An Assessment of the Scientific Merits of Action Research' by Susman, G.I. & Evered, R.D., published in *Administrative Science Quarterly* (23), pp. 582–603, December 1978, by permission © Johnson Graduate School of Management, Cornell University.

domain. Second, the therapeutic stage involves collaborative change. In this stage changes are introduced and the effects are studied.

A more comprehensive model is provided by Susman and Evered (1978). They suggest that action research can be viewed as a cyclical process with five phases: diagnosing, action planning, action taking, evaluating, and specifying learning. They argue that all five phases are necessary for a comprehensive definition of action research. The infrastructure within the client system (the research environment) and the action researcher maintain and regulate some or all of these five phases jointly. Susman and Evered's cyclical process is represented in Figure 6.1.

In Susman and Evered's model, the first phase, called diagnosing, involves the identification of primary problems that are to be addressed within the host organization. The second phase, action planning, specifies the organizational actions that should be taken to relieve or address these problems. These planned actions are guided by the theoretical framework of the action researcher. The third phase, called action taking, implements the planned actions. The fourth phase, evaluating, includes analysing whether the planned actions achieved their intended effects. The last phase, specifying learning, specifies what was learnt during the action research project. This is when the knowledge gained is applied within the organization and communicated to the scientific community. It may well lead to a change in the theoretical framework or model used in the second phase. This last phase may lead to the start of a new action research cycle, especially if the action research project was unsuccessful.

Elden and Chisholm (1993), in their introduction to the special issue on action research in *Human Relations*, provide a brief review of earlier action research in management studies. They say that a broadly shared definition of action research has existed since Lewin's seminal (1946) work.

Lewin and most subsequent researchers have conceived of action research as a cyclical process that involves diagnosing a problem situation, planning action steps, and implementing and evaluating outcomes. Evaluation leads to diagnosing the situation anew based on learnings from the previous activities' cycle. A distinctive feature of action research is that the research process is carried out in collaboration with those who experience the problem, or their representatives. The main idea is that action research uses a scientific approach to study important organizational or social problems together with the people who experience them (Elden & Chisholm, 1993: 124).

Elden and Chisholm (1993) suggest five elements which would need to be present in some degree for any research to be classified as action research. These are as follows:

1 *Purpose and value choice.* While the purpose of scientific enquiry is to contribute to general knowledge, action research aims at scientific enquiry plus practical problem solving. Action research is change oriented and seeks to bring about change that has positive social value.
2 *Contextual focus.* Since the action researcher is concerned with solving 'real-world', practical problems, action research must focus on the wider context, as in case study and ethnographic research.
3 *Change-based data and sense-making.* Since action research is change oriented, it requires data that help track the consequences of intended changes. Action researchers need to have data collected systematically over time, and they need to interpret and make sense of these data.
4 *Participation in the research process.* Action research requires those who experience or 'own' the real-world problem to be actively involved with the researcher. This involves, at a minimum, the participants being involved in selecting the problem and sanctioning the search for solutions. They may also be involved with validating the results. Action research, by definition, is collaborative.
5 *Knowledge diffusion.* For action research to be regarded as research, it must be written up and diffused according to the canons of accepted social science practice. This involves relating the topic to the existing research literature in the attempt to generate general knowledge. This is typically the job of the researchers alone.

Although these five elements can be regarded as essential features of action research, Elden and Chisholm (1993) suggest that there is great diversity in contemporary action research. I discuss various approaches to action research below.

PETER CHECKLAND AND SOFT SYSTEMS METHODOLOGY

In the United Kingdom, Peter Checkland used action research in the development of soft systems methodology (SSM) at Lancaster University (Checkland, 1991; Checkland & Holwell, 1998; Checkland & Scholes, 1990). SSM is a methodology for enquiry into 'soft' or ill-structured situations. SSM has been used in information systems and operations management to understand problem situations, and then to recommend taking action to improve them.

Some indication of Checkland's influence on information systems research in the United Kingdom can be gauged from the fact that a special issue of the *Journal of Information Systems* was devoted to the impact of SSM on information systems research in 1993 (now renamed *Information Systems Journal*). Also, both SSM and the action research method were used and adapted by Avison and Wood-Harper in their development of the Multiview information systems development methodology (Avison & Wood-Harper, 1990).

APPROACHES TO ACTION RESEARCH

There are three main types of action research. These three types correspond to the three main philosophical approaches to research discussed in Chapter 3. That is, action research can take positivist, interpretive, or critical forms.

The first type of action research is positivist action research. Positivist action research, sometimes called 'classical action research' (Elden & Chisholm, 1993), sees action research as a social experiment and attempts to meet the requirements of positivist social science. Work of this kind is often justified in positivistic terms – action research is seen as a method for testing and refining hypotheses in the real world. For example, Clark (1972) says that action research can be used to test out and/or replicate theory in a new setting by immediate involvement in the implementation phase of a situation. Payne and Payne say that action research is primarily designed to provide an empirical test of a possible solution: 'Action research is one type of applied research that is essentially a social experiment, introducing some new policy and then monitoring its effects' (2004: 9).

The second type of action research is interpretive action research. Interpretive action research, called 'contemporary action research' by Elden and Chisholm (1993), tends to rely on an underlying interpretive and constructivist epistemology, i.e. social reality is socially constructed. An example of this approach is Greenwood, Whyte, and Harkavy (1993), who argue that action research is always an emergent process, since it is largely controlled by local conditions.

The third type of action research is critical action research. In education, there has been a strong movement towards combining action research with the critical social theory of Habermas (1984). Carr and Kemmis, for example, define action research 'as a form of self-reflective enquiry undertaken by participants in social situations in order to improve the rationality and justice of their own practices, their understanding of these practices, and the situations in which these practices are carried out' (1986: 162). They argue that action research should be participatory and aim for emancipation. They say that action research is based 'on a view of truth and action as socially constructed and historically-embedded' (Carr & Kemmis, 1986: 182). While interpretive educational researchers adopt a similar view of knowledge, they say that action researchers are distinctive in adopting a more activist view of their role; unlike interpretive researchers who aim to understand the significance of the past to the present, action researchers aim to change the present situation to produce a different future. They suggest that action research must aim towards social justice, involve critical reflection on current practices, question the taken-for-granted assumptions which underlie those practices, and aim towards collective action.

As well as these three main types of action research, there are other kinds. One type of action research is called *participatory action research* (Whyte, 1991). In participatory action research, the practitioners are involved as subjects and co-researchers. As co-researchers, practitioners have control over the research process, by setting their own research agenda, helping to collect and analyse data, and controlling the use of the results. Participatory action research is very similar to *collaborative practice research.*

Another type of action research is called *action science.* Action science emphasizes understanding the difference between the behaviour of practitioners (theories-in-use) and their beliefs (espoused theories), and recommends the use of single- and double-loop learning for self-improvement (Argyris & Schön, 1991).

An espoused theory represents the world view and values that people believe their behaviour is based on. An espoused theory is what they think they are doing and this is what they will tell you in interviews. A theory-in-use, by contrast, is the world view and values implied by their behaviour, or the maps they use to take action. A fundamental assumption of action science is that there is usually a difference between what people say and what they do. Argyris and Schön (1991) suggest that people are unaware that their theories-in-use are often not the same as their espoused theories, and that people are often unaware of their theories-in-use. Of course, a theory-in-use can only be discovered by studying what people do (as opposed simply to hearing what they say they do).

Single-loop learning occurs when a correction is made to the process through changes in espoused theories and/or assumptions; however, the norms themselves do not undergo change. Double-loop learning, on the other hand, involves changes in norms as well as espoused theories or assumptions. Double-loop learning is thus much more important and extensive than single-loop learning.

How to Get Started

Finding a company in which you can do action research can be difficult. A good way of finding a suitable company is to explore existing personal or corporate friendships. For example, companies which already support your university in various ways are probably more likely to be receptive to the idea of action research. Previous graduates of the university (your alumni) are also likely to be more receptive than complete strangers. Of course, it is much easier if a company approaches the university asking for a research project to be carried out.

CRITIQUE OF ACTION RESEARCH

Advantages and Disadvantages of Action Research

One of the main advantages of doing action research is that it helps to ensure that your business research is practically relevant. Business research is often criticized as being too theoretical; business people will sometimes say that the research results are not useful. It is true that most research articles published in top research journals are read by a few hundred people at most, and these people are almost all academics. However, since action research aims to solve a practical business problem and involves working with people in business organizations from the start, action research, by definition, can help to improve the impact and image of business research within the business community.

One of the main disadvantages of doing action research is that it is very difficult for many people to do the *action* and *research*. It is very difficult to do research that contributes to solving a practical business problem while at the same time ending up with a research article that contributes to theory and is publishable in a research journal. Many action research articles tend to be published in more practitioner-oriented journals and magazines, which tend to be less highly ranked in business schools than pure research journals. However, it can be done, as the special issue of *MIS Quarterly* has shown (Baskerville & Myers, 2004).

Another disadvantage of action research is that there is a tendency for action researchers to overstate the importance of the intervention in the organization and the contribution to academic research. Oates (2006) says that action researchers, perhaps subconsciously, want to show that the exercise is useful, and that their theory or method is valid. She calls this phenomenon 'self-delusion and group-think'. She recommends the use of a 'devil's advocate' procedure to guard against this (Oates, 2006).

Action Research Is Not Consulting

To do action research, you need to combine both action and research – action without research is consulting, research without action is some other research method altogether. As Baskerville and Wood-Harper (1996) point out, you need to have a clear understanding of the differences between action research and consulting. Consulting or applied problem solving is not action research.

The first part – the action – means that you need to have a company or a person with a problem to be solved. The person must believe that their problem is important and that it needs a researcher to help solve it. They must be willing for a researcher to ask (sometimes tricky) questions, and to let the researcher probe into current business practices. The person must also be willing to sponsor the research in a company. Sponsorship can take many forms, including money for research expenses or a scholarship, but at the very least the person has to be willing to give you access to the company (e.g. people, documents, and projects). Without their full support the action is unlikely to be successful. I recommend walking away from a company when this full support is not forthcoming. You are better off trying to find another company where that support is willingly provided.

The second part – the research – means that you need to make sure that the practical problem to be solved is something that is of interest to other researchers in your field. That is, the immediate practical problem is simply one instance of a much wider set of issues and problems that are of current interest in the current research literature. The lessons learned from the action must be generalized to relevant theory in your particular field.

How To Evaluate Action Research Studies

There are many ways to evaluate action research studies. However, there are two basic requirements.

First, all action research studies must demonstrate a contribution or a potential contribution to practice (the 'action'). Some kind of intervention in a business process or an organization must have been attempted (even if the attempt was a failure).

Second, all action research studies must demonstrate a clear contribution to research (the 'theory'). It is important that the action research study is situated within a wider problem domain (usually via a literature review of your topic within a particular field) and the write-up specifies how the research contributes to that wider domain (Baskerville & Myers, 2004).

With regard to the first requirement, the best way to demonstrate a contribution to practice is if the sponsor in the organization agrees that the intervention was worthwhile. Some kind of documentation to this effect (a letter or a report) is a good idea.

As for the second requirement, the most convincing way to demonstrate a contribution to research is if the write-up of your action research project ends up being accepted as a research contribution by the examiners of your Masters thesis or PhD dissertation. It is even better if you are able to get an article published in a peer-reviewed conference or journal. By definition, an article published in a peer-reviewed research outlet of some kind has been reviewed by scholars who believe that your project makes an original contribution to the field. Of course, if your article is rejected many times, it is perhaps rather late in the day to start trying to ensure that your project contributes to a wider problem domain within your field. Therefore a much better way to ensure this kind of contribution is to get feedback from scholars early on, when you are engaged in the research design. The sooner you are able to present your research proposal to a wider audience, the better. You could present your proposal at a departmental seminar, at a doctoral consortium, or at a qualitative research workshop of some kind. Whichever option you choose, it is vitally important to ensure that your proposed action research is seen by your supervisors and other interested colleagues/faculty members as a potential contribution to research.

EXAMPLES OF ACTION RESEARCH

An Action Research Study of Management Accounting and Supply Chains

Seal, Cullen, Dunlop, Berry, and Ahmed (1999) conducted an action research project in management accounting, focusing on supply chains. They found that the existing work on supply chain performance was dominated by the industrial dynamics and logistics literatures. There was relatively little research that looked at the nature, type, and roles of accounting information in the formation, management, and functioning of supply chains. Furthermore, much of the published research had been heavily influenced by data from Japanese manufacturing firms where the role of the accountant was traditionally less prominent than that of the engineer.

As a response to these perceived gaps, the authors conducted a study looking at the accounting issues in supply chain management. Crucially, the researchers had access to the points of view of both parties in a dyadic relationship. Although the academic focus was on the role of management accounting in such relationships, the researchers became involved in the negotiation process partly in order to suggest solutions to specific accounting problems but mainly because they had come to be perceived by both parties as 'honest brokers', i.e. interested but impartial participants.

One of the key contributions of the action research project was to show that the specification and sharing of cost data can play a central role in inter-organizational negotiations as both sides in a manufacturing partnership learn about and respect each other's financial and commercial constraints and objectives. They suggest that accounting may play a constitutional role in the establishment and management of trusting and collaborative business relationships that go beyond the technical to a more symbolic level. However, technical idiosyncrasies in a firm's management accounting systems, difficulties in understanding their internal cost drivers, and an emphasis on financial accountability may make it harder for accountants to play a proactive role. They say that an ideal role for management accounting would seem to be in an open-book agreement whereby both parties can inspect each partner's revenues and costs. An important area of the strategic partnership can then become self-enforcing.

The underlying epistemology in this study was interpretivism. The research was based on meetings, visits, and interviews conducted on numerous occasions over an 18-month period with executives of both companies involved in a proposed strategic alliance. Contact with the executives ranged from short interviews to factory visits and meetings which lasted a full day. The ongoing nature of the negotiations offered the researchers an opportunity to act as 'honest brokers' if and when required. The researchers had a desire to see the agreement succeed but, apart from a wish to further the research, they had no vested interests. The researchers' role involved winning the trust and confidence of both partners. As active participants, the researchers were able to record what was happening because they were involved in the continuing dialogue with regard to the drafting of the proposed alliance agreement and the setting of agendas for meetings.

This action research project was unusual to some extent in that the researchers were actually involved with participants from more than one organization. The researchers were primarily interested in the partnership between the two organizations, rather than the organizations per se. However, the researchers were well placed to observe and experience the continuous changes that were taking place inside the organizations to the extent that these changes were relevant to the development of the partnership arrangement. Since there was no legal or joint equity basis to the partnership, the 'spirit' rather than the 'letter' of the relationship was particularly important, with the former only accessible through close involvement with the ongoing negotiations (Seal et al., 1999).

An Action Research Study in Marketing of Using the Internet for Customer Relationship Management

O'Leary, Rao, and Perry (2004) say that many firms at that time had not yet fully capitalized on the interactive marketing capabilities of the Internet. As very little academic research had been conducted on integrating the Internet/database marketing for customer relationship management (CRM), the purpose of their study was to develop a framework for integrating the Internet and database marketing to help marketers improve CRM. The authors believe that their study was one of the first to look at this topic.

Using action research, the researchers adopted a cyclical process methodology that incorporates the four-step process of planning, acting, observing, and reflecting on results generated from a particular project or body of work. Two action cycles were incorporated into the project to determine how the Internet might be integrated with database marketing within an Australian Internet portal. These action cycles, in conjunction with reconnaissance focus groups and convergent interviews, led to the development of the final framework of the integration of Internet and database marketing strategies.

Action research was used in this study for two reasons. First, as very little research had been conducted on integrating Internet/database marketing for CRM, the process by which this could be done was unclear. Thus, they believed exploratory research was required, and action research provided this capability better than other alternatives. Second, the authors were attracted by the degree of flexibility afforded by action research, particularly within an evolving information technology project that concerned a problem about which little was known.

The authors say that their research confirmed the usefulness of action research in that it provided the opportunity to build theory rather than test theory, with the end result being the actual effective implementation of integrated Internet/database marketing within a major Australian organization. Thus, their research contributed to solving a practical problem in a business setting and contributed to building theory for future marketing research.

An Action Research Study of Leadership

The last decade has seen a worldwide movement towards collaborative governance, collaborative public service provision, and collaborative approaches to addressing social problems. Huxham and Vangen (2000) looked at collaborative leadership and what it takes to make things happen in collaborative ventures.

The authors conducted a number of action research interventions in the United Kingdom. These included work with three partnerships concerned with health promotion, four partnerships concerned with economic and social regeneration, one partnership concerned with environmental issues, one concerned with community collaboration, and work with civil servants and others concerned with designing, implementing, and supporting.

The authors found that carrying any one of the 'leadership activities' through to completion requires much energy, commitment, skill, and continual nurturing on the part of a 'leader'. Successful leaders devoted significant personal attention to championing their causes. The authors found it paradoxical that the single-mindedness of leaders appears to be central to collaborative success (Huxham & Vangen, 2000).

Exemplars of Action Research in Information Systems

A special issue of *MIS Quarterly* on action research was published in 2004 (Baskerville & Myers, 2004). As *MIS Quarterly* is the top research journal in information systems, all the articles published in this issue can be regarded as exemplars of action research in a business discipline. The special issue illustrates some of the different types of action research. All the articles suggest criteria for how their own action research projects should be evaluated.

The first article, entitled 'Networks of action: sustainable health information systems across developing countries', looks at the pivotal importance of networks in ensuring the sustainability of action research interventions. The authors base their analysis on an ongoing, large-scale action research project within the health care sector in a number of developing countries (Braa, Monteiro, & Sahay, 2004).

The second article, entitled 'Informating the clan: controlling physicians' costs and outcomes', reports on the successful attempt by a hospital's management to 'informate the clan' of physicians to reduce clinical procedural costs and adopt better practices. This paper contributes to a better understanding of how to 'informate' autonomous professionals (Kohli & Kettinger, 2004).

The third article discusses a particular form of action research, called *collaborative practice research*, to study software process improvement initiatives in four Danish software organizations. Entitled 'Managing risk in software process improvement: an action research approach', the article proposes an approach to understanding and managing risks in software process improvement teams (Iversen, Mathiassen, & Nielsen, 2004).

The fourth article, entitled 'Design principles for competence management systems: a synthesis of an action research study', uses *canonical action research*. The authors developed and tested design principles for competence management systems (Lindgren, Henfridsson, & Schultze, 2004).

The fifth article used *participatory action research* to study the ways in which a small business management team developed an information-systems-enabled solution to address their growth needs. Entitled 'Small business growth and internal transparency: the role of information systems', the article proposes the concept of 'Internal Transparency' as an important outcome of organizational effectiveness (Street & Meister, 2004).

The sixth article, entitled 'Dialogical action research at Omega Corporation', uses *dialogical action research*. In dialogical action research, the intervention takes the form of one-on-one dialogues between the researcher and practitioner (Mårtensson & Lee, 2004).

Exercises

1 How actively involved should a researcher be in an action research project? Do you think it is acceptable for an action researcher to become politically involved in a situation?

2 What are the differences between action research and consulting? Do you think it would be possible for one to merge into the other? Discuss the pros and cons of that happening.

3 Conduct a brief literature search using Google Scholar or some other bibliographic database and see if you can find some action research articles in your chosen field. What kinds of topics appear?

4 Evaluate some of the articles you found in the previous exercise. Did the authors solve a practical problem? Did the authors make a contribution to theory? Was the research both rigorous and relevant?

5 Consider some of the theories used in your chosen field of study. Do you think any of these theories could be explored or tested using action research? If so, how would you design your action research study?

6 Brainstorm to come up with a list of four or five possible practical research topics. How could these topics be studied using action research?

7 Find one or more faculty members at your institution or at a conference who conduct action research. Ask them what topics they are working on right now, and why.

Further Reading

Articles

A brief introduction to the action research method is provided by the article entitled 'An assessment of the scientific merits of action research' by Susman and Evered (1978). For a more in-depth look at the method, see the special issue on action research in *Human Relations* (Elden & Chisholm, 1993) and the special issue on action research in *MIS Quarterly* (Baskerville & Myers, 2004).

Websites on the Internet

- The Centre for Action Research in Professional Practice is based in the School of Management at the University of Bath. The focus is on approaches to action research which integrate action and reflection, so that the knowledge gained in the enquiry is directly relevant to the issues being studied, and in which there is increased collaboration between all those involved in the enquiry project. See the website at http://www.bath.ac.uk/carpp/
- The Action Learning, Action Research Association (ALARA) is an international networking and resourcing organization incorporated in Australia. The website can be found at http://www.alara.net.au. ALARA holds a World Congress every few years and also publishes a journal.
- More references are available at www.qual.auckland.ac.nz

7

CASE STUDY RESEARCH

```
┌─────────────────────────────────────────────────────────────────┐
│                          Objectives                               │
│                                                                   │
│  By the end of this chapter, you will be able to:                 │
│                                                                   │
│    • Understand the purpose of case study research                │
│    • Appreciate the difference between teaching cases and research cases │
│    • Distinguish between different approaches to conducting case study research │
│    • Be more confident in doing case study research               │
│    • Identify the advantages and disadvantages of case study research │
│    • Evaluate case study research                                 │
│    • See how case study research has been used in business and management │
└─────────────────────────────────────────────────────────────────┘
```

INTRODUCTION

In all of the business disciplines, case studies are used in many different ways. The two most popular uses of case studies in business schools are, first, in teaching, and, second, in research.

In teaching, case studies are tremendously helpful to students in allowing them to understand better the theory and principles that are relevant to business. Case studies illustrate a principle or a particular point that the instructor wishes to make. They show that the theory has a practical application and bring the subject matter to life. Probably the most famous case studies of this type – in business schools at least – are the Harvard cases published by the Harvard Business School. These cases describe actual situations that the instructor and students explore together. The idea is for the students to figure out by themselves the 'correct' answer or answers to the discussion

Table 7.1 A comparison of teaching and research cases

Teaching cases	Research cases
Written primarily for students	Written primarily for researchers
Designed to illustrate an existing theory or principle	Designed to contribute to a new theory or explore/test an existing theory
Published on its own as a teaching case, often with notes for the instructor	Published as part of a research article in a journal, conference, or book

questions. As students study more cases, hopefully they get better at identifying current business problems and solutions, and how such solutions might be implemented.

Teaching case studies are thus written for students of business. They are designed to illustrate a more general point or a theory that is already well known to most, if not all, instructors in the subject. The purpose of teaching cases is to help students learn. The cases themselves may be based on real life or they may be fictional.

By contrast, research case studies are written primarily for researchers, not students. Research cases are used as empirical evidence to convince other researchers of the applicability (or inapplicability) of a particular theory or proposition. If the case is first published as part of a research article, the particular point that the research article makes is likely to be new to those reviewing the paper (i.e. other experts in the same field). The purpose of research cases is thus to contribute to knowledge in a particular field. Teaching and research cases are compared in Table 7.1.

This chapter is concerned with the use of case studies in research, but does not deal with the use of case studies in teaching. Although the writing of teaching cases for business students is a very worthwhile activity and one that I fully support, the preparation and writing of case studies for teaching purposes is outside the scope of this book. Instead, this book focuses on the use of case studies for research in business, hence the name of this chapter.

Writing a research case requires different skills and knowledge than when writing a teaching case. To write a teaching case, an author needs to be familiar with the subject matter of the course being taught: for example, the textbook and readings that are used in that course. The author also needs to gain access to or to create an interesting scenario that illustrates the point to be made. However, the theory or the guidelines that the case is designed to illustrate may or may not be explicitly mentioned in the write-up of the case itself. As a general rule, the write-up will include few, if any, citations of the relevant research literature. This is because the very idea of a teaching case is often for students to 'discover' the applicable theory or principles for themselves. One of the key things about creating teaching cases is that the case needs to be written in an engaging manner such that students are inspired and encouraged to learn.

To write a research case, the author needs to have a much higher and more detailed knowledge of the subject matter. The author needs to be familiar with, and cite, the latest research on the particular topic in question. The author also needs to write up a case that directly relates to that research topic. The case needs to be written in such a way that the story is plausible and convinces other researchers that the research article is indeed a new contribution to knowledge in the field. The case also needs to be written in an engaging manner, such that fellow researchers will find the story interesting.

THEORY BUILDING FROM CASE STUDIES IN MANAGEMENT

Following the logic of inductive case study methods, Dutta, Zbaracki, and Bergen (2003) analysed the data collected from a study of the pricing process of a large manufacturing firm in an iterative manner: first, they analysed the data and compared the data with existing theory; second, they developed a new theory; third, they returned to the data to see how the emergent theory matched the data; lastly, they returned to the theory for yet another revision (Dutta et al., 2003).

Research case studies can be used in the exploratory phase of a research topic, to discover the relevant features, factors, or issues that might apply in other similar situations. In this way, case studies are used in the early stages of research on a particular topic. Research cases can also be used in explanatory research, when there is already a large body of literature on the subject. In this way, case studies can be used to test theory, to develop causal explanations, or even to compare theories. It is mistake to suggest, as some do, that research cases can only be used in an exploratory way.

RESEARCH CASES CAN BE USED:

- In exploratory research – to discover.
- In explanatory research – to test, to explain, or to compare.

Case study research is thus applicable at any stage of the research on a particular topic. The key defining feature of case study research is not *when* in the research process it should be used, but *what* is studied. The 'what' are contemporary real-life situations where there is no control on the part of the researcher and where everything might happen all at once. Real life is sometimes messy, but then business theories that are unable to deal with messy real-life situations are probably of little value.

In a business discipline, case study research uses empirical evidence from real people in contemporary real-life organizations. The specific topics vary widely, from current marketing practices in marketing through to the implementation of enterprise resource planning (ERP) systems in the field of information systems. But a defining feature of case study research is its focus on asking 'how' and 'why' questions. The case study researcher seeks to understand how and why a particular business decision was made, or how and why a business process works the way it does. Unlike action research, the case study researcher does not deliberately intervene in a situation but seeks, at least in the first instance, simply to describe it. And as was mentioned earlier, as distinct from teaching cases, the primary audience for the case study write-up is fellow researchers in a particular discipline, not students. The case study write-up has to convince these fellow researchers that the case study is an original contribution to knowledge. These fellow researchers might be the examiners of your Masters or PhD thesis, or reviewers from a peer-reviewed research conference or journal.

> The purpose of case study research in business and management is to use empirical evidence from real people in real organizations to make an original contribution to knowledge.

A CLASSIC THEORY-TESTING CASE STUDY

One of the most cited articles in the field of information systems is a theory-testing case study written by Markus (1983). Markus compared three theories of resistance with the implementation of computer-based information systems (IS), using an in-depth case study to test the predictions of each theory.

The first theory of IS implementation is what she calls a 'people-determined' theory. This theory assumes that people resist IS because of factors internal to the person or group. An example of this is when it is said that 'people resist change'.

(Cont'd)

> The second theory of IS implementation is what she calls a 'system-determined' theory. This theory assumes that people resist IS because of factors inherent in the system itself. In this second theory, resistance is determined externally by the environment or the technology.
>
> The first theory thus suggests that 'people' are the primary cases of resistance, whereas the second theory suggests that 'systems' or the technology are the primary cases of resistance.
>
> Markus suggested a third theory – a theory of interaction. The third theory holds that people resist IS because of an interaction between characteristics related to the people and characteristics related to the system.
>
> Using empirical data from a case study of the implementation of a financial information system, Markus showed that the interaction theory has superior explanatory and predictive power (Markus, 1983).

Defining Case Study Research

The word 'case study' has multiple meanings. The simplest idea of 'a case' is that the phenomenon described is of a more general category. That is, the description of a particular case or situation is used to draw some conclusions about the phenomenon more generally. For example, a medical journal might describe the case of an asthma patient who showed certain symptoms after taking a particular medication. The particular case might be new and unique, but the case is still an example of a more general phenomenon (e.g. asthma).

A somewhat narrower definition of a case study, one that is more applicable for the social sciences, is that it is a detailed study of a single social unit: 'The social unit is usually located in one physical place, the people making up the unit being differentiated from others who are not part of it. In short, the unit has clear boundaries which make it easy to identify' (Payne & Payne, 2004: 31). A case study can be of a social process, an organization, or any collective social unit.

Along similar lines, Yin (2003) defines a case study in two parts, as follows:

1. A case study is an empirical inquiry that

   - Investigates a contemporary phenomenon within its real-life context, especially when
   - The boundaries between phenomenon and context are not clearly evident

- Copes with the technically distinctive situation in which there will be many more variables of interest than data points, and as one result
- Relies on multiple sources of evidence, with data needing to converge in a triangulating fashion, and as another result
- Benefits from the prior development of theoretical propositions to guide data collection and analysis. (pp. 13–14)

The first part of Yin's definition specifies the scope of a case study. The real-life context of a case means that the phenomenon of interest is not studied divorced from its context. In case study research, it is in fact very difficult to separate the phenomenon of interest from the context, because the context itself is part and parcel of the story. Also, in a case study the researcher has no control over the situation. This contrasts with the use of some other research methods such as a laboratory experiment, where the whole idea is for the researcher to maintain control of certain specified variables and to separate clearly the context from the phenomenon.

The second part of Yin's definition specifies the data collection and data analysis strategies. Yin advocates using multiple sources of evidence, triangulating these data, and using theoretical propositions from the research literature to guide the research.

Although Yin's definition of a case study is very helpful – and I thoroughly recommend his book as one of the best books available on case study research – the definition does not necessarily fit all case studies within the business disciplines. In one respect it is too broad, in another it is too narrow.

Yin's definition is too broad in the sense that case studies in business are usually restricted to studies of one or more business organizations. A 'case study' in business is almost always synonymous with a study of some business aspect of an organization. This organizational focus is an important identifying feature of most case studies in the business disciplines, and distinguishes case study research in business from case study research in other fields. In other fields, there can be case studies of educational programmes, or case studies of communities in a local neighbourhood. But as these are not studies of a business-related issue in an organization, they would not qualify as being called case study research in business.

Yin's definition is too narrow in the sense that he advocates just one type of case study research. This is perhaps best described as a positivist approach to case study research. Like most positivist researchers, Yin recommends the prior development of theoretical propositions or hypotheses. He also suggests that the quality of case study research designs can be judged by paying attention to four design tests, namely, construct validity, internal validity, external validity, and reliability. However, there are other types of case studies such as interpretive and critical case study research that do not require or recommend the use of propositions or hypotheses in research. Also, these other types of case study research do not use the words 'validity' or 'reliability' as part of their quality assessment.

> The aim of Buxey's (2005) research project was to document how the Australian textiles, clothing, and footwear industry has responded to the forces of globalization. Given the high level of competition within the industry, the objective of the study was to discover what strategies the survivors employed.
>
> Buxey conducted three representative cases of firms in the industry. He describes the strategy that each firm employed in responding to the forces of globalization (Buxey, 2005).

Hence, while Yin's (2003) book can be regarded as one of the most useful books on case study research – and it is widely cited by researchers in most business disciplines – his definition of case study research is not entirely appropriate for all qualitative researchers in business. Therefore I propose my own definition of case study research as follows:

> Case study research in business uses empirical evidence from one or more organizations where an attempt is made to study the subject matter in context. Multiple sources of evidence are used, although most of the evidence comes from interviews and documents.

There are three important points to note about this definition:

1   This definition draws attention to the fact that case study research in business *almost always involves a firm or organization*, even if the main issue, topic, or subject matter being studied is something else. For example, a case study of a joint venture might focus primarily on the joint venture – its governance, its financial or marketing success – but the researcher would still use empirical evidence from one or more of the organizations concerned; a case study in information systems might focus on an information systems development project, but the project will be situated within one or more organizations; or a case study in marketing might focus primarily on the development of brands, but these brands would still involve one or more firms. The most common

research cases in business, therefore, have an explicit organizational focus and tell the story of that organization.

2   This definition also distinguishes case study research from ethnographic research. Case study research, even in-depth case study research, *does not normally involve participant observation or fieldwork*. Most of the empirical evidence in case study research in business comes from interviews and documents. Ethnographic research, on the other hand, relies extensively on data from fieldwork. Fieldwork is the defining feature of ethnography.

3   Lastly, this definition of case study research is philosophically neutral. That is, it allows for the fact that *case study research can be conducted according to positivist, interpretive, or critical tenets* of what is considered to be 'good' research. These different types of case study research are discussed next.

APPROACHES TO CASE STUDY RESEARCH

Just like action research, case study research can take positivist, interpretive, or critical forms. These three types correspond to the three main philosophical approaches to research discussed in Chapter 3.

Positivist case study research was the norm in business schools some 10 or 15 years ago. However, interpretive case studies have become more accepted over the past decade and now appear on a reasonably regular basis in the top journals and conferences of most business disciplines. There are still very few critical case studies, but I predict that these will increase over the next decade.

The first type of case study research, positivist case study research, attempts to meet the requirements of positivist social science. Work of this kind is often justified in positivistic terms – case study research is seen as a method for testing and refining hypotheses or propositions in the real world. An example of this approach is Yin (2003), who discusses the importance of propositions and emphasizes construct validity, internal validity, external validity, and reliability. The concern with 'validity' and 'reliability' represents an attempt to ensure that the case meets the quality standards expected of a positivistic study. Another example of a positivistic approach to case study research is Benbasat, Goldstein, and Mead's (1987) approach to case study research in information systems. Essentially, they apply Yin's approach to the field of information systems and advocate case study research along positivistic lines.

The second type of case study research is of an interpretive nature. Interpretive case study research relies on an underlying interpretive and constructivist epistemology, i.e. social reality is socially constructed. Interpretive case studies generally attempt to understand phenomena through the meanings that people assign to them. Unlike positivist case studies, which define quality in terms of validity and reliability, interpretive case studies define quality in terms of the plausibility of the story and the overall argument. An example of an interpretive case study in business is Corley and Gioia's study of organizational identity change in the spin-off of a Fortune 100 company's top-performing organizational unit into an independent organization (Corley & Gioia, 2004). Another example is Walsham and Waema's study of information systems strategy development in a building society in the United Kingdom (Walsham & Waema, 1994). Both case studies focus on the social construction of reality – how and why people see the world the way they do. Both cases are plausible, and the authors do not justify their research in positivistic terms.

The third type of case study research, critical case study research, involves critical reflection on current practices, questions taken-for-granted assumptions, and critiques the status quo based on the theories of one or more critical theorists. An example of a critical case study is Myers' study of the failed implementation of an information system in the health sector. Myers (1994) used the critical hermeneutics of Gadamer and Ricoeur to help explain the findings. Like interpretive case studies, the author does not justify the quality of the research in positivist terms. Words such as 'validity' and 'reliability', which imply an objective reality independent of social reality, are not normally used in interpretive or critical studies.

Some Practical Suggestions

One of the most important things in doing case study research is finding an 'interesting' case in the first place. If your case is boring, then it does not matter how well you do the research, or how meticulous you are in recording your interviews, or how well you write it up; a boring case is really just a waste of everyone's time. So what makes an interesting case?

An interesting case study is one which tells us something new. That is, it tells researchers in a particular field something that they did not know before. For example, if it is an exploratory case, then it provides the vehicle for exploring a new subject area. If it is a theory-testing case, then perhaps it is a critical case which disconfirms existing theory and suggests an alternative. At the very least both you and your supervisors should find the story and the implications of the case interesting.

One of the biggest challenges in doing case study research is to find a company in which you can do the research. Some of my students have found that it can take a good few attempts before permission is obtained.

One way of finding a suitable company is to read the local newspaper or business magazines. If the story in a magazine includes quotations from some of the people in a relevant organization, then you already have one or more contact names. Another way is to explore existing personal or corporate friendships. For example, if you have already worked for a company or have friends or relatives working there, they might be more likely to be receptive to the idea of case study research. In particular I have found that previous graduates of the university are much more likely to be receptive to case study research than complete strangers. I suspect this is because they feel some obligation to the university which educated them, and because they are more open to the idea of research being done on them. Also they may be less threatened by the idea of the researcher finding out some bad news about the organization. In fact, they may well welcome such findings and treat them as an opportunity to learn and improve.

Once you have been given access to an organization, then you need to gather as much evidence as possible that is relevant to your topic. There are various techniques for gathering data (these are discussed in more detail in Part IV); however, the most common technique – and probably the most important – used for gathering data in business is the interview. Interviews are an excellent 'window' into an organization, and can help you to find out what people are thinking. They are particularly useful for finding out people's motivations, and their rationale as to why they did certain things.

Of course, there is a need for those doing interviews to have good people skills. If you are not good at relating to people or empathizing with them, then it is highly unlikely that you will learn much. Not everyone is suited to doing case study research. Although people skills can be taught, it might be easier and less time consuming for some budding researchers to choose another research method altogether, one that does not rely so heavily on people interaction. Case study research is not a soft option, particularly for those who are socially challenged.

It is possible to conduct a case study that is based almost entirely on a few interviews with key people. However, a more in-depth case study will rely on interviews with many people in the organization, and these people will represent diverse perspectives.

Either way, it is extremely important to identify and interview 'key' informants. Key informants are those who know the most about a particular topic in the organization and have decision-making authority for the general area in which you are interested. For example, if you are doing a case study about the marketing strategy of a particular company, then you will definitely want to interview the marketing manager. The marketing manager is the one who is likely to know the most about the whys and wherefores of the company's approach.

A more in-depth case study will use other sources of evidence besides interviews. Written documents can be extremely valuable as they often provide evidence for things which people sometimes have difficulty remembering, e.g. exact dates of a particular event, or the attendee list at a particular meeting, and so forth. Documentary evidence includes items such as annual reports, newspaper clippings, reports, memos, organization charts, and minutes of meetings. In some cases, physical artefacts such as devices, tools, or systems might provide additional sources of evidence.

> ## TIPS FOR SUCCESS IN DOING CASE STUDY RESEARCH
>
> - Find an interesting case.
> - Make sure you have good people skills.
> - Gather rich data and try to establish the context.

CRITIQUE OF CASE STUDY RESEARCH

Advantages and Disadvantages of Case Study Research

Case study research is the most popular qualitative research method used in the business disciplines. It is popular because one of the main advantages of case study research is what I would call its 'face validity'. By 'face validity', I mean that a well-written case study based on empirical research in an organization represents a real story that most researchers can identify with. This is especially the case with well-known organizations, where everyone is already familiar with the company or its products. Most cases are also contemporary stories, which means that the case documents one or more firms' attempt to deal with issues of current importance to other firms, many of which are likely to be in the same boat.

Another advantage of case study research is that it allows researchers to explore or test theories within the context of messy real-life situations. These situations are never as neat and tidy as our theories. For example, there may be multiple, equally valid interpretations of the same situation, or a chief executive officer (CEO) may have many reasons for doing a particular action, some personal, some professional, and some based on rational business principles (this is not to say that personal reasons are not rational reasons). These kinds of complexities can only be brought out in a research method that allows a researcher to get 'close to the action', as the case study research method does.

IMPLEMENTING ACTIVITY-BASED COSTING: A CASE STUDY IN MANAGEMENT ACCOUNTING

Consultants, business schools, and the business media have promoted activity-based accounting (ABC), claiming that it gives more accurate product costs and helps managers understand cost causation. However, there have been few empirical studies of the implementation of ABC. Doubts about the benefits and impact of ABC remain.

Therefore Major and Hopper (2005) decided to conduct an in-depth, interpretive case study of Marconi, a Portuguese telecommunications company, investigating ABC implementation and usage. They decided they wanted to identify and explore issues from the perspective of the actors involved, cast light on previous findings, and aid theory development. Like most case study research, they focused on exploring 'how' and 'why' research questions.

The data were obtained mostly from interviews and documents. Semi-structured interviews were conducted with managers and employees of Marconi, its parent company, the consultants that implemented ABC, the Portuguese telecommunications regulator, and managers from other telecommunication companies in Portugal. Their aim was to gain a rich description of Marconi's ABC system, its implementation, and managers' usage and evaluation of ABC.

Their research case makes three important contributions to the management accounting literature on ABC implementation:

1   Technical issues arose, in that there were technical problems associated with joint and common costs. These are significant in telecommunications. The ABC system did not meet the stringent conditions for providing valid data.
2   Implementing ABC in firms beset by conflict is difficult. As it turned out, only parts of the company used ABC. The production engineers resisted using ABC. They saw ABC as threatening their autonomy, threatening their employment prospects, and increasing their work load. Generally, they regarded it as a confusing and meaningless exercise.
3   Outside production the ABC implementation was judged a 'success' (in terms of evaluations and usage). This was associated with top management support, adequate resources, clear goals, and employee commitment. The implementer tried to give employees ownership of the project (Major & Hopper, 2005).

One of the main disadvantages of doing case study research, particularly in business settings, is that it can be difficult to gain access to the particular company or group of companies that you want to study. This is because firms may be sceptical of the value of the research for themselves. In fact they may worry that not only will the researcher take up too much of their valuable time in interviews, but also that the findings may be unflattering and lead to some unwelcome publicity. The last thing a company wants is bad PR. For these reasons it can sometimes take you months to find a suitable company and one that gives you the required permissions.

Another disadvantage of case study research is that the researcher has no control over the situation. In practice, this means that if the company you are studying is suddenly taken over by another company halfway through your study, there is very little that you can do about it. Alternatively, if your key sponsor (e.g. the chief operating officer) resigns just as you are starting to conduct your interviews, you may find that you have too few friends within the firm to continue your research.

Yet another disadvantage of case study research is that it can be difficult, particularly for younger, inexperienced researchers, to focus on the most important issues. As the context of the study can be as large or as small as you want, a real danger is that an inexperienced researcher will think everything is relevant. Therefore such a person ends up with a huge amount of data, most of which turns out to be irrelevant in the final analysis.

The last disadvantage of case study research is that it takes a long time, even for experienced researchers. It takes time to gain access, it takes time to do the empirical research, and it takes even more time to do the write-up. From start to finish, case study research is time consuming.

If we put all these disadvantages together, it means that only those who are enthusiastic and committed, and only those who have the required people skills, should consider doing case study research. It is a serious mistake to think that case study research is an easy or a soft option. It is not easy at all.

However, for those who are keen, case study research can be very rewarding. It gives you the opportunity to find out at first hand whether or not your concepts or theories have any value in the business world.

How to Evaluate Case Study Research

Like all qualitative research methods, it is important that case study research should be evaluated in an appropriate way. In other words, it is important to evaluate case study research according to its fundamental tenets, and not by the assumptions or tenets of some other method. It would be inappropriate to evaluate case study research by criteria used in evaluating survey research, just as it would be inappropriate to evaluate survey research by criteria used in evaluating a case study.

Keeping this comment in mind, it is important to note that conducting just one case study is fine. Many budding qualitative researchers make the mistake of thinking that one case study is not enough. They think that if only they had three or more cases, then this would increase the 'validity' of the findings.

However, this way of thinking confuses things. Researchers who think this way are making the common mistake, of using sampling logic to judge the validity of the case method. But case study research does not use sampling logic. Sampling logic is based on statistics. Sampling logic and statistical theory are what are used when you conduct a survey.

In a survey, the larger your sample size, the better. The larger the sample, the more sure you can be that the results truly reflect the population as a whole. Most statistical concepts such as significance tests and confidence intervals assume you have a truly random sample.

But in case study research, statistical concepts such as confidence levels and confidence intervals are meaningless. Using three or four cases is no better than using one case when it comes to increasing the confidence in your findings. First of all, the sample size is still far too small; second, you do not have a truly random sample in the first place. A case study is not one instance of a much larger random sample!

Instead of using sampling logic to justify case study research, which generalizes from a sample to a population, it is much better to generalize one or more cases to theory, as Yin (2003) points out. Just as it is possible to generalize from a single experiment, so it is possible to generalize from a single case (Lee, 1989; Yin, 2003).

So what makes an exemplary case study? The following criteria are offered as general guidelines for evaluating a research case in business:

1   The case study must be 'interesting'.
2   The case study must display sufficient evidence.
3   The case study should be 'complete'.
4   The case study must consider alternative perspectives.
5   The case study should be written in an engaging manner.
6   The case study should contribute to knowledge.

First of all, the case study must be 'interesting'. As was mentioned earlier, this means that the case study should tell the researchers in a particular field something new that they did not know before. At the very least both you and your supervisors should find the story of the case interesting.

Second, the case study must display sufficient evidence. If you are writing a research article for a journal, this means that it is usually a good idea to include some supporting quotations from those who were interviewed. Quotes that are verbatim bring the case to life. The general idea is that you need to include sufficient evidence such that your argument makes sense and is plausible.

Third, the case study should be 'complete'. By complete, I do not mean that everything that it is possible to say about the case has been said. Rather,

I mean that all the relevant evidence to prove or disprove a particular theoretical point has been collected.

Fourth, the case study must consider alternative perspectives. This may mean considering different theories, alternative cultural views, or disagreements among the subjects. The key point here is that cases that document real-life situations should reflect real life. Since real life is never neat and tidy, the story that is presented in your case study should not be so neat and tidy either. A 'perfect story' where there is a hero or heroine and everyone lives happily ever after is a fairy story, not a research case. Hence it may be advisable to include evidence which does not necessarily support your own theory.

Fifth, the case study should be written in an engaging manner. The key test here is whether you are enthusiastic about it. If you are not captivated by the story, then it is almost guaranteed that others will not be enthusiastic either. The write-up requires some creative energy.

Sixth, the case study should contribute to knowledge. This is fairly similar to the first criterion, except that it emphasizes the contribution to scientific knowledge rather than the case's intrinsic interest value. As a general rule, this means that a research case will be generalized to one or more theories or concepts.

These six criteria for evaluating a research case apply to all kinds of case study research. However, it is also possible to add additional quality criteria for evaluating case study research depending upon the type of such research that is conducted. These quality criteria will vary depending upon whether this research is positivist, interpretive, or critical.

For positivist research, good case study design is vital (Dubé & Paré, 2003; Yin, 2003). Yin (2003) suggests five components of good case study design:

1 A study's questions.
2 Its propositions, if any.
3 Its unit(s) of analysis.
4 The logic linking the data to the propositions.
5 The criteria for interpreting the findings.

For interpretive research, the plausibility of the case is far more important than its design. That is, fellow researchers in a particular field will need some confidence in the case, and its story should be believable. The plausibility of a case is improved by many things, such as using multiple sources of evidence, and having a clear description of what you did and how.

Klein and Myers (1999) suggest seven principles for evaluating interpretive case studies (although these principles also apply to interpretive ethnographies):

1 The Fundamental Principle of the Hermeneutic Circle
2 The Principle of Contextualization
3 The Principle of Interaction between the Researchers and Subjects
4 The Principle of Abstraction and Generalization
5 The Principle of Dialogical Reasoning
6 The Principle of Multiple Interpretations
7 The Principle of Suspicion.

These seven principles are summarized in Figure 7.1. They apply to interpretive work that is of a hermeneutic nature, but other criteria or principles might be more applicable to interpretive work that takes a different approach.

For critical research, the case should question taken-for-granted assumptions, and open to scrutiny possible hidden agendas, power centres, and assumptions that inhibit, repress, and constrain (cf. Thomas, 1993). Most critical case studies will use one or more critical theories such as from Habermas or Foucault.

EXAMPLES OF CASE STUDY RESEARCH

Open-Book Accounting in Networks: A Case Study in Management Accounting

Many manufacturing companies have developed close cooperative relationships with their key suppliers and buyers in recent years. This has led to the emergence of manufacturing networks, where there is a more comprehensive sharing of information among supply chain members.

In their research, Kajuter and Kulmala (2005) looked at the issue of manufacturing networks providing a platform for inter-organizational cost management. Compared with traditional cost management in single companies, they say that additional opportunities for cost reduction arise through collaborative efforts of network members. However, in order to reveal such opportunities, transparency of cost structures is essential. Open-book accounting can play a key role in inter-organizational cost management.

The authors, using an interpretive type of case study research, investigated the reasons why open-book accounting is successful in some cases and often fails in others. They examined the main obstacles hindering firms from exchanging cost data in networks.

This interpretive study consisted of two parts. First, a single case study of a German car manufacturing network – the Eurocar case – was conducted. Second, a multi-site case study of three Finnish manufacturing networks was

1 The Fundamental Principle of the Hermeneutic Circle

Suggests that all human understanding is achieved by iterating between considering the interdependent meaning of parts and the whole that they form. This principle of human understanding is fundamental to all the other principles.

Example: Lee's (1994) study of information richness in email communications. It iterates between the separate message fragments of individual email participants as parts and the global context which determines the full meanings of the separate messages to interpret the message exchange as a whole.

2 The Principle of Contextualization

Requires critical reflection on the social and historical background of the research setting, so that the intended audience can see how the current situation under investigation emerged.

Example: After discussing the historical forces which led to Fiat establishing a new assembly plant, Ciborra, Patriotta, and Erlicher (1996) show how old Fordist production concepts still had a significant influence despite radical changes in work organization and operations.

3 The Principle of Interaction Between the Researchers and the Subjects

Requires critical reflection on how the research materials (or "data") were socially constructed through the interaction between the researchers and participants.

Example: Trauth (1997) explains how her understanding improved as she became self-conscious and started to question her own assumptions.

4 The Principle of Abstraction and Generalization

Requires relating the idiographic details revealed by the data interpretation through the application of Principles 1 and 2 to theoretical, general concepts that describe the nature of human understanding and social action.

Example: Monteiro and Hanseth's (1996) findings are discussed in relation to Latour's actor–network theory.

5 The Principle of Dialogical Reasoning

Requires sensitivity to possible contradictions between the theoretical preconceptions guiding the research design and actual findings ("the story which the data tell") with subsequent cycles of revision.

Example: Lee (1991) describes how Nardulli (1978) came several times to revise his preconceptions of the role of case load pressure as a central concept in the study of criminal courts.

6 The Principle of Multiple Interpretations

Requires sensitivity to possible differences in interpretations among the participants as are typically expressed in multiple narratives or stories of the same sequence of events under study. Similar to multiple witness accounts even if all tell it as they saw it.

Example: Levine and Rossmore's (1993) account of the conflicting expectations for the Threshold system in the Bremerton Inc. case.

7 The Principle of Suspicion

Requires sensitivity to possible 'biases' and systematic 'distortions' in the narratives collected from the participants.

Example: Forester (1992) looks at the facetious figures of speech used by city planning staff to negotiate the problem of data acquisition.

Figure 7.1   The seven principles of interpretive research as suggested by Klein and Myers (1999)

conducted. In these studies the contextual factors influencing the implementation, utilization, and outcome of open-book accounting in networks were
analysed.

Most of the data were obtained by conducting 61 semi-structured interviews with key personnel. At Eurocar and at the Finnish main contractors,
manager-level personnel responsible for product development, purchasing,
production, and accounting were interviewed. In the Finnish networks, at
least one person from each supplier's top management, either the managing
director or the entrepreneur, was interviewed. These people were assumed to
have a good overview of their entire company and its relationships to network partners.

The interviews included mainly open questions. Due to the confidential
nature of some of the issues discussed, the interviews were not recorded on
tape. Non-recording was expected to encourage the respondents to answer as
freely and openly as possible. The interviews took from 1.5 to 3 hours each.

All firms were visited at least once in order to gain an understanding of the
operations and business environment. In addition, content analysis was used
for both official and internal documents.

The authors' analysis was based upon the contingency theory of management accounting. As this theory suggests, many, or even most, of the changes
and improvements in management accounting can be explained through con-
tingencies in the external environment and internal structure, strategy, and
culture of companies.

On the basis of a contingency model, the authors found that open-book
accounting is most likely to work in long-term hierarchical networks that
manufacture functional products, provide a sound infrastructure for open-
book practice, and comprise trust-based network relationships (Kajuter &
Kulmala, 2005).

Mergers and Acquisitions: Multiple Interpretive Cases
Telling the Seller's Side of the Story

Graebner and Eisenhardt (2004) say that most of the research literature in the
area of corporate governance in management has taken the buyer's perspective. Most acquisition studies have focused on the acquirer as the decision
maker of importance and have ignored the seller.

Therefore, the authors chose to explore acquisition from the seller's perspective. Specifically, they wanted to know when and to whom company
leaders sell their firms. Given that this research was exploratory, they
decided to conduct 12 case studies of entrepreneurial firms. They chose
entrepreneurial firms because they say these firms 'are a primary engine of

growth' whose acquisition has emerged as central to the corporate strategy of many corporations.

The research design they chose to use was a multiple case, inductive study involving 12 entrepreneurial firms in the United States. Four firms (three acquired, one not acquired) were chosen in each of three industries: networking hardware, infrastructure software, and online commerce. These industries have significant entrepreneurial activity and yet differ along key dimensions such as cost structure, sales and distribution channels, and customer characteristics. The time period was 1999–2000.

Most of the data were obtained from semi-structured interviews with key acquisition decision makers from both sellers and buyers. The authors also used emails and phone calls to follow up interviews and track real-time acquisition processes, and used archival data, including company websites, business publications, and materials provided by informants. Lastly, the authors used quantitative data on financing rounds. This study illustrates that interpretive case study research can use quantitative as well as qualitative data.

More than 80 interviews were conducted over 14 months. The interviews were 60–90 minutes long. All interviews were tape recorded and transcribed.

The first phase included 15 pilot interviews with managers who had sold their companies, managers who had purchased companies, investors in companies that were sold, and acquisition intermediaries. The pilot interviews indicated that the selling firm's acquisition decisions are usually made by a very small set of people, typically the CEO and two or three key executives and/or board members. Other individuals at the selling firm will have limited, if any, awareness of the events taking place. This pattern reflects the sensitive nature of acquisition decisions and is consistent with prior evidence that awareness of a firm's strategy declines rapidly below the top management team.

In the second phase, multiple senior-level informants in the selling and buying firms were interviewed. The pilot interviews provided guidance in identifying the most influential informants in the acquisition process. To ensure further that the sample included the most important individuals, 'snowball sampling' was used. The initial entry was made through either the CEO of the selling firm or the head of business development at the buying firm, if applicable. This contact then identified other individuals who had been actively involved in the acquisition with both the buyer and seller. These individuals then identified others, as appropriate.

As is typical in inductive research, the data were analysed by first building individual case studies synthesizing the interview transcripts and archival data. A central aspect of case writing was 'triangulation' between each interview and archival sources to create a richer, more reliable account.

The case histories were used for two analyses: within-case and cross-case. The within-case analysis focused on developing constructs and relationships to describe the process experienced by a single focal firm. A core aspect of the inductive process was that it allowed constructs to emerge from the data during this process, rather than being guided by specific hypotheses.

Cross-case analysis began after all cases were finished. Using standard cross-case analysis techniques, similar constructs and relationships across multiple cases were looked for. Tentative propositions were developed by grouping the firms according to the potential variables of interest. Case pairs were compared to identify similarities and differences. Emerging relationships were refined through replication logic, revisiting the data often to see if each separate case demonstrated the same pattern, using charts and tables to facilitate comparisons. The analysis process was iterative and lasted six months. From this process a framework emerged describing when acquisitions occur from the seller's perspective.

The key contribution of this study was to propose an emergent framework of when acquisition occurs from the seller's perspective. The authors framed acquisition as a courtship, emphasizing that acquisition is a process of mutual agreement between buyer and seller, and encompasses timing and strategic and emotional factors, not just price (Graebner & Eisenhardt, 2004).

Responding to Schedule Changes in Supply Chains: Multiple Case Studies in Operations Management

A supply chain is a network of plants and logistical resources producing the materials, components, assemblies, and final product for various customers. With the trend of mass customization and personalization, more and more products – from personal computers and customized bicycles to automobiles – are being made through build-to-order (BTO) supply chains. Krajewski, Wei, and Tang (2005) say that, unlike a typical assembly-to-order environment where customers can only choose from a small set of pre-configured end products, a BTO supply chain allows each customer to configure a final product from a personalized subset of components.

In this study, the authors focused on the short-term dynamics in BTO supply chains brought on by changes in the replenishment shipping schedules of members in the chain. They explored the reaction strategies that suppliers use to respond to short-term dynamics in BTO supply chains, and also looked at the power relations between a buyer and supplier.

The authors studied five firms in the microcomputer industry involved in the production of notebook computers and their components in Taiwan. The microcomputer industry was selected because of the prevalent use of BTO supply chains and because short-term dynamics in this industry create a challenging environment.

As can be seen, the authors decided to use multiple cases to address the research question. In this multiple case study design, the cases were treated as a series of experiments that confirm or disconfirm the emerging conceptual insights. Data were obtained primarily via structured interviews.

With regard to their data analysis, the authors first of all conducted within-case analysis, where members of the research team discussed the elements of reaction strategies and the short-term process flexibility and supplier power relationships. Then a cross-case analysis was conducted to denote the differences and similarities between the cases. The cross-case analysis provided the basis for developing the study's propositions.

In their research article, the authors describe the various reaction strategies of the various firms in the BTO supply chain and make some recommendations for best practice. In summary, the study shows that high short-term process flexibility can be used to competitive advantage by offering flexible supply contracts and supporting that linkage with frequent schedule revisions, even though finished goods inventories must be maintained (Krajewski et al., 2005).

EXERCISES

1   Look in the business pages of your local newspaper and find an interesting story about a new company, product, or service. Try to find other related articles in the paper and obtain as much publicly available information related to your story as you can (e.g. the latest annual report of the company). Are there one or more theories that you think might be relevant to the story? Write up a mini-case that attempts to explain your data in the light of your chosen theory.

2   Conduct a brief literature search using Google Scholar or some other bibliographic database and see if you can find some case study research articles in your chosen field. What kinds of topics appear?

3   Now narrow your search to one of the top journals in your field that has a reputation for publishing qualitative research (e.g. *Academy of Management Review, Accounting, Organizations and Society, Journal of Consumer Research, MIS Quarterly,* etc.). How many articles using case study research can you find over the past 2–3 years?

4   Evaluate some of the articles you found earlier. Do the articles adopt a positivist, interpretive, or critical approach?

5   Evaluate some of these same articles. Did the authors rely mostly on data from interviews? Did the authors use data from the use of other data-gathering techniques? What approach to data analysis did they use?

6   Brainstorm to come up with a list of three or four possible practical research topics. How could these topics be studied using case study research?
7   Find one or more faculty members at your institution or at a conference who conducts case study research. Ask them what topics they are working on right now, and why.

Further Reading

Articles

An article by Walsham (1995) discusses how interpretive case studies can be evaluated. The article by Klein and Myers (1999), as mentioned earlier, suggests a set of principles by which interpretive field studies (both case studies and ethnographies) can be evaluated.

Books

One of the best books on case study research is the classic book entitled *Case Study Research: Design and Methods* by Yin (2003). This book provides an excellent introduction to the case study research method. However, you should keep in mind that Yin, by and large, adopts a positivistic approach to case study research.

Another book by Yin entitled *Applications of Case Study Research* provides a companion to the first (Yin, 2002). This book discusses numerous completed case studies on a variety of topics and includes examples using specific case study techniques and principles.

Websites on the Internet

- The Qualitative Report includes a few useful articles on case study research. This resource is freely available at http://www.nova.edu/ssss/QR/index.html
- More references are available at www.qual.auckland.ac.nz

ETHNOGRAPHIC RESEARCH

Objectives

By the end of this chapter, you will be able to:

- Understand the purpose of ethnographic research
- Appreciate the unique features of ethnographic research
- Be more confident in doing ethnographic research
- Identify the advantages and disadvantages of ethnographic research
- Evaluate ethnographic research studies
- See how ethnographic research has been used in business and management

INTRODUCTION

Ethnographic research is one of the most in-depth research methods possible. As the researcher is there for a reasonable amount of time – and sees what people are doing as well as what they say they are doing – ethnography is well suited to providing researchers with rich insights into the human, social, and organizational aspects of business organizations. Ethnography provides a researcher with the opportunity to get close to 'where the action is'. It enables a researcher to understand the broader context within which people work (Myers, 1999).

Spradley (1980) describes the value of ethnography as follows:

> Ethnography is an exciting enterprise. It reveals what people think and shows us the cultural meanings they use daily. It is the one systematic approach in the social sciences that leads us into those separate realities which others have learned and which they use to make sense out of their worlds ... Ethnography offers us the chance to step outside our narrow cultural backgrounds, to set aside our socially inherited ethnocentrism, if only for a brief period, and to apprehend the world from the viewpoint of other human beings who live by different meaning systems. (pp. vii–viii)

Ethnographic research should be the research method of choice if you are planning to study organizational culture. This is because organizational culture includes not just the explicit values and behaviours of the members of an organization, but also taken-for-granted assumptions that are virtually impossible to discover if you are there for only a short time. If you obtain your data primarily from interviews, as in case study research, you will only ever scratch the surface of the culture of an organization. Hence the need for ethnographic research: it is the only method that enables a researcher to spend long enough in the field such that he or she can start to discern the unwritten rules of how things work or how they are supposed to work. These unwritten rules are seldom verbalized, but can be discovered by patient ethnographic fieldwork.

The method of discovery is one where everything is seen in its context. Context is crucial for an ethnographer. In many quantitative research methods, context is treated as either a set of interfering variables that need controlling, or as 'noise' in the data. In other words, the context gets in the way and is something of a nuisance. In ethnographic research, however, context is the very thing that is being sought after (Harvey & Myers, 1995). Understanding actions and beliefs in their proper context provides the key to unravelling the unwritten rules and taken-for-granted assumptions in an organization. In a sense, context is thus the glue which holds our socially constructed reality together. The key task of the ethnographer is to observe and analyse this context so that meaning in context can be obtained.

The main purpose of ethnographic research in business settings is thus to obtain a deep understanding of people and their culture. The distinguishing feature of ethnography is fieldwork. The ethnographer 'immerses himself in the life of people he studies' (Lewis, 1985: 380) and seeks to place the phenomena studied in their social and cultural context.

IN THE AGE OF THE SMART MACHINE

Shoshana Zuboff, a professor at Harvard Business School, published what is regarded by many as one of the most insightful books that has ever been written about the nature of work, information technology, and organizations (Zuboff, 1988). This book is so insightful because Zuboff used ethnographic research to immerse herself in the life of the companies she studied.

Zuboff suggested that information technology could be used in two different ways. First, it could be used to automate work, leading to dull jobs with lack of meaning. However, it could also be used to 'informate', leading to more stimulating, challenging jobs, with greater satisfaction on the part of employees. When her book was first published in 1988, the 'informating' potential of IT was not really appreciated.

A Brief History of Ethnographic Research

Ethnographic research comes from the discipline of social and cultural anthropology. Ethnographers seek to place the phenomena studied in their social and cultural context. Given that much recent business research has focused on the social, organizational, and cultural aspects of business, ethnographic research has emerged as one important means of studying these contexts.

The first anthropologist to adopt the ethnographic research method was Bronislaw Malinowski, who in 1922 published his now famous book *Argonauts of the Western Pacific*. This book was based on Malinowski's fieldwork among the Trobriand Islanders. It is useful to understand why Malinowski adopted this approach (for more detail, see Darnell, 1974; Kuper, 1973).

Before Malinowski, anthropologists had collected volumes of material from non-Western cultures and societies all around the world. However, despite this vast collection of material, very little of it made any sense to Western observers. The social and cultural practices in other cultures seemed strange and 'primitive', if not frightening. An anthropologist would typically document a particular cultural practice (e.g. sorcery), and then try to explain it by comparison with other practices of the same kind in other cultures. Thus, Frazer's *The Golden Bough*, first published in 1890, was an encyclopedic collection of various cultural practices from around the globe (Frazer, 1980).

Where Malinowski departed from previous researchers was in suggesting that cultural practices from other societies could only be understood by studying the context in which they took place. All previous research had simply taken various cultural practices out of context – and that is why they appeared strange. By learning the local language and living in a society for at least one year, by trying to understand the meaning of particular cultural practices in context, only then would other cultures and societies start to make sense to Western observers (Harvey & Myers, 1995).

After Malinowski's lead, the ethnographic research method involving intensive fieldwork became established in anthropology as the dominant form of research. Anthropologists coined the term 'ethnocentrism' to refer to the tendency of people in most cultures to think of their own culture as the best and most sensible. A good ethnography, however, was one which 'sensitized' the reader to the beliefs, values, and practices of the natives in another society. If, after reading the ethnography, actions which were previously seen as absurd, strange, or irrational 'made sense', then that ethnography had achieved its purpose (Harvey & Myers, 1995).

We can see, then, that there are significant differences between ethnographic research and case study research. The main difference is the length of time that the investigator is required to spend in the field and the extent to which the researcher immerses him- or herself in the life of the social group under study. In anthropology, an ethnographer is usually expected to spend at least one year doing fieldwork, living with the people, and learning about their way of life. For someone doing ethnography in a business or organizational setting, the time required for fieldwork may not be as much as one full year, since the researcher will normally speak the same language as those who are studied. However, the researcher will normally spend at least six months during fieldwork. This compares with a case study researcher, who might spend only a few weeks or months investigating one or more companies.

Another difference between case study research and ethnographic research is the orientation of the researcher. Whereas a case study researcher *studies* people, an ethnographer *learns from* people. An ethnographer learns the way other people see, hear, speak, think, and act (Spradley, 1980). The ethnographer becomes a student of other people's culture.

A third difference between case study research and ethnographic research is the type of data collected. In a case study, the primary source of data is interviews, supplemented by documentary evidence such as annual reports, minutes of meetings, and so forth. In ethnography, these data sources are supplemented by data collected through participant observation or fieldwork. Ethnographies usually require the researcher to spend a long period of time in the 'field' and emphasize detailed, observational evidence (Yin, 2003).

The difference between a case study and ethnography can be illustrated from the research literature. The in-depth case study method was used by Walsham and Waema (1994), who studied a building society. The principal method of data collection was in-depth interviews with a range of organizational participants. The researchers did not use participant observation. The ethnographic research method was used by Orlikowski (1991), who studied a large, multinational software consulting firm over eight months. Data were collected via participant observation, interviews, documents, and informal social contact with the participants.

APPROACHES TO ETHNOGRAPHIC RESEARCH

There are many different schools or types of ethnography (see Clifford & Marcus, 1986; Van Maanen, 1988). Sanday (1979) divides ethnography into the holistic, semiotic, and behaviouristic schools of thought, and she further divides the semiotic school into thick description and ethnoscience. Each school of thought has a different approach to doing ethnography.

The Holistic School

Most ethnographers of the holistic school say that empathy and identification with the social grouping being observed are needed; they insist that an anthropologist should 'go native' and live just like the local people (e.g. Evans-Pritchard, 1950). The assumption is that the anthropologist has to become like a blank slate in order to fully understand local social and cultural practices. The anthropologist acts like a sponge, soaking up the language and culture of the people under study (Harvey & Myers, 1995).

The Semiotic School

On the other hand, Clifford Geertz, the foremost exponent of the 'thick description' (semiotic) school, says that anthropologists do not need to have empathy with their subjects (Geertz, 1973; 1988). Rather, the ethnographer has to search out and analyse symbolic forms – words, images, institutions, behaviours – with respect to one another and to the whole that they comprise. Geertz argues that it is possible for an anthropologist to describe and analyse another culture without having to empathize with the people. He says that anthropologists need to understand the 'webs of significance' which people weave within the cultural context, and these webs of significance can only be communicated to others by thickly describing the situation and its context (Harvey & Myers, 1995).

Critical Ethnography

Yet another approach is called 'critical ethnography' (Myers, 1997a). Critical ethnography sees ethnographic research as an emergent process, in which there is a dialogue between the ethnographer and the people in the research setting. Critical ethnography also sees social life as constructed in contexts of power (Noblit, 2004). Critical ethnographers tend to 'open to scrutiny otherwise hidden agendas, power centers, and assumptions that inhibit, repress, and constrain. Critical scholarship requires that commonsense assumptions be questioned' (Thomas, 1993: 2–3). For example, Forester (1992) used the critical social theory of Habermas in the development of an approach called critical ethnography. Forester used critical ethnography to examine the facetious figures of speech used by city planning staff to negotiate the problem of data acquisition.

Netnography

Kozinets has suggested the term 'netnography' to describe the study of culture and communities on the Internet (Kozinets, 1997; 1998). Instead of conducting fieldwork in the 'real' world, netnography involves the study of culture through computer-mediated communications. The data are gathered via participant observation and interaction with members of an online community. Kozinets used this particular research method to study consumer behaviour in marketing (Kozinets, 1997; 1998).

HOW TO DO ETHNOGRAPHIC RESEARCH

As we have just seen, there are various approaches to doing ethnographic research. At the one extreme are the more positivistic researchers who see ethnography as a way of describing the real world. An example of this kind of approach is Ellen (1984), who discusses various approaches to doing ethnographic research, preparation for fieldwork, the fieldwork experience, ethical issues, and writing up. At the other extreme are post-modern ethnographers, who treat the writing up of ethnography as akin to writing a novel (Harvey, 1997). Somewhere in between lies the majority of anthropologists, who see ethnography as both a method and a genre (Atkinson, 1990).

Regardless of which kind of ethnographic research you choose to undertake, I have a few practical suggestions that apply to them all.

First, as a general rule you should write up your field notes on a regular basis. These notes can include observations, impressions, feelings, hunches, questions which emerge, and so forth. Hammersley and Atkinson say: 'It is difficult to overemphasize the importance of meticulous note taking. The memory should never be relied upon, and a good maxim is "If in doubt, write it down". It is absolutely essential that one keeps up-to-date in processing notes' (1983: 150). I heartily agree with this advice. In fact I have always found it extremely valuable to be able to go back over my field notes later to see what I was thinking at the start. I have often found that what I considered 'strange' or unusual at the start was no longer so at the end. It is good practice to keep a careful record of one's field notes, otherwise it is possible to forget what was so interesting at an earlier stage of the research.

Another general rule is that an ethnographer should write up an interview as soon as possible. I agree with Patton who suggests that this should be on the same day as the interview itself (Patton, 1990). This is perhaps not quite so important if the interview was taped, but even so, writing a brief summary of the interview is a good idea. If you leave it any longer than one day, then the mind quickly forgets all the details.

Third, I believe it is important for you to be regularly reviewing and developing your ideas as the research progresses. Hammersley and Atkinson suggest the use of analytic memos. They describe these memos as periodic written notes whereby progress is assessed, emergent ideas identified, research strategy is sketched out, and so on. It is all too easy to let one's field notes, and other types of data, pile up day by day and week by week ... it is a grave error to let this work pile up without regular reflection and review. (Hammersley & Atkinson, 1983: 164)

Lastly, since an ethnographer ends up with a huge amount of data, the researcher has to develop strategies to deal with this right from the start. At every step of the way the ethnographer should be summarizing, indexing, and classifying the data as appropriate. One way of doing this would be to use one of the many software tools that are available for analysing qualitative data.

CRITIQUE OF ETHNOGRAPHIC RESEARCH

Advantages and Disadvantages of Ethnographic Research

Like any other research method, ethnography has its advantages and disadvantages.

First, one of the most valuable aspects of ethnographic research is its depth. Because the researcher is 'there' for an extended period of time, the ethnographer sees what people are doing as well as what they say they are doing. Over time the researcher is able to gain an in-depth understanding of the people, the organization, and the broader context within which they work. As Grills points out, by going to 'where the action is' the field researcher develops an intimate familiarity with the dilemmas, frustrations, routines, relationships, and risks that are part of everyday life (Grills, 1998a). The profound strength of ethnography is that it is the most 'in-depth' or 'intensive' research method possible (Myers, 1999).

Second, knowledge of what happens in the field can provide vital information to challenge our assumptions. Ethnography often leads the researcher to question what we 'take for granted'. For example, Hughes, Randall, and Shapiro (1992) show how their ethnographic studies led them to question some widely held assumptions about systems design. They found that the information provided by the ethnography provided a deeper understanding of the problem domain and that conventional principles normally thought of as 'good design' could be inappropriate for cooperative systems. Likewise, Orlikowski's ethnographic (1991) research showed how the use of new information technology led to the existing forms of control in one professional services organization being intensified and fused. This went against much of the information systems research literature at that time which assumed that information technology would transform existing bureaucratic organizational forms and social relations.

One of the main disadvantages of ethnographic research is that it does take a lot longer than most other kinds of research. Not only does it take a long time to do the fieldwork, it also takes a long time to analyse the material and write it up. For most people, this means that probably the best time to do ethnographic research is during their doctoral studies (although I am aware of people in business schools who started their ethnographic research afterwards). Although ethnographic research is very time consuming, it is nevertheless a very 'productive' research method considering the amount, and likely substance, of the research findings (Myers, 1999).

Another disadvantage of ethnographic research is that it does not have much breadth. Unlike a survey, an ethnographer usually studies just the one organization or the one culture. In fact this is a common criticism of ethnographic research – that it leads to in-depth knowledge only of particular contexts and situations. Some would go further and argue that it is impossible to develop more general models from just one ethnographic study. While I agree with the first criticism, I take issue with the second. This latter criticism can be answered in one of two ways. First, the lack of generalizability is more of a limitation due to the novelty of the approach in business and management than it is a limitation per se. Over time, as more ethnographies are completed, it might be possible to develop more general models of the meaningful contexts of various aspects of business organizations. Second, just as it is possible to generalize from one case study to theory (Walsham, 1995; Yin, 2003), so it is possible to generalize from one ethnography to theory. The arguments that have been made in favour of generalization from case studies apply equally well to ethnographies (Klein & Myers, 1999; Myers, 1999).

Yet another disadvantage of ethnographic research is that it can be very difficult to write up the research for publication in a peer-reviewed journal. Ethnographic research leads to the gathering of a significant mass of data, and all of it tends to be holistically related to a specific context. This means that a doctoral dissertation using ethnography will have many related points. The preferred publication format for ethnography is a book.

However, as a general rule, journal articles are regarded much more highly than books in business schools. Singular findings are supposed to be presented in each paper, i.e. each journal article should have just one main 'point'. This means that it is a significant challenge for ethnographers to write up their results within the space constraints of a 20-page journal article.

I discuss writing up in more detail in Chapter 17; however, I will briefly mention one point. One possible solution to this problem is for ethnographic researchers to treat each paper as a part of the whole. That is, an ethnographer has to devise a way to carve up the work in such a way that parts of it can be published separately. Then the issue becomes which part of the story is going to be told in one particular paper. A qualitative researcher has to come to terms with the fact that it is impossible to tell the 'whole story' in any one paper, so he or she has to accept that only one part of it can be told at any one time. One advantage of such a strategy is that there is potential for an ethnographer to publish many papers from just the one period of field-work. Usually it is possible to tell the same story but from different angles.

How to Evaluate Ethnographic Research Studies

Klein and Myers (1999) suggest a set of principles for the conduct and eval-uation of interpretive field studies in information systems (including case studies and ethnographies). While these principles might not apply to all kinds of ethnography, they can at least give some idea of how ethnographic research which takes an interpretive stance can be evaluated. Of course, the only practical way for ethnographic research to be evaluated is by looking at the written report, since it is generally impractical for anyone other than the ethnographer to visit the original fieldwork site.

Rather than summarize the whole Klein and Myers' (1999) article in detail, I will highlight just a few general aspects here. These are important questions to be considered in evaluating the quality of ethnographic research.

Is This a Contribution to the Field?   This is one of the most important aspects to be considered. The worth of an ethnographic study can be judged by the extent to which the author has told us something new. Of course, what is new for one person might not be new for another. The key thing is that the ethno-grapher must convince the publishers of a book or the reviewers and editors who serve on the editorial boards of journals that the findings are new. The ethnographer's main challenge is to convince this audience in particular of the worth of his or her research (Myers, 1999).

Does the Author Offer Rich Insights?   It is vital that any paper purporting to be based on ethnographic research should offer rich insights into the subject mat-ter (Myers, 1999). One way of doing this is to consider whether or not the man-uscript contradicts conventional wisdom. A good example of one paper that does this is the article by Bentley et al. (1992). These researchers found that their ethnographic studies contradicted conventional thinking in information systems design. They found that the conventional principles normally thought of as 'good design' could be inappropriate for cooperative systems.

Has a Significant Amount of Material/Data Been Collected?   As was men-tioned earlier, one of the distinguishing features of ethnographic research is fieldwork. The researcher needs to have been there and lived in the organization for a reasonable length of time. This means that a sufficient amount of empirical material data must have been collected during the period of fieldwork. There should be some evidence of this in any article produced. We would expect to see the subject matter set in its social and historical context, multiple viewpoints expressed, and so forth (Klein & Myers, 1999). Also, it is essential for an article to go beyond the 'official line' promoted by the organization. We need to know if there were any 'hidden agendas', disagreements, and so forth (Myers & Young, 1997). This is because an ethnographer goes behind the scenes, so to speak, and sees the difference between what people say and what they do.

Is There Sufficient Information about the Research Method?   This last aspect is discussed in more detail by Klein and Myers (1999). In essence we need to know how the research instrument (the ethnographer) was calibrated. Anyone reading the published article should be able to evaluate for themselves the 'validity' of the findings. It is vitally important that we know what the researcher did and how.

All of the above aspects help reviewers and editors to evaluate the quality of an ethnographic study. Overall, the most important consideration is for ethnographers to write an account that is convincing and 'plausible' (Prasad, 1997).

EXAMPLES OF ETHNOGRAPHIC RESEARCH

Efficiency in Auditing

Radcliffe (1999) looks at the concept of efficiency in auditing. He says that auditors are called upon to investigate a wide array of government practices, categorizing activities as efficient or inefficient, and then publicly report their findings. However, the concept of efficiency is not a tangible concept. At best it is a concept that can be subject to a wide variety of interpretations.

Radcliffe therefore decided to conduct ethnographic research to look at how efficiency auditing is carried out in practice. He conducted ethnographic fieldwork looking at three audits of varying complexity conducted by the Office of the Auditor General of Alberta, Canada, in the health area. He used a variety of data collection techniques, including interviews, passive observation, and documentary analysis, and also used analytic notes to help systematize the data and analysis. He says that one of the significant benefits of ethnography is its capacity for discovery and surprise.

Radcliffe's ethnographic research provides us with deep insights into efficiency auditing. He says that auditors are very much socially situated, despite the tone of detachment and calm that pervades an audit report. Auditors both reacted to and acted upon their environment. As Radcliffe (1999) explains:

> They attempted to estimate the kind of change which was attainable at a given time, and to encourage that, even though the auditors might themselves prefer a higher ideal or standard. The result was a very practical sort of efficiency audit, one which relied on a sophisticated reading of the environment so as to gauge attainable change. In these cases one year's audit had to be understood in the context of other audits, with knowledge that the auditors were, in many cases, aiming to progressively change their client institutions. (p. 357)

Radcliffe found that efficiency audit reports are strategic reports in that they are written to promote action: 'Yet the Auditor cannot compel change; they merely advise, persuade and monitor' (1999: 359). The efficiency that is recommended is very much a 'contingent efficiency', one which recognizes organizational and social dynamics as much as it does technical procedures of financial administration (Radcliffe, 1999).

Power and Control in International Retail Franchising

International retail companies are increasingly using franchising as a means of entering foreign markets. In this particular research project, Quinn and Doherty (2000) used ethnographic research to provide deep insights into the nature of the international retail franchise relationship, and, in particular, the mechanisms used by the franchiser to control and co-ordinate the international retail franchise network.

The researchers studied a British retail company which used franchising as its principal method of international expansion. An intensive nine-month period was spent within the company whereby participant observation was adopted as the main method of data collection (Quinn & Doherty, 2000). As well as participant observation, the researchers also used in-depth interviews with key decision makers and documentary analysis.

The key contribution of their paper is an examination of the importance of the nature of power and control in the international retail franchise relationship and the ability of the marketing channels and agency theory literatures to explain these issues. They found that where a defined concept and brand are present, coercive sources of power, as advocated by agency theory, can explain power and control in the international retail franchise relationship. Coercive sources of power include such things as enforcing the franchise contract. Conversely, where such conditions are not present, predominantly non-coercive sources of power, as promoted by the marketing channels literature, provide the only source of control (Quinn & Doherty, 2000).

The Speed Trap: Making Ever Faster Decisions to Survive

There is much focus on the part of both managers and scholars on the importance of fast action. The popular business press continually admonishes organizations to move more quickly, labelling those that do not as 'dinosaurs'. Perlow, Okhuysen, and Repenning (2002), however, say that despite the competitive benefits of fast action, achieving such increases in speed can be problematic. It remains unclear how a focus on speed actually affects organizational processes, and whether such a focus actually improves performance.

Therefore the researchers decided to conduct an ethnographic study of how an emphasis on speed affects organizational processes. The setting for the study was a start-up in the Internet industry, a competitive environment in which speed is considered to be essential for success (Perlow et al., 2002). Data were drawn from a 19-month ethnography of the life of Notes.com as it went from four students working out of a fraternity house, to a $125 million enterprise – located in the heart of Silicon Valley, with venture capital funding and a professional CEO – to bankruptcy. Using interviews, observation, and documentary analysis, the authors collected over 10,000 pages of field notes along with many other types of material.

The central contribution of their research was the identification of the 'speed trap', a potential pathology for organizations attempting to make fast decisions. They found that fast decisions were initially quite effective in helping Notes.com achieve its stated growth objectives. However, the early focus on speed – by changing both the internal operations and the competitive environment – trapped Notes.com in a pathological context in which members believed they had to make ever faster decisions to survive (Perlow et al., 2002).

Star Trek's Culture of Consumption

Star Trek is perhaps one of the great consumption phenomena of our time. As Kozinets (2001) describes, *Star Trek* became enormously popular with four spin-off series, nine major motion pictures, and billions of dollars in licensed merchandise revenues.

Kozinets, a marketing researcher, decided to use ethnography to study *Star Trek*'s sub culture of consumption. He collected data from three sites over a period of 20 months, including participant observation at various fan gatherings and fan-related meetings. He also used a variety of data gathering techniques, including the use of email interviews with 65 self-proclaimed *Star Trek* fans (Kozinets, 2001).

Kozinets's findings inform our understanding of entertainment and mass media consumption. His ethnography portrays a group of devoted consumers socially constructing reality, rather than merely passively consuming a product. He suggests that entertainment products are key conceptual spaces that consumers in contemporary society use to construct their identities and their sense of what matters in life. The findings of his research indicate that articulations of morality and community are not only important marketing acts, but also essential components of the meanings and practices that structure consumption practices on a cultural and sub cultural level (Kozinets, 2001).

Exercises

1 Become an ethnographer for a few hours and conduct some fieldwork. Attend a cultural, entertainment, or sports event that you would not normally attend (so that you are an 'outsider') and observe carefully what happens. To help you in your fieldwork, think of questions such as: What kind of people are attending? What are people wearing? What are they doing and saying (write down specific quotes or phrases that you consider important)? Are there any ceremonies or rituals being performed? If so, what do they mean? Why are people doing this? To answer the last question you may need to ask someone! (Note: Please ask your instructor if you need ethics permission for this exercise.)

2 Write up your field notes from the first exercise. Can you think of one or more theories that help to explain what you found? Which one do you think is the best?

3 If you were to conduct ethnographic research in a company, how would you go about gaining entry into the company? What difficulties might you encounter, and how might these be overcome?

4 Conduct a brief literature search using Google Scholar or some other bibliographic database and see if you can find some ethnographic research articles in your chosen field. What kinds of topics appear?

5 Evaluate some of the articles you found in the previous exercise. What type of ethnographic research are they? Did the authors rely mostly on data from their fieldwork? Did the authors use data from the use of other data gathering techniques?

6 Brainstorm to come up with a list of three or four possible research topics. How could these topics be studied using ethnographic research?

7 Find one or more faculty members at your institution or at a conference who conduct ethnographic research. Ask them what topics they are working on right now, and why.

Further Reading

Books

Two books which give an excellent introduction to the ethnographic research method are those by Geertz (1973) and Van Maanen (1988). The first is entitled *The Interpretation of Cultures* and the second *Tales of the Field: On Writing Ethnography*. Both are written by anthropologists.

There are quite a few books which give much practical guidance with regard to the doing of ethnography (e.g. Atkinson, 1990; Ellen, 1984; Fetterman, 1998; Grills, 1998b; Hammersley & Atkinson, 1983; Thomas, 1993). Of these, I believe that the book by Hammersley and Atkinson (1983) entitled *Ethnography: Principles in Practice* is one of the best. My own article entitled 'Investigating information systems with ethnographic research' (Myers, 1999) gives a brief overview of the potential of ethnographic research for information systems.

Zuboff's (1988) book entitled *In the Age of the Smart Machine* is regarded by many as the best and most insightful book that has ever been written about the impact of IT on organizations.

Websites on the Internet

There are quite a few useful websites on ethnographic research:

- The Wikipedia entry on ethnography is useful. See http://en.wikipedia.org/wiki/Ethnography
- The Social Science Information Gateway has a section on ethnography and anthropology at http://www.intute.ac.uk/socialsciences/
- Further references are available at www.qual.auckland.ac.nz

GROUNDED THEORY

Objectives

By the end of this chapter, you will be able to:

- Understand the purpose of grounded theory
- Appreciate how grounded theory differs from other qualitative research methods
- Identify various approaches to grounded theory
- Be more confident in using grounded theory
- Recognize the advantages and disadvantages of grounded theory
- Evaluate grounded theory research studies
- See how grounded theory research has been used in business and management

INTRODUCTION

Grounded theory is a qualitative research method that seeks to develop theory that is grounded in data systematically gathered and analysed. According to Martin and Turner (1986), grounded theory is 'an inductive, theory discovery methodology that allows the researcher to develop a theoretical account of the general features of a topic while simultaneously grounding the account in empirical observations or data'. One of the main differences between grounded theory and other qualitative research methods is its specific approach to theory development – grounded theory suggests that there should be a continuous interplay between data collection and analysis (Myers, 1997c).

Grounded theory is very useful in developing context-based, process-oriented descriptions and explanations of organizational phenomena (Myers, 1997c). It offers relatively well-signposted procedures for data analysis (Urquhart, 1997; 2001) and potentially allows for the emergence of original and rich findings that are closely tied to the data (Orlikowski, 1993). It is this last feature that provides researchers with a great deal of confidence, because for each concept produced, the researcher can point to many instances in the data that relate to it (Urquhart, Lehmann, & Myers, 2006).

Many qualitative researchers in business and management use grounded theory solely as a way of coding their data. As a coding technique, grounded theory is certainly very useful. However, there is more to grounded theory than this; it is also a comprehensive method of theory generation. In fact, one of the attractions of grounded theory for researchers in business and management is the promise that it will help to develop new concepts and theories of business-related phenomena, theories that are firmly grounded in empirical phenomena. Hence, the true potential of grounded theory is only realized if researchers use the method to progress from coding to theory generation (Urquhart et al., 2006).

However, I must admit that I am not a purist when it comes to grounded theory or qualitative research more generally. Thus, if all you want to do is use some of the grounded theory coding techniques for your qualitative data analysis, and some other theory as an overarching framework for your study, then I believe that is acceptable. All qualitative research methods require the researcher to be critical and creative and grounded theory studies are no exception.

> The purpose of grounded theory research in business and management is to develop new concepts and theories of business-related phenomena, where these concepts and theories are firmly grounded in qualitative data.

Defining Grounded Theory

In 1967 Barney Glaser and Anselm Strauss published a seminal work in grounded theory entitled *The Discovery of Grounded Theory* (Glaser & Strauss, 1967). This book outlined a research methodology that aimed at systematically deriving theories of human behaviour from empirical data. It was a reaction against 'armchair' functionalist theories in sociology (Dey, 1999). Subsequently, grounded theory became an accepted qualitative research method within the social sciences, nursing, and many other fields (Annells, 1996; Dey, 1993; Glaser, 1978; Strauss, 1987).

Originally Glaser and Strauss defined grounded theory as '*the discovery of theory from data – systematically obtained and analysed in social research*' (1967: 1).

Some years later Strauss (1987) provided a more detailed definition as follows:

> The methodological thrust of grounded theory is toward the development of theory, without any particular commitment to specific kinds of data, lines of research, or theoretical interests ... Rather it is a style of doing qualitative analysis that includes a number of distinct features ... and the use of a coding paradigm to ensure conceptual development and density. (p. 5)

Strauss and Corbin (1990) describe the kind of theory produced as one which emerges in an iterative fashion:

> A grounded theory is one that is inductively derived from the study of the phenomenon it represents. That is, it is discovered, developed, and provisionally verified through systematic data collection and analysis of data pertaining to that phenomenon. Therefore, data collection, analysis, and theory stand in reciprocal relationship with each other. One does not begin with a theory then prove it. Rather, one begins with an area of study and what is relevant to that area is allowed to emerge. (p. 23)

It can be seen from these various descriptions and definitions that a grounded theory researcher does not start with a set of hypotheses that he or she seeks to test. Grounded theory is not really designed for hypothesis testing. Rather, the concepts and the theory are supposed to emerge from the data. To ensure that the concepts do indeed emerge from the data, as a general rule the researcher should make sure that he or she has *no preconceived theoretical ideas* before starting the research.

This injunction to have no preconceived theoretical ideas before starting the research is sometimes interpreted as meaning that the researcher using grounded theory should not conduct a literature review before starting the empirical research. If this were the case, this would go against the advice of almost every other kind of research including qualitative research. However, the originators of grounded theory did not argue against conducting a literature review per se; they only argued that the grounded theory researcher should make sure that a reading of the prior literature does not stifle creativity (Urquhart et al., 2006). As Strauss and Corbin (1998) explain:

> The researcher brings to the inquiry a considerable background in professional and disciplinary literature ... [But] the researcher does not want to be so steeped in the literature that he or she is constrained and even stifled by it. It is not unusual for students to become enamored with a previous study (or studies) either before or during their own investigations, so much so that they are nearly paralyzed. It is not until they are able to let go and put trust in their abilities to generate knowledge that they finally are able to make discoveries of their own. (pp. 48–9)

From this we can see that it is fine to conduct a literature review before starting a grounded theory study. However, a grounded theory researcher must be careful to avoid having preconceived theoretical ideas about what he or she might find. The key thing is to be creative and have an open mind, particularly in the early stages of the research.

Once the qualitative data have been obtained, the researcher moves on to qualitative data analysis.

APPROACHES TO GROUNDED THEORY

Generally speaking, there are two distinct variants of grounded theory, one advocated by Glaser, the other advocated by Strauss. These two co-founders of grounded theory publicly disagreed about the nature of grounded theory when Strauss and Corbin published their book in 1990.

This book was intended as a 'how to' manual of grounded theory, and contains clear guidelines and procedures. In Glaser's view, however, this formalization is far too restrictive. He believes that the prescriptions may strangle any emergent conceptualizations and force the concepts into a preconceived mould. He felt so strongly about the book that he wrote a rejoinder entitled *Emergence vs. Forcing: Basics of Grounded Theory Analysis* (Glaser, 1992). In this book he claims that Strauss and Corbin are no longer using grounded theory as it was originally intended.

Glaser (1992) sums up his critique as follows:

> If you torture the data long enough, it will give up! ... [In Strauss and Corbin's method] the data is not allowed to speak for itself as in grounded theory, and to be heard from, infrequently it has to scream. Forcing by preconception constantly derails it from relevance. (p. 123)

Urquhart et al. (2006) say that Glaser disagreed with Strauss and Corbin on two fundamental issues. First, Strauss and Corbin (1990) suggested breaking down the coding process into four prescriptive steps (open, axial, selective, and 'coding for process'), whereas Glaser uses just three (open, selective, and theoretical coding). Second, Glaser objected to the use of a coding paradigm and the 'conditional matrix' which are designed to provide ready-made tools for the conceptualization process. Glaser pointed out that to 'force' coding through one paradigm and/or down one conditional path was not grounded theory, but conceptual description, which ignored the emergent nature of grounded theory (Glaser, 1992).

Kendall (1999) provides a good discussion of using both versions; however, the Strauss and Corbin version is arguably the most widely known and used (Strauss & Corbin, 1998). This is probably because many people find the 'ready-made' tools provided by Strauss and Corbin to be quite helpful.

How to Do Grounded Theory Research

After you have collected and transcribed your data, the first stage of qualitative data analysis in grounded theory is called *open coding*. Open coding involves analysing the text (e.g. a sentence or paragraph) and summarizing this text by the use of a succinct code. Open codes are descriptive: that is, they identify, name, and categorize phenomena found in the text. Descriptions are the most basic of conceptual constructs, where analysis has not proceeded beyond identifying concepts at the level of 'categories'.

To avoid simply paraphrasing, Bohm (2004) recommends the use of 'theory-generating' questions when a researcher is doing open coding. Some of his suggested questions are as follows:

- **What?** What is at issue here? What phenomenon is being addressed?
- **Who?** What persons or actors are involved? What roles do they play? How do they interact?
- **How?** What aspects of the phenomenon are addressed (or not addressed)?
- **When?** How long? Where? How much? How strongly?
- **Why?** What reasons are given or may be deduced? (Bohm, 2004: 271)

As you continue to do the open coding, one of the most important activities is one of constant comparison. Grounded theory suggests that you should constantly compare and contrast qualitative data in the search for similarities and differences. This is done by comparing the codes that you produce. To start with, the codes and concepts that are produced have a provisional and tentative character, but as the analysis progresses they become more settled and certain. The differentiated concepts become categories. Categories may have detailed 'properties'.

After open coding, the second stage is the interpretation of categories and properties. This stage is sometimes called *axial coding* or *selective coding* (depending upon which version of grounded theory is being used). The main activity of this stage is to refine the conceptual constructs that might help explain whatever interaction occurs between the descriptive categories (Glaser, 1978).

The third stage, *theoretical coding*, involves the formulation of a theory. The aim is to create inferential and/or predictive statements (often in the form of hypotheses) about the phenomena. This is achieved by specifying explicit causal and/or correlational linkages between individual interpretive constructs. The system of inferences covers the whole of the area under investigation (Urquhart et al., 2006).

Throughout every stage it is important that you put on your critical and creative thinking cap. I have come across quite a few students who assume that, because the grounded theory method provides such detailed procedures for analysing qualitative data, it virtually guarantees the production of results that are valid and rigorous. It is tempting to think that an excellent thesis can be guaranteed, as long as you use the grounded theory method. This idea, however, is a grave mistake. While the grounded theory method helps to bring some standardization and rigour to qualitative data analysis, the use of grounded theory does not guarantee that you will come up with original and interesting results. As Strauss and Corbin (1998) point out, creativity is essential and grounded theory procedures should not be followed in a dogmatic and inflexible manner.

It is important, therefore, to follow the grounded theory procedures carefully, while at the same time trying to foster your own critical and creative inspiration.

CRITIQUE OF GROUNDED THEORY

Advantages and Disadvantages of Grounded Theory

There are many advantages to using grounded theory. Grounded theory is particularly useful for studying regular, repeated processes. If you want to study, for example, the ways in which business investment analysts communicate with their clients, then grounded theory should help you to discover the regular patterns of communication.

The advantages of grounded theory can be summarized as follows:

- It has an intuitive appeal for novice researchers, since it allows them to become immersed in the data at a detailed level.
- It gets researchers analysing the data early.
- It encourages systematic, detailed analysis of the data and provides a method for doing so.
- It gives researchers ample evidence to back up their claims.
- It encourages a constant interplay between data collection and analysis.
- It is especially useful for describing repeated processes, e.g. the communications processes between doctors and patients, or the communications processes between information systems analysts and users.

The main advantage of using grounded theory is perhaps the third one, i.e. it encourages systematic, detailed analysis of the data and provides a method for doing so. For the novice researcher in particular, the detailed guidance provides a certain level of comfort that the data are being analysed in a systematic and rigorous manner. Grounded theory is a 'bottom-up' approach to coding data (Dey, 1993).

However, this advantage of grounded theory is at one and the same time its main disadvantage. My experience is that first-time users of the grounded theory method tend to get overwhelmed at the coding level. The attention to word and sentence-level coding naturally focuses the mind on the detail. Younger, more inexperienced researchers in particular tend to find it difficult to rise above the detail. This means that it can be difficult to 'scale up' to larger concepts or themes; it can be difficult to see the bigger picture. The net result is often the generation of what I would call lower level theories. In fact, the use of grounded theory never leads to grand social theory, nor should it be expected to do so, but this can be frustrating for some people.

It is this aspect of grounded theory that probably explains the tendency, particularly in the business and management disciplines, for researchers to use grounded theory as a coding technique only. I can imagine some people might get frustrated at the level of detail, and as a consequence will choose an existing higher level social theory to help explain their findings. The final written report (a published paper or a thesis) thus combines grounded theory as a research method with the use of some other theory as an overarching framework for the study.

This somewhat limited use of grounded theory might be frowned upon by some grounded theory purists, and I agree with them that it is not using grounded theory to its full potential. I agree that grounded theory, used to its full extent, should be used to generate theories that are well grounded in the data (Urquhart et al., 2006). However, in the final analysis, if the researcher is able to make an original contribution to knowledge and come up with some interesting findings by using the techniques of grounded theory for coding only, then I believe this somewhat limited use of grounded theory can be justified.

How to Evaluate Grounded Theory Research Studies

Generally speaking, there are two fundamental criteria by which all grounded theory studies should be evaluated. The first criterion relates to the rigour and validity of the qualitative data analysis. The second relates to the extent to which the researcher has produced theory.

Some questions with regard to the rigour and validity of the data analysis are:

- Is there a clear chain of evidence linking the findings to the data?
- Are there multiple instances in the data which support the concepts produced?
- Has the researcher demonstrated that he or she is very familiar with the subject area or, as Glaser puts it, is steeped in the field of investigation (Glaser, 1978)?

Some questions with regard to the extent to which the researcher has produced theory are:

- Has the researcher created inferential and/or predictive statements about the phenomena? These statements might be in the form of hypotheses.
- Has the researcher suggested theoretical generalizations that are applicable to a range of situations?

If a grounded theory study demonstrates rigour in the data analysis and makes a theoretical contribution, then we can conclude that the study is an excellent example of the use of the grounded theory method.

EXAMPLES OF GROUNDED THEORY RESEARCH

Management Control Systems in Strategic Investment Decisions

Capital investments create the foundations of the value creation process in organizations and are vital to the enactment of their strategy. In one particular study, Slagmulder (1997) looks at the use of management control systems (MCSs) in the process of making strategic investment decisions (SIDs). Strategic investments are intended to help firms achieve their long-term goals and sustain or reinforce their competitive position by developing new product-market activities and enhancing their capabilities.

Slagmulder says that most previous research on investment decision making has concentrated on the techniques used for project selection and has largely ignored the broader managerial and organizational context in which these decision processes are embedded (Slagmulder, 1997). The purpose of this study, therefore, was to describe and model the design and use of firms' MCSs with regard to SIDs. To limit the scope of the study to a reasonable domain, she focused on one class of business decisions: those concerning strategic capital investment in manufacturing plant and equipment made in decentralized companies.

Slagmulder studied ten research sites at six companies. She conducted a series of in-depth, tape-recorded interviews with 68 individuals. These people were senior executives and operational managers who had been closely involved in particular investment projects. She also obtained data from documents such as investment proposals and strategic plans.

She then analysed these qualitative data using grounded theory procedures. She started with open coding, developing a preliminary set of categories and subcategories in a highly iterative process. Once the categories and subcategories were identified, she then moved to axial and then selective coding. She says the objective at this stage was to code the qualitative data into causal conditions, phenomena, contexts, intervening conditions, action/interaction strategies, and consequences. Finally, a theory was developed which attempts to capture the full richness of the role of MCSs for SIDs in the strategic alignment process (Slagmulder, 1997).

This theory identifies the primary role of the MCSs for SIDs as achieving alignment between the firm's investment stream and its strategy. The theory postulates a process of continuous change in the environmental conditions faced by the firm. These environmental changes require that the firm's MCSs for SIDs be modified to maintain strategic alignment. Thus Slagmulder's main contribution is in showing how a firm's MCSs must not remain static, but rather need to change over time to help achieve the strategic alignment of SIDs (Slagmulder, 1997).

Informal Resource Exchanges Between R&D Researchers Across Organizational Boundaries

Bouty (2000) looks at how R&D scientists regularly exchange proprietary resources across organizational boundaries in order to do their work. She says that individuals meet at conferences or annual meetings or are classmates. They know each other and belong to networks, and they call on each other for assistance in their daily work. On the one hand, past research has proved these informal exchanges across organizational boundaries to be major learning processes that are of great consequence for innovation. On the other hand, resources also flow out of firms through these exchanges. These resources might represent critical breaches of confidentiality from the standpoint of the organization. Bouty says that a tension therefore builds between fostering innovation and retaining intellectual capital. Interpersonal exchanges and the individual decisions that underlie them are at the heart of this tension.

Bouty therefore decided to study these informal exchanges between R&D scientists using grounded theory.

She obtained her data using interviews with researchers who worked in France. These researchers were from different organizations and industrial sectors. These qualitative data were obtained over a nine-month period.

Interviews were carried out in two steps. In an introduction, the purpose of the research was explained and interviewees were asked to describe briefly their jobs, their internal and external networks, and their publication/communication habits. This conversation enabled the development of mutual trust and established a friendly climate. Then the researchers were asked to describe in detail past experiences of resource exchanges with external partners. A total of 128 incidents were recorded (Bouty, 2000).

Bouty says that these incidents were identified and then categorized by theme. Following the principle of constant comparison, each new incident was systematically compared with former ones, in order to decide whether it belonged to an existing category or was the first of a new one. In an emergent, cumulative, and data-driven fashion, fundamental regularities emerged and started to constitute the theoretical framework (Bouty, 2000).

Bouty's study makes a few important theoretical contributions.

First, she found that from an organizational learning perspective, equitable exchanges are preferable: they are richer than profitable ones, and their negative consequences with regard to opportunistic behaviours are limited. Equitable exchanges are richer because needs are openly and accurately taken into account from the start. They also enable key resources to flow in (Bouty, 2000).

Second, from a social capital perspective, informal acquisition of external resources by scientists is essential to firms, but rests on personal considerations. There is no universal rule, no uniform line between individual and organizational interest. The economic interest of a firm and employees' social capital are intertwined.

Third, the resources are imported: they are neither in the scientist's employing firm, nor in any intermediate formal arrangement. These resources reside in the community, where they are shared (Bouty, 2000).

Fourth, the idea of community emerges as a key concept, as important as the concepts of organization and market.

Bouty says there are a few managerial implications of her study. One is that management should not guard against leaks by prohibiting exchanges (Bouty, 2000). These exchanges are very important to the life blood of the firm.

Customers' Desired Value Change

Marketing managers are pushed to adopt customer value strategies in order to grow profits and ensure long-term survival. These strategies require that managers understand what customers want or value from products, services, and supplier relationships.

However, Flint et al. (2002) say that customers periodically change what they value, and for some customers in certain industries, this happens quite rapidly and extensively. Therefore, suppliers cannot depend on what they currently know about customer value to hold into the future. To retain key customers, suppliers are forced either to anticipate what customers will value next, or to be ready to react faster than competitors do to these changes. Both approaches demand that managers recognize and understand the implications of customers' desired value change (CDVC) when they see it (Flint et al., 2002).

Flint and colleagues therefore decided to conduct a grounded theory study in an area they describe as 'emerging customer value research', which focuses mainly on what customers currently value from suppliers.

The authors conducted interviews with influential decision makers involved in purchasing and supplier management. The final sample consisted of 22 participants from nine manufacturing organizations. Interviews took place in participants' offices, all but two of which were located in the upper mid-western United States. The interviews were open-ended and discovery oriented. They were supplemented, when possible, by observation and by analyses of documents provided by participants (Flint et al., 2002).

The authors' analyses of the interview transcripts followed traditional grounded theory procedures. Flint et al. began these analyses early, after the first few interviews, allowing interpretations to inform and direct subsequent interviews. The authors used open, selective, and axial coding, The coding was done using a qualitative data analysis software package called QSR NUD*IST.

Flint et al. found that CDVC is a complex phenomenon, encompassing three interrelated subphenomena: CDVC form/intensity, tension management, and action/interaction strategies (Flint et al., 2002).

Exercises

1 Practice doing open coding. First, find a recent interview of a business person in your local newspaper. Second, analyse the interview line by line. Closely examine each word or phrase. Are there similarities and differences in the data? Are there labels or concepts that can be applied to similar events, objects, actions? Make sure that the label or concept you use is suggested by the context in which the event/object/action occurs.

2 Continue the open coding you started in the previous exercise. This time, examine an entire paragraph. Can you think of categories, codes, or labels that neatly summarize the key point of the paragraph?

3 Continue the open coding you started in the previous exercise. This time, examine the entire interview. Can you think of categories, codes, or labels that summarize the key point of the interview?

4 Brainstorm to come up with a list of three or four possible research topics. Now come up with one or two research questions per topic.
5 Can you think of how some of these topics could be studied using grounded theory? What kinds of data could you use?
6 Conduct a brief literature search using Google Scholar or some other bibliographic database and see if you can find grounded theory articles in your chosen field. What kinds of topics appear?
7 Find one or more faculty members at your institution or at a conference who you know use grounded theory. Ask them what topics they are working on right now, and why.

Further Reading

Books

One of the early classics in grounded theory is the book by Glaser and Strauss (1967). More recently, Glaser and Strauss have disagreed about what grounded theory 'really' is. One view is represented in the book by Strauss and Corbin: the first edition was published in 1990 and the second in 1998. The other view is represented in the book by Glaser (1992).

Two books by Dey (1993; 1999) provide an excellent introduction to grounded theory and explain the data analysis methods in some detail.

Websites on the Internet

There are a few useful websites on grounded theory:

- The Grounded Theory Institute is dedicated to Glaser's view of grounded theory at http://www.groundedtheory.com/. It is a very useful site and provides additional references and materials.
- A short introduction to grounded theory is provided by Steve Borgatti at http://www.analytictech.com/mb870/introtoGT.htm
- More references on grounded theory are available at www.qual.auckland.ac.nz

PART FOUR

DATA COLLECTION TECHNIQUES

Part IV discusses three qualitative data collection techniques, as illustrated in Figure IV.1. Chapter 10 discusses interviews; Chapter 11 discusses participant observation and fieldwork; and Chapter 12 discusses the use of documents. Examples are provided of the use of these techniques in business and management.

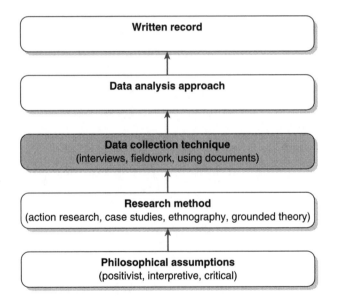

Figure IV.1 Qualitative research design

10 _____ *INTERVIEWS*

Objectives

By the end of this chapter, you will be able to:

- Appreciate the importance of interviews
- Understand different types of interviews
- Recognize potential problems in using interviews
- See how a model of the interview can be used
- Be more confident in using interviews

INTRODUCTION

Interviews are one of the most important data gathering techniques for qualitative researchers in business and management. They are used in almost all kinds of qualitative research (positivist, interpretive, or critical) and are the technique of choice in most qualitative research methods. Interviews allow us to gather rich data from people in various roles and situations. It has been said that qualitative interviews are like night goggles, 'permitting us to see that which is not ordinarily on view and examine that which is looked at but seldom seen' (Rubin & Rubin, 2005).

A good interview helps us to focus on the subject's world. The idea is to use their language rather than imposing one's own. The role of the interviewer is to listen, prompt, encourage, and direct. Overall, the more comfortable interviewees are, and the more they are prepared to open up and talk, the better the disclosure is likely to be. From the perspective of qualitative research, the more interesting the story, the better it is (as long as it does not move into the domain of fiction).

Of course, interviews are just one of many ways to gather data about the world of business and management. Other data collection techniques include the use of participant observation and fieldwork, or some kind of library or archival research. The question then arises: how do you know which data collection technique to use?

Well, some data collection techniques are almost mandatory with certain kinds of research methods. For example, if you are planning to conduct case study research in business and management, then it is almost certain that you will conduct interviews (although the type of interview is up to you). If you are planning to conduct ethnographic research, then it is mandatory to do some fieldwork. This is because fieldwork is one of the defining characteristics of the ethnographic research method. But in many instances, it is up to you to decide which particular data collection techniques to use. It is not obligatory for you to do any archival research with either case study or ethnographic research, but you may decide on the basis of prior knowledge that it is worthwhile to do so. You may consult documents in an archive if you believe that there are relevant documents there.

In summary, the choice of a particular data collection technique will depend upon your earlier choice of a research method, your research topic, and the availability of data. However, another important criterion is the extent to which you are proficient with a particular qualitative data collection technique. The more proficient you are with this particular technique, the most likely you are to use it, and the more valuable it is likely to be. When you are collecting qualitative data, you are the research instrument, and as any experienced musician will tell you, all instruments need to be tuned.

Hence, the next few chapters are designed to tune you up as a qualitative researcher – to help you become proficient with a few data collection techniques. This first chapter in this part of the book is concerned with the use of interviews to gather qualitative data.

Primary and Secondary Data

In the social sciences an important distinction is made between primary and secondary sources of data. Primary sources are those data which are unpublished and which the researcher has gathered directly from the people or organization. Primary data include data from interviews, fieldwork, and unpublished documents such as minutes of meetings and so forth. Secondary data refer to any data which you have gathered that have been previously published. Secondary data include previously published books, newspaper articles, journal articles, and so forth.

An important point I wish to make here is that *primary data add richness and credibility to qualitative manuscripts*. Primary data – data that you have gathered yourself – represent part of the added value that you bring to the table. This is because the primary data you have gathered are unique to you and your particular research project.

Hence, it is very important for you to become familiar with the use of one or more qualitative data collection techniques. It is also important for you to use these techniques well, since your proficiency with them will determine to a large extent the richness of your data. A qualitative researcher should study and practise the techniques before using them, since it is often the case that the researcher might only get one opportunity to attend an important event (if doing fieldwork), or conduct an interview (with a specific person) during the course of the research project.

However, let us assume that you do not take my advice. Imagine that you are tense and ill prepared for a specific interview. How will the interviewee feel during the interview? I would think that at best he or she might feel uncomfortable; at worst, the interviewee might be wishing that the interview would end as soon as possible. If so, then the reality is that you are unlikely to obtain much useful qualitative data from him or her. If your interviewee does not open up during the conversation, then the primary data you collect may be of limited value. Both the quantity and quality of your data will be affected negatively. Of course, if all of your interviews tend to fall into this same pattern, then it might be best to think about doing something else rather than qualitative research! Not everyone is suited to being a qualitative researcher.

On the other hand, if you are prepared to study and practise the use of one or more qualitative data collection techniques, I believe it is possible for most people to become proficient in their use. In this chapter, then, we will discuss how you can become proficient in the use of qualitative interviews. As a general rule, the more proficient you can become, the better your qualitative data will be. The better your qualitative data, the more chance you have of writing an interesting story; and the more interesting the story, the greater chance you have of its being accepted for publication.

TYPES OF INTERVIEWS

Although there are many different kinds of interviews, all interviews can be classified into three basic types. These three types are summarized in Table 10.1.

Structured interviews involve the use of pre-formulated questions, usually asked in a specific order, and sometimes within a specified time limit. Structured interviews require considerable planning beforehand in order to make sure that all the important questions are included in the script from day 1. Conversely, structured interviews minimize the role of the interviewer

Table 10.1 Types of interviews

Structured interviews	The use of pre-formulated questions, strictly regulated with regard to the order of the questions, and sometimes regulated with regard to the time available
Semi-structured interviews	The use of some pre-formulated questions, but no strict adherence to them. New questions might emerge during the conversation
Unstructured interviews	Few if any pre-formulated questions. In effect interviewees have free rein to say what they want. Often no set time limit

during the interview itself, since there is no need for improvisation during the interview. In fact, any departure from the script is usually looked upon with disdain. The whole idea of structured interviews is to ensure consistency across multiple interviews. Structured interviews tend to be used in telephone interviews, with survey research, market research, and political polling, and with intercept research in public places such as shopping malls.

Unstructured interviews are just the opposite. Unstructured interviews involve the use of very few (if any) pre-formulated questions. There may or may not be a time limit (usually not), and interviewees have a free rein to say what they want. In a narrative interview, for example, the key idea is to get the interviewee to narrate freely. Questions are only used to jog his or her memory. However, if the interviewee stops talking and there is a break in the conversation, then the interviewer has to be prepared to improvise. He or she may have to invent a few new questions on the spot, hopefully ones that are related in some way to the subject at hand. There is no attempt to maintain consistency across interviews.

Semi-structured interviews sit somewhere in between structured and unstructured interviews. Semi-structured interviews involve the use of some pre-formulated questions, but there is no strict adherence to them. New questions might emerge during the conversation, and such improvisation is encouraged. However, there is some consistency across interviews, given that the interviewer usually starts with a similar set of questions each time.

One of the major advantages of the structured interview is consistency across interviews. However, this is also one of the major disadvantages of this technique. If you stick religiously to your prepared set of questions, by definition you are unable to pursue any new lines of enquiry that might emerge during the course of the interview. Hence you might miss out on one or more new insights that the interviewee would have given you if only you had been prepared to ask.

One of the major advantages of the unstructured interview is that it allows the interviewee to talk freely and tell you everything that he or she considers to be important. However, this is also one of its major disadvantages. If the interviewee is not in a talkative mood, then he or she may end up saying very little. If the interviewee is too talkative, then you may end up being there all day, while gathering lots of data that may be irrelevant to the topic at hand.

The semi-structured interview is thus the type of interview that tries to take the best of both approaches, while minimizing the risks. It gives you some structure, while allowing for some improvisation. It thus gives the interviewee the opportunity to add important insights as they arise during the course of the conversation, while your previously prepared questions provide some focus as well. The semi-structured type of qualitative interview is the one that is most commonly used in business and management.

Focus Groups

Another way to classify types of interviews is to make a distinction between individual interviews and group interviews. By far the majority of interviews conducted by qualitative researchers in business and management are individual one-on-one interviews (whether in person or over the phone). However, focus group interviews can be used as well.

Although focus group interviews are most commonly used in marketing research, focus groups can be used in almost any disciplinary area.

The purpose of a focus group interview is to get collective views on a certain defined topic of interest from a group of people who are known to have had certain experiences. The interviewer or moderator directs the enquiry and the interaction among respondents. Focus groups allow participants to engage in thoughtful discussion. In fact, 'the method depends on the interaction of the group to stimulate participants to think beyond their own private thoughts and to articulate their opinions. It is in having to formulate, represent, give evidence, receive feedback, and then respond that individuals move beyond the private' (Kleiber, 2004: 91).

Kleiber (2004) also says that focus groups typically bring together between 7 and 12 people for an hour or so to discuss a specific topic. Usually five to six general questions are posed to the group. Focus group moderators should encourage participants to express their points of view in an atmosphere of mutual respect and to facilitate interaction among the participants. It is usually considered mandatory to hold at least three if not more sets of interviews on the same topic with different groups to ensure that themes common across the groups emerge. However, consensus is never a goal of focus groups (Kleiber, 2004).

There are many advantages to focus groups. First, they enable a researcher to elicit opinions, attitudes and beliefs held by members of a group: 'The data generated are typically very rich as ideas build and people work to explain why they feel the way they do' (Kleiber, 2004: 97). Second, they enable a researcher to have more control than in participant observation, but less control than in face-to-face interviewing (Kleiber, 2004).

One disadvantage of focus groups is that they are often time intensive and expensive to run (Kleiber, 2004).

Fontana and Frey (2005), citing Merton and colleagues, note three specific problems with focus groups:

(a) The interviewer must keep one person or small coalition of persons from dominating the group,

(b) The interviewer must encourage recalcitrant respondents to participate, and

(c) The interviewer must obtain responses from the entire group to ensure the fullest coverage of the topic. (p. 704)

FOCUS GROUP INTERVIEWS IN MARKETING

In a case study of wedding planning, three marketing researchers explored the concept of consumer ambivalence. Same-sex focus group interviews were conducted with brides and grooms (two each of brides and grooms). Group sizes ranged from six to ten. The focus group interviews lasted 60–90 minutes, were videotaped, and the conversations from the videotapes were transcribed and analysed. The focus group interviews helped the authors to explore wedding artefacts, scripts, performance roles, and the role of the audience, and also to generate questions for the in-depth phases of the study.

As well as focus group interviews, the researchers used in-depth interviews and shopping trips to gather qualitative data (Otnes, Lowrey, & Shrum, 1997).

POTENTIAL PROBLEMS USING INTERVIEWS

Although many interviews will turn out to be unproblematic, there are potential difficulties, problems, and pitfalls that can arise. Some of these potential difficulties, as listed by Myers and Newman (2007), are summarized in Table 10.2.

A MODEL OF THE INTERVIEW

In an effort to overcome some of the potential difficulties listed in the table, some qualitative researchers have suggested using a dramaturgical model of the interview (Gubrium & Holstein, 2002; Hermanns, 2004; Holstein &

Table 10.2 Potential difficulties, problems, and pitfalls of interviews (adapted from Myers & Newman, 2007)

Artificiality of the interview	The qualitative interview involves interrogating someone who is a complete stranger; it involves asking subjects to give or to create opinions under time pressure
Lack of trust	As the interviewer is a complete stranger, there is likely to be a concern on the part of the interviewee with regard to how much the interviewer can be trusted. This means that the interviewee may choose not to divulge information that he or she considers to be 'sensitive'. If this is potentially important information for the research, the data gathering remains incomplete
Lack of time	The lack of time for the interview may mean that the data gathering is incomplete. However, it can also lead to the opposite problem – of subjects creating opinions under time pressure (when these opinions were never really held strongly to start with). In this case more data are gathered but the data gathered are not entirely reliable
Level of entry	The level at which the researcher enters the organization is crucial (Buchanan, Boddy, & McCalman, 1988). For example, if a researcher enters at a lower level, it may prove difficult if not impossible to interview senior managers at a later date. In some organizations, talking to union members can bar access to management and vice versa. Additionally, gatekeepers may inhibit the researcher's ability to access a broader range of subjects
Elite bias	A researcher may interview only certain people of high status (key informants) and will therefore fail to gain an understanding of the broader situation. Miles and Huberman (1994) talk about the bias introduced in qualitative research by interviewing the 'stars' in an organization
Hawthorne effects	Qualitative interviews are intrusive and can potentially change the situation. The interviewer is not an invisible, neutral entity; rather, the interviewer is part of the interactions he or she seeks to study and may influence those interactions (Fontana & Frey, 2000)
Constructing knowledge	Naive interviewers may think that they are like sponges, simply soaking up data that are already there. They may not realize that, as well as gathering data, they are also actively constructing knowledge (Fontana & Frey, 2000). In response to an interviewer, interviewees construct the story – they are reflecting on issues that they may have never considered so explicitly before. Interviewees usually want to appear knowledgeable and rational, hence the need to construct a story that is logical and consistent

(Cont'd)

Table 10.2

Ambiguity of language	The meaning of the interviewer's words is often ambiguous, and it is not always certain that subjects fully understand the questions. Fontana and Frey say that: 'Asking questions and getting answers is a much harder task than it may seem at first. The spoken or written word has always a residue of ambiguity, no matter how carefully we word the questions or how carefully we report or code the answers' (2000: 645)
Interviews can go wrong	Interviews are fraught with fears, problems, and pitfalls. It is possible for an interviewer to offend or unintentionally insult an interviewee, in which case the interview might be abandoned altogether (Hermanns, 2004).

Table 10.3 The qualitative interview as a drama (adapted from Myers & Newman, 2007)

Concepts	Description
Drama	The interview is a drama with a stage, props, actors, an audience, a script, and a performance
Stage	A variety of organizational settings and social situations, although in business settings the stage is normally an office. Various props might be used such as pens, notes, or a tape recorder
Actor	Both the interviewer and the interviewee can be seen as actors. The researcher has to play the part of an interested interviewer; the interviewee plays the part of a knowledgeable person in the organization
Audience	Both the interviewer and the interviewee can be seen as the audience. The researcher should listen intently while interviewing; the interviewee(s) should listen to the questions and answer them appropriately. The audience can also be seen more broadly as the readers of the research paper(s) produced
Script	The interviewer has a more or less partially developed script with questions to put to the interviewee to guide the conversation. The interviewee normally has no script and has to improvise
Entry	Impression management is very important, particularly first impressions. It is important to dress up or dress down depending upon the situation
Exit	Leaving the stage, possibly preparing the way for the next performance (finding other actors – snowballing) or another performance at a later date
Performance	All of the above together produce a good or a bad performance. The quality of the performance affects the quality of the disclosure which in turn affects the quality of the data

Gubrium, 1995; Myers & Newman, 2007). The dramaturgical model treats the individual interview as a drama.

The drama (the interview) has a stage, props, actors, an audience, a script, an entry, and an exit. The quality of the performance affects the extent to which the interviewee discloses important information which in turn affects the quality of the data (Myers & Newman, 2007). The various dramaturgical concepts as applied to the qualitative interview are summarized in Table 10.3.

The Drama

The entire qualitative interview can be seen as a drama. As in a drama, the interviewer has to give stage directions and pay attention to stage management. This means that the interviewer should clearly explain the purpose of the interview and what he or she hopes to achieve. However, the interviewer must be careful not to over-direct the performance, as he or she has to allow for some improvisation (Myers & Newman, 2007). This is especially the case with semi-structured or unstructured interviews, where the main idea is to allow the interviewee to talk freely about the subject in question. As a stage director, the interviewer has to learn to deal with different kinds of behaviour from interviewees:

> Interviewees may show off (the subject exaggerates their importance to you or their company), on the other hand they may be shy (the subject that answers in mono syllables) or awed (e.g. may perceive a high social gulf between the researcher and themselves). Interviewees may treat the interview as a confessional/cathartic experience (some subjects reveal sensitive, confidential information, either about themselves or their company), on the other hand they may be bored (with a disinterested subject, it may be impossible to penetrate their front) or fatigued (e.g. over-researched subjects). Lastly, interviewees may try to reverse roles and probe the interviewer for information about others in the organization. (Myers & Newman, 2007: 12–13)

The key point here is that the interviewer is the stage director, and he or she should attempt to keep the interview under a reasonable amount of control.

The Stage

The stage is the location in which the interview takes place. The stage can be a variety of organizational settings and social situations. In qualitative research concerning business and management, the stage is usually an office.

The first thing that needs to be done is to set the stage. When you are in the process of organizing the interview, it is important to set clear expectations as to what the interview is about with the person you are planning to interview. The setting usually involves the physical layout of the office and other stage props (e.g. the office furniture).

It is important that the stage itself helps to create a productive atmosphere. Usually, an informal, quieter setting is best. You should also be aware of the difference between the front stage and back stage:

> The back stage is all the informal activity and chatting that happens before or after the interview per se (e.g. if a tape recorder was used, the informal chats

would normally not be taped). Once the interview begins, and the tape rolls, then both parties are front stage. The trick is to ensure that all the backstage activities beforehand help both parties to move seamlessly into a solid performance once the tape starts to roll. (Myers & Newman, 2007: 13)

If the interviewee asks me if I would like some coffee or tea, my usual response is to say yes. This is because it already sets a more relaxed tone to the interview. It also allows for more informal interaction to take place before the formal part of the interview begins.

The Actor(s)

Both the interviewer and the interviewee can be seen as actors. The researcher has to play the part of an interested interviewer; the interviewee plays the part of a person knowledgeable about the subject matter. It is very important for the interviewee to take the researcher seriously. The researcher can help matters by dressing appropriately, making sure that he or she is knowledgeable about the organization beforehand, and by conducting the interview in a professional manner (Myers & Newman, 2007).

In the interview it is important for the interviewer (the actor) to show empathy, understanding, and respect to the interviewee. The interviewer also has to create space for the interviewee, since the whole idea of an interview is for the interviewee to describe the world in his or her own words. An interviewer who talks too much is likely to stifle the interviewee and to call into question the purpose of the interview.

The Audience

Both the interviewer and the interviewee can be seen as the audience (depending upon who is acting at the time). The researcher should listen intently while interviewing; the interviewee(s) should listen to the questions and answer them appropriately (Myers & Newman, 2007).

More broadly, the academic community and the readers of the research paper(s) produced may be seen as the audience, although in practice the academic community may only see a short excerpt from each interview (e.g. a quotation in the published article).

The Script

Depending upon the type of interview, the interviewer has a fully or partially developed script with questions to be put to the interviewee. If the interviewer is using an unstructured interview, then much more improvisation is required on his or her part. Improvisation is required to ensure that the interview flows freely and there are no major gaps in the conversation. The interviewee normally has no script and has to improvise throughout the interview.

No matter what type of interview you use, you should at the very least prepare the opening (introducing yourself), prepare the introduction (explain the purpose of the interview), and prepare a few key questions. Esterberg (2002) says a qualitative researcher can legitimately ask people questions about the following:

- Their experiences or behaviours
- Their opinions or values
- Their feelings
- Their factual knowledge
- Their sensory experiences
- Their personal background. (p. 95)

However, you should not over-prepare the script, since the qualitative interviewer should usually be reasonably open and flexible. You should be prepared to explore interesting lines of research if such opportunities arise (Myers & Newman, 2007), unless, of course, you are using structured interviews.

The Entry

One's entry to the stage is important. First impressions can dramatically affect the rest of the interview (either positively or negatively). It may be important to dress up or dress down depending upon the situation. The key point is to make the interviewees feel comfortable as soon as possible, and to minimize social dissonance. If interviewees feel uncomfortable, they are unlikely to take you into their confidence.

The Exit

The exit involves leaving the stage and closing the interview. The researcher may want to mention at this point that he or she will provide feedback to the subjects. Also, it might be a good idea to ask permission to follow up, if needed. Additionally, it is usually a good idea to ask who else the interviewee recommends that might be interviewed. This technique (called snowballing) is a very useful one, where interviewing one person leads to another, which in turn leads to another. Snowballing helps the researcher to gain access to other interviewees and to obtain a critical mass of interview data (Myers & Newman, 2007).

The Performance

All of the elements of the drama together produce a good or a bad performance. The quality of the performance affects the quality of the disclosure, which in turn affects the quality of the data.

Limits of the Dramaturgical Model

Although I believe that the dramaturgical model of the interview is very helpful, particularly for those who are new to qualitative research and qualitative interviewing, the model does have its limitations.

The dramaturgical model could potentially encourage manipulative and cynical behaviour for one's own ends. Manning (1992) suggests that the dramaturgical model sees the world as one in which 'people, whether individually or in groups, pursue their own ends in a cynical disregard for others'. The individual can be seen as 'a set of performance masks hiding a manipulative and cynical self' (Manning, 1992: 44). The interviewer could become an actor whose sole aim is to manipulate the interviewee into disclosing important information.

I acknowledge that, if taken to extremes, the dramaturgical model could lead to unethical behaviour. Hence, I believe that this chapter should be read in conjunction with Chapter 5, where the ethical principles related to research are discussed. Seeing the interview as a drama is a useful metaphor, but it should not be taken too far.

Ensuring a Good Performance

The two most important interviewing skills are eliciting and listening skills. The term 'eliciting' is used rather than questioning, because the questions are merely a prompt. Often it is better to avoid direct questioning (Chrzanowska, 2002).

Eliciting Skills

All interviewers should be very familiar with the difference between open and closed questions. Generally speaking, you should try to use open questions in interviews. Open questions take the form 'who', 'what', 'why', 'where', 'when', 'how', and usually lead to answers that are open ended and more descriptive.

Closed questions usually lead to 'yes or no' answers, and quickly stifle the conversation. They take the form 'are', 'have', 'do', or 'did'.

For example, let us assume I asked you the following question: 'Do you play football?' As this is a closed question, your answer is likely to be just 'yes' or 'no'. You may add an additional sentence, but this is optional. On the other hand, let us assume I asked you: 'Why do you play football?' As this is an open question, it invites a more open-ended and descriptive answer.

Hence, you will obtain much more qualitative data if you use open questions. However, closed questions are useful for confirming factual information or for bringing the interview to a close.

Listening Skills

Listening is much more difficult than it might seem at first. It takes much effort and skill to become a good listener. Chrzanowska (2002) comments:

> An interviewer needs to follow the content of what is being said, listen to the meaning underneath the words, and then gently bring this into the conversation. He or she offers or reflects back what they have heard, so that the respondent can confirm, deny, or elaborate. This way of working creates empathy, deepens the conversation and ensures the meaning has been understood. (p. 112)

PRACTICAL SUGGESTIONS FOR INTERVIEWING

As well as using the dramaturgical model in interviews, I have a few additional practical suggestions for interviewing:

- In qualitative research it is a good idea to try to interview a variety of people representing diverse views. Finding different subjects is called 'triangulation of subjects' (Rubin & Rubin, 2005: 67) where the idea is to obtain a certain breadth of opinion. Not all respondents think alike. Triangulation of subjects is a broader version of Miles and Huberman's injunction to avoid elite bias (Miles & Huberman, 1994).
- It can be helpful to construct an interview guide for use in talking with interviewees. Even if you are intending to use unstructured interviews, you should still be well prepared beforehand. DeMarrais (2004) suggests three guidelines for constructing interview questions:

1 Short, clear questions lead to detailed responses from participants.
2 Questions that ask participants to recall specific events or experiences in detail encourage fuller narratives.
3 A few broad, open-ended questions work better than a long series of close-ended questions.

- In qualitative interviews it is usually a good practice to use mirroring. Mirroring involves taking the words and phrases the subjects use in order to construct a subsequent question or comment. This technique allows you to focus on their world and their language, rather than imposing your own (Myers & Newman, 2007).
- You should be flexible and open to new ideas and lines of enquiry. This is often where the added value of interviews lies. The one exception to this is if you are using structured interviews.
- As a general rule it is a good idea to tape interviews. The main benefit of taping is that you have a record of the exact words spoken by the interviewee. If you have the exact words, then it is possible to provide a quote of what the interviewee said in your thesis or article. An exact quote is so much more credible than a paraphrase of what someone else said. However, there are two possible disadvantages of taping interviews. One disadvantage is that it can take a long time to transcribe the tapes – my experience is that it takes most people, on average, about eight hours to transcribe a one-hour interview. This can be mitigated if you can get research funding to pay for transcription (although I recommend that all qualitative researchers should transcribe some of their own tapes, mostly for the experience of doing so). The second disadvantage is that if the subject matter is highly sensitive, the person you are interviewing may be reluctant to talk about some of the matters on tape. If you tape the interview, you may end up with little qualitative data of value. On the other hand, if you do not tape the interview, the person may open up and provide a free and frank discussion of the topic.
- If you decide for whatever reason not to tape the interview, it is always a good idea to take brief notes during the interview (as long as you check that this is all right with the interviewee) and to write up as full an account as possible immediately afterwards. If you are not taping, your aim should be to write up the interview as soon as you get back to the office. You should not let anything interfere with your writing up. If you write up straight away, using your brief notes as a guide, you will find that you can remember most of the conversation including many of the details. However, if you delay writing up, even for a few hours, it is amazing how quickly your mind can forget the details. The longer you leave it, the less you will remember. One rule you should always follow is to write up an interview on the same day that the interview took place (at the latest by the end of the day). If you leave it until the following day, it is questionable as to whether the interview will provide any value at all. Even if you tape an interview, you may find it valuable to write up a brief summary of the interview on one page. This is because, if you are conducting many interviews, there may be some delay in transcribing them, or you may not have sufficient funds to transcribe them all, in which case a brief summary helps to jog your memory about the content of each tape.

Exercises

1   Team up with one other person. Take turns to interview each other, taking about ten minutes per interview. If you are the interviewer, interview the other person about one or more of their hobbies or interests. Question the person to find out about their hobby/interest (e.g. cars, sport, movies, dogs, knitting, etc.). Find out why they pursue this particular hobby or interest.

2   If possible, it is a good idea to have a third person as a silent observer of the interviews in the first exercise. At the end of the interviews, the observer should comment on the *quality of the process* of the interview (not the content). For example, comment on the use of open or closed questions.

3   Discuss the advantages and disadvantages of structured interviews as compared with unstructured interviews.

4   Discuss the advantages and disadvantages of taping interviews.

5   Write an interview guide (the script) for an interview on a general topic that interests you. Test the script on a friend. Can you think of ways in which your script could be improved?

6   After you have conducted the interview described in the previous question, write down a summary of the interview immediately afterwards. How much can you remember? Do you wish you had taped the interview?

7   Find one or more faculty members at your institution who are qualitative researchers. Ask them how they go about conducting interviews. For example, do they always tape record interviews?

Further Reading

Articles

The article by Fontana and Frey (2005) provides a good overview of the different types of interviews, and some of the historical background as to the use of interviews. Hermanns (2004) provides stage directions for those conducting interviews. Myers and Newman (2007) discuss the dramaturgical model of the interview in some depth.

Books

A more detailed treatment of the qualitative interview can be found in the books by Kvale (1996) and Rubin and Rubin (2005).

If you are planning on conducting qualitative market research, the seven-volume Sage series on *Qualitative Market Research: Principle and Practice* will be very useful. One volume of the series has many practical suggestions for interviewing groups and individuals (Chrzanowska, 2002).

Websites on the Internet

There are a few useful websites about the qualitative interview:

- A website at Arizona State University entitled 'What is Qualitative Interviewing': http://www.public.asu.edu/~ifmls/artinculturalcontextsfolder/qualintermeth.html
- A website at the University of Florida entitled 'Qualitative interviewing': http://web.clas.ufl.edu/users/ardelt/Aging/QualInt.htm

11

PARTICIPANT OBSERVATION AND FIELDWORK

Objectives

By the end of this chapter, you will be able to:

- Understand the purpose of participant observation and fieldwork
- Appreciate various fieldwork concepts
- Distinguish between the main types of fieldwork
- Recognize the advantages and disadvantages of fieldwork
- Be more confident in doing fieldwork
- See how fieldwork has been used in business and management

INTRODUCTION

As well as interviews, another way in which you can gather qualitative data is to use fieldwork. Fieldwork is defined by Hughes (2005) as the

> observation of people *in situ*; finding them where they are, staying with them in some role which, while acceptable to them, will allow both intimate observation of certain parts of their behavior, and reporting it in ways useful to social science but not harmful to those observed. (p. 3).

Wolcott (2005a) adds that

> fieldwork is a form of inquiry in which one is immersed personally in the ongoing social activities of some individual or group for the purposes of research. Fieldwork is characterized by personal involvement to achieve some level of understanding that will be shared with others. (p. 44)

Depending upon the disciplinary background and aims of the researcher, fieldwork is sometimes called participant observation and/or fieldwork. In this chapter I treat participant observation and fieldwork as synonymous – both words describe a technique or a particular way of gathering qualitative data. Hence I will mostly use the word 'fieldwork' from now on. Of course, there are different kinds of fieldwork, as I will describe shortly, but the overall goal is the same no matter which words are used: to gather qualitative data about the social world by interacting with people and observing them in their own 'natural' setting. The data obtained by participant observation and fieldwork can be of much value and can often provide an additional dimension to your understanding that you could never have obtained by interviews alone.

Some of the main differences between interviews and fieldwork can be summarized as follows:

- Whereas an interview requires setting aside a specific time and place for the express purpose of questioning someone, fieldwork does not; the conversations and observations that occur while you are doing fieldwork can happen anywhere and at any time.
- Whereas the period of engagement with someone during an interview is relatively short (a few hours at most), fieldwork usually involves an extended period of engagement with the group or organization under study.
- Whereas an interview is a relatively formal occasion in which interviewees are in effect performing on a stage, fieldwork often allows a researcher to engage in numerous informal conversations with people.
- Whereas in an interview informants will normally tell you what they think you want hear (the 'official' story), fieldwork allows a researcher to hear the unofficial story and to observe what people actually do.

Given these differences between interviews and fieldwork, the data gathering techniques that you need for each are very different. Hence a separate chapter is devoted to this.

Observation and Participant Observation

Although I regard the terms 'participant observation' and 'fieldwork' as synonyms, there is a difference between observation and participant observation. The differences between them can be explained as follows.

Observation is when you are watching other people *from the outside*. For example, you may attend an annual meeting of a company, and watch the meeting as an observer. However, you will take no part whatsoever in the activities of the annual meeting – you are essentially a spectator. There is little, if any, interaction between you and the people you are studying.

Participant observation is when you not only observe people doing things, but participate to some extent in these activities as well. The main idea is that you are talking with people and interacting with them in an attempt to gain an understanding of their beliefs and activities *from the inside*. For example, anthropologists will often go and live in the same community or village as the people they are studying. The idea is that by immersing themselves in the society and culture, a better understanding will be gained – they will start to see things from the people's point of view. As another example, one of my students took up a part-time job in the hospital where he was doing his ethnographic research on the development of an information system. He did this so he could participate in the life of the hospital as a staff member.

Of course, these two categories are not completely different. A qualitative researcher may end up being solely an observer in some situations, while interacting with people in others. Also, even though you might be participating and attempting to observe people's activities from the inside, you might still be regarded by them as an outsider. You are still a researcher no matter how much you might try to 'go native' and become one of them. Hence, these categories are more a matter of degree than a hard and fast distinction.

However, most fieldwork of a qualitative nature tends to involve participant observation rather than observation. Since qualitative researchers are mostly interested in understanding meanings, observation without any social interaction is not particularly helpful. It is only by talking to people that you find out the meaning or importance of a particular thing or activity in their culture. This chapter, therefore, focuses only on participant observation and fieldwork, not observation by itself.

Unless you are doing auto-ethnography or something similar (where you are doing fieldwork in familiar surroundings), most fieldwork involves moving into unfamiliar territory. Fieldwork usually involves observing people who have a different culture or sub culture. Traditionally in anthropology, fieldwork involved going to a completely different culture from your own, such as an African village if you were a European, or an Eskimo village if you were an American. You would then try to learn the language and understand the people's cultural beliefs and practices. However, even if you are doing fieldwork in a bank in your own home town, and you speak the same language, you might still have the feeling of being in unfamiliar territory, and you might also need to learn many new words (the jargon of banking). Hence, all fieldwork usually involves a period of enculturation, a time where you learn to become a member of another culture or sub culture. This process will take more or less time depending upon the extent of the difference between your culture and theirs, and your own adaptability.

FIELDWORK CONCEPTS

There are some important concepts with which you need to become familiar if you are to conduct fieldwork in a social situation. I will now discuss each of these concepts in turn.

A Place, Actors, and Activities

Spradley (1980) says that all participant observation takes place in social situations. Every social situation can be identified by three primary elements: a *place*, *actors*, and *activities*. As a participant observer, 'you will locate yourself in some place; you will watch actors of one sort or another and become involved with them; you will observe and participate in activities' (Spradley, 1980: 39–40).

A *place* is any physical setting where people are engaged in social activities. For example, streets, offices, or villages can all be seen as places.

People become *actors* when they play a role in a certain situation. For example, on a bus there are passengers and a driver. Obviously, these same people may take on a different role when they are engaged in a different activity in another place.

Activities are recognizable patterns of behaviour that people perform. For example, people might select a seat on a bus or be engaged in answering email.

Hence, Spradley (1980) says that a participant observer observes and records the activities of actors in a particular place.

Object, Act, Event, Time, Goal, Feeling

As well as a place, actors, and activities, Spradley (1980) says that all social situations have six additional dimensions. He describes all nine dimensions as follows:

1 *Space*: the physical place or places
2 *Actor*: the people involved
3 *Activity*: a set of related acts that people do
4 *Object*: the physical things that are present
5 *Act*: single actions that people do
6 *Event*: a set of related activities that people carry out
7 *Time*: the sequencing that takes place over time
8 *Goal*: the things people are trying to accomplish
9 *Feeling*: the emotions felt and expressed. (Spradley, 1980: 78)

People might use objects in the performance of an act (e.g. rings might be exchanged during a particular part of a wedding). Sets of activities might be linked together into events. Events are occasions such as a wedding. At a wedding, certain acts are put into a sequence to accomplish a certain goal (e.g. the groom is 'permitted', or rather requested, to kiss the bride – but only after the exchange of vows). At a wedding, feelings are felt and expressed.

Spradley suggests that these nine dimensions can serve as guides for the participant observer. For example, you can ask questions about each of these dimensions. (Can you tell me about the people, activity, event, and so forth?) The dimensions help the participant observer to take comprehensive notes and record everything in detail (Spradley, 1980).

Gaining Access

In conducting fieldwork the qualitative researcher is the research instrument. Hence, the level of access significantly affects the quality and nature of the data gathered. If you are given only limited opportunities to attend meetings and develop close relationships with people, then by definition the qualitative data you obtain will be so much the poorer. On the other hand, if you are given free rein to observe whatever you like, then your data will be so much richer (as long as you are in the right place at the right time, of course).

However, one of the biggest problems for qualitative researchers can be gaining access to the research site. You have to get past the gatekeepers (senior managers, secretaries, personal assistants) to do the research. Even if you are able to talk to a manager of a company on the phone, you might not have much success. If you say, 'I would like to observe the people in your company for four months, see how things work, and then write it up for publication', I doubt if you will get very far. Most likely managers will say they are too busy to have someone around for that length of time. They might also worry about the possible disruption to their work, and what you might write. How do they know that you will not write up something that is critical of the company? The last thing they need is bad publicity on the front page of a newspaper.

In my experience, therefore, I have found it essential to have a clear plan with regard to how to gain access to the research site. A few practical suggestions are as follows.

First, you should learn as much as possible about the potential research site beforehand. When you first make contact with the people, you do not want to appear completely ignorant; you want them to know that you have done your homework and that you are able to engage in a reasonably intelligent conversation. Of course, you do not have to know everything. As

Jackson points out, 'Being less knowledgeable than your informants is always acceptable – if you knew more than they did about everything you were discussing, they would be superfluous – but being downright ignorant is inexcusable' (1987: 23). Hence, you should learn as much as possible about them beforehand. You can probably find some information from the Internet, newspapers, magazines, and possibly journal articles and books.

Second, if you are a PhD student, I suggest that your thesis supervisor should make the first contact with the organization (if you do not have any contacts there). It is important for the organization to know that you have the backing of the university for your research project, and a call or a letter from a lecturer or professor who is an employee of the university tends to give people a lot more confidence than a call from a postgraduate student. Hence, I always try to make sure that I accompany my students for the very first meeting at the research site with a senior manager. In my field (information systems), this manager is normally the chief information officer or the equivalent. This person is the one with the authority to approve or decline the proposed research project. In your field this might be the marketing manager or the chief financial officer. By attending this first meeting, your supervisor is demonstrating that your research project is an official research project of your institution. People might find it harder to say no to a professor or lecturer than a student.

Third, I have found it useful at the first meeting to present a letter outlining the nature of the research project and how the results will be used. This letter should clearly state the conditions under which the results will be published, e.g. perhaps stating that a representative of the organization will have the opportunity to review any articles for publication before they are submitted, or that pseudonyms might be used to protect the confidentiality of any informants if this is deemed appropriate. This letter might also state that a 20-page summary of the research will be presented to management. I think it is important to highlight how the organization might benefit from the research – otherwise, why should they bother having you around?

Fourth, as a general rule you will have much more success if there is already some pre-existing relationship between the university and the company or organization. For example, a company might be a sponsor of the business school, it might fund scholarships for postgraduate students, or one or more of the senior managers might be alumni of the university. In all these cases, the organization is likely to be much more receptive to the idea of a research project. The project can be described as one way in which the organization can contribute to the university and to the development of new knowledge. All of my students have had a very high success rate in gaining access when such a company has been chosen as the research site. The senior managers are already positively disposed towards the university in these cases and if they are graduates of the university might feel some obligation to help. If the topic of your research is directly relevant to the company (e.g. perhaps you are studying the challenges faced by small start-up companies), then of course the chances of gaining access are greater still.

Becoming Accepted

Just because you have managed to get past the gatekeeper this does not guarantee that other members of the organization will want to talk to you. Hence, the next challenge after gaining access is to build a rapport and relationships of trust with those in the organization. Obviously, you need to get invited to any important meetings that are relevant to your research project. You also want the people to share their knowledge and their experiences with you. How can this be done?

One way to build trust is to make sure that you keep to yourself any information that is shared with you in confidence. If someone finds out that you have been divulging sensitive information to others, then they are unlikely to want to share any further information with you.

Another way to build trust is to share some of your most important findings with the people in the company. As long as the findings you share are reasonably high level, there should be no need to break any confidences (in fact, you should make sure that you do not divulge any sensitive information, as mentioned in the previous paragraph).

You also have to build confidence in yourself. When you first start your fieldwork, often you will be treated like a stranger. You will not know the culture, the regular routines, or the jargon. Over time, however, you should become more knowledgeable about the organization and how things work. As you learn more, people might start to ask you for advice. If you can provide good advice, then their confidence in you will grow. The more confident they are in you, the more likely they are to open up. Wolcott (2005b) says that a fieldworker needs to have personal determination coupled with faith in him or herself.

Reciprocity

One important principle in maintaining good relationships with people is reciprocity. If a friend gives us a Christmas present, then most of us will feel obliged to reciprocate in order to maintain good relations. A quick way to lose friends is to receive gifts but never give any back in return.

Hence, it is incumbent upon the researcher to provide something in return for the time and knowledge he or she is receiving from people. However, as

Wolcott points out, there is an art to gift giving: 'fieldwork entails a subtle kind of exchange, one that often involves gifting across cultural boundaries where exchange rates may be ambiguous or one wonders what to offer in exchange for intangibles such as hospitality or a personal life history' (2005b: 106).

There are no simple answers with regard to what an appropriate gift should be, except I think it is important to be aware of the requirement for some kind of reciprocity. The nature of the gift will depend upon the context. For example, if you are studying a company in a developed country, the most valuable thing you can provide might be a high-level report on your findings. For a business venture, another gift could be consulting advice.

Key Informants

As well as gatekeepers, key informants are very important. Payne and Payne (2004) describe key informants as follows:

> Key informants are those whose social positions in a research setting give them specialist knowledge about other people, processes or happenings that is more extensive, detailed or privileged than ordinary people, and who are therefore particularly valuable sources of information to a researcher, not least in the early stages of a project. (p. 134)

In conducting their fieldwork, anthropologists often gain much of their understanding of the local culture via their key informants. These key informants are often important political leaders within the society being studied who can enable the anthropologist to understand and navigate the local situation.

Hence, it is important to try to identify key informants early on in your project. Not only do they provide much valuable information, they can also advise you on how you ought to behave in certain situations.

Length of Fieldwork

In anthropology it is considered that anthropologists should spend a substantial period in the field, ideally at least 12 months (Wolcott, 2005a). Often they will go back for a second or third visit. This period of time is needed to understand those taken-for-granted features of a culture that the people themselves may not explicitly verbalize. A longer period may be required if it is necessary to learn the language.

In business and management, however, the period of fieldwork tends to be much shorter. Often there is no need to learn a completely new language, and the culture may be similar (e.g. an American who studies a US company). Also, the subject matter may be reasonably familiar to the researcher. For example, if a researcher in operations management conducts fieldwork in a company, then presumably he or she would be studying some aspect of the operations of the company. Hence, a year of fieldwork in such a situation is probably overkill. In my experience, most fieldwork in business and management is conducted for between four and eight months.

Also, it is usually not feasible to live on site in urban situations. Most researchers simply conduct their fieldwork from 9 to 5, while the company is open for business. Of course, if you are able to attend an informal social gathering after work, then it is probably advisable to do so. Also, if you are studying something else, such as a hospital or sports team, then your daily time schedule might vary.

When should you finish your fieldwork? A general rule of thumb is that it is time to conclude your period of fieldwork when what initially appeared strange is now taken for granted. When you find that you understand almost everything that is going on, and that you are not discovering any new insights, it is probably a good time to consider leaving.

Esterberg (2002) gives similar advice:

> Ideally, you should leave when you feel you have little more to gain by observing longer. Perhaps the field notes seem to be saying the same things over and over, or additional informants seem to be telling you the same kind of things... Or perhaps you feel you have learned all you can, at least for the time being. If this is the case, it's probably a good time to leave. (p. 78)

Before you leave, however, you should just make sure that you have sufficient data to answer your original research questions. In some situations, you may be forced to leave for some other reason (e.g. your research funding runs out, or the deadline for completion draws near).

Equipment

Most people doing fieldwork will use some kind of recording equipment – a camera, a video camera, a tape recorder, and/or a digital voice recorder. The data you can capture by means of these devices potentially add tremendous richness to your story. Some topics, of course, may require the use of a particular device such as a video recorder almost exclusively.

There are a few important general guidelines that you should bear in mind when using any recording equipment.

First, you should be very familiar with your equipment. You should know that it works and how to use it appropriately. You should check that your camera takes good photos in various conditions, and that your tape recorder or voice recorder produces clear recordings. There is nothing worse than finding out that your recordings are of such poor quality that you cannot hear much of what was said. This use of recording equipment is discussed in more detail shortly.

Second, you should take only as much equipment as you need. In fact, it is usually best to try to take as little as possible. This is because your equipment can be a distraction and can actually get in the way of what you are supposed to be there for – listening and observing. If you are too busy setting up and operating your equipment, you may miss out on observing some important incident or activities.

Third, you should try to make your equipment as invisible as possible. The less obtrusive and noticeable your equipment is, the better your data will be. The fundamental idea of fieldwork is to study people in their own natural setting; hence, if your equipment is very noticeable and becomes a distraction, your natural setting soon becomes unnatural. The quality of your data is likely to be compromised.

Fourth, you should always make sure that you have permission beforehand to take photos or use your recording equipment. The ethics of fieldwork and of qualitative research in general were discussed in more detail in Chapter 5.

Field Notes

As well as using various kinds of recording equipment, you should also take field notes. In fact, you should write down as many notes as possible even if you are making a recording. This is because your field notes are in effect another source of data – they are a commentary on what was happening at the time. Just like a diary, field notes can record what you were thinking and feeling. These notes can be a source of deep insight later, particularly if you find that your understanding has changed over time. Some suggest that field notes represent the major part of any ethnographic record (Spradley, 1980), although I think it depends on the topic and the kind of research you are doing.

You should always label or annotate your recordings with the time and date of recording, the place the recording was made, and some details about the event. This meta-information is absolutely essential. It allows you to catalogue and index all your data later, making it easier to search for and retrieve information when needed.

As a general rule, you should write up your field notes at the end of each day. This is because you will soon forget many important details about what happened if you leave it too long.

Spradley (1980) emphasizes the point that the participant observer must make a verbatim record of what people say:

> The native terms must be recorded verbatim. Failure to take these first steps along the path to discovering the inner meaning of another culture will lead to a false confidence that we have found out what the natives know. We may never even realize that our picture is seriously distorted and incomplete. (pp. 67–8)

Payne and Payne (2004) say that a qualitative researcher should record as much as possible in the field notes, as it is not possible to tell what will be relevant later. They also say that field notes should cover the participants' own personal reactions:

> Feelings, initial impressions, half ideas, possible leads, even admissions of tactical errors or things missed during the day, should all be included. Fieldwork is a reflexive experience, researchers bringing themselves into contact with real-life situations (Reflexivity). The researcher is part of the things being studied. The researcher's own reactions are an essential element of participation. (Payne & Payne, 2004: 168–9)

However, notes should not be left as a stream of consciousness, but should be organized and indexed systematically (Payne & Payne, 2004).

APPROACHES TO FIELDWORK

Although there are many different kinds of fieldwork, the two main approaches are those stemming from the British anthropological tradition and the Chicago sociological tradition. I will discuss each of these approaches in turn.

The British Anthropological Tradition

As I mentioned in Chapter 8, Malinowski was one of the first anthropologists to use the ethnographic research method in the early part of the twentieth century. He, along with other British anthropologists such as Radcliffe-Brown and Evans-Pritchard, pioneered the technique of intensive fieldwork. The idea was that an anthropologist should live in a completely different culture or society for an extended period (such as a tribe in Africa, or a village in Polynesia). He or she should learn the language and participate in and observe the activities of the people. The researcher should take extensive field notes, in an attempt to provide as full a description as possible of their way of life, their beliefs, and cultural practices. Fieldwork was seen as the only way to gather detailed empirical data of this kind.

For example, Raymond Firth, an anthropologist at the London School of Economics, published many volumes documenting in great detail the social structure, cultural practices, and beliefs of the people of Tikopia (Firth, 1983). Tikopia is a Polynesian island in the South Pacific. Firth says that one of the reasons for publishing in such detail was so as to preserve as much as possible of the culture, given the rapid changes and breakdown of ancient cultures that were occurring.

Much of the early fieldwork conducted by British anthropologists had positivistic tendencies. They assumed that they were documenting a single, relatively stable reality for audiences in the West. However, there is now tremendous variety in the approaches that anthropologists take to fieldwork. The most common approaches can be described as interpretive, although some adopt a critical approach.

The Chicago Sociological Tradition

Whereas anthropologists studied non-urban cultures that were unfamiliar and 'strange', sociologists at the University of Chicago studied urban cultures that were often already partially known to the observer (Manning, 1987). The city became the social laboratory for the researcher, who would examine people and their social behaviour in Chicago (Burgess, 2005). As some observers were former or current members of the social groups they studied, and often continued to live in their own homes, the challenge was not so much to become acculturated as to maintain one's 'limbo' status or marginality (Manning, 1987). Manning (1987) describes this as follows:

> The proper attitude (for sociologists doing fieldwork) was one of a 'limbo member,' or a 'marginal man,' someone who understands and empathizes with the group under study, but who retains an alternative perspective. Something of a binocular vision is required. There was the overall aim of creating an empathetic understanding of the unfolding nature of the cultural life of the group, mainly focused on a small segment, and with the purpose of maintaining a role (either fully participant through to full observer) throughout the course of the study. (p. 16)

Most of the early fieldwork conducted by the sociology faculty at the University of Chicago was positivistic, 'firmly located in the realist tradition' (Preissle & Grant, 2004: 169). However, there is now a much greater variety of fieldwork approaches in sociology.

HOW TO CONDUCT FIELDWORK

Punch (1986) says that 'infiltration' constitutes a key skill in doing field-work, especially if the fieldwork involves a prolonged period of immersion in the life of a group, community or organization. Fieldwork is a craft 'requiring both tenacity of purpose and competence in a number of social skills' (Punch, 1986: 16).

Wolcott (2005b) says that fieldworkers should participate more, and play the role of the aloof observer less. He advises against thinking of oneself as needing to wear a white lab coat and carry a clipboard to study human behaviour; rather, a fieldworker should genuinely participate and engage with people.

Jackson (1987) says that fieldwork consists of three phases: the planning, collecting, and analysing phases. All three phases are linked. These phases are summarized in Table 11.1.

Table 11.1 The planning phases of fieldwork (adapted from Jackson, 1987)

Phase	Description
Planning	You decide what you want to do, why you want to do it, what resources you need, and what research may have already been done on the same subject
Collecting	You gather the information, make notes and observations about the information, its character, and the collecting events
Analysing	You need to index the field-collected materials for an archive, summarize them, and write them up

The planning phase includes setting goals, determining what resources you need (budget, equipment), and organizing your tools. For example, if you are planning to use a video recorder, then you should know exactly how it works beforehand. It is not acceptable to be amateurish in your use of equipment, as Jackson (1987) explains:

> Fumbling while loading or focusing the camera or fidgeting with the controls of the tape recorder draws excess attention to those machines, and that's the last thing you want. Most people (and especially those who work with machines or instruments themselves) tend not to think well of people who spend an inordinate amount of time talking about or fussing with the tools of their trade. Think of how you'd feel if you were at the dentist's office and he or she kept puttering with the drill, turning it on and off, and then said, 'I'll get it right soon, don't you worry.' (p. 24)

Hence, good planning involves testing your equipment beforehand and making sure you are very familiar with how it works.

The collecting phase means that you have to pay attention to watching, listening, and asking questions. You need to find the right people and document as much as possible. You will probably end up collecting many different kinds of data, e.g. photos, videos, tape or digital sound recordings, documents, as well as your own field notes.

The analysing phase involves classifying and indexing all of your field-collected materials. Since you are likely to end up with hundreds if not thousands of items, it is a good idea to get into the habit of summarizing them for easy retrieval later. It is a mistake to think that you do not need to summarize anything because 'I have it on tape anyway'. The problem is that when you come to write up your research report or thesis, you may not remember exactly what happened or what someone said, and you may not have the time to go back and listen to all of your tapes. Hence it is so much better to get into the habit of summarizing your field-collected materials as soon as possible after you have collected them.

ADVANTAGES AND DISADVANTAGES OF FIELDWORK

The main advantage of fieldwork is that it enables an in-depth understanding of the attitudes, beliefs, values, norms, and practices of the social group or organization being studied. It is the best way to get an understanding of social situations 'from the inside'.

One limitation of fieldwork is that you can only study a small group or one organization at a time. Hence, the domain of analysis can be somewhat limited and the topics narrow (Manning, 1987). Another limitation is the tendency to be purely descriptive and to make little contribution to theory (Manning, 1987). Additionally, fieldwork requires the qualitative researcher to have excellent social skills. Not everyone may be suited to doing fieldwork.

EXAMPLES OF FIELDWORK IN BUSINESS AND MANAGEMENT

Advertising to Adolescents

Ritson and Elliott (1999) used fieldwork along with interviews to study the social uses of advertising by adolescent consumers. They say that consumer research in marketing generally focuses on the solitary subject rather than the role that advertising plays within the social contexts of group interaction. Their article looked at adolescents as social viewers and reported on the context and socio-cultural setting of their consumption activity.

The authors conducted fieldwork at six schools over a period of six months. They decided to study adolescents because this group is particularly active in the social use of a variety of different forms of popular media. They are also 'advertising literate'.

In order to gain access to the research sites, six schools in the north-west of England were approached by the first author who volunteered to teach a nationally required media studies class lasting six weeks in return for field-work access to each school. All the schools that were approached agreed to the proposed research, and all six were included in the study.

The media class being taught typically occupied one hour per day. The researcher spent the rest of the school day immersed in a variety of activities. In effect, the researcher used the teaching role to gain a backstage pass to the rest of the school.

Their article shows how advertising can form the basis for a wide variety of social interactions. The adolescents in the study were able to use advertising texts independently from the product that the ads were promoting (Ritson & Elliott, 1999).

Information Technology and the Control of Work

Orlikowski (1991) studied a large, multinational software consulting firm, looking at the implications of information technology for forms of control and forms of organizing. She studied the organization for eight months, collecting data from participant observation, interviews, and documents. She studied five different software application development projects, spending an average of four weeks on each project. She observed and interviewed project team members in their daily development work and in their interaction with each other. She also attended meetings and identified other key informants.

Her article shows how the information technology used in this firm reinforced established forms of organizing and facilitated an intensification and fusion of existing mechanisms of control. This finding was surprising, given that software consultants are often thought of as knowledge professionals and as having a certain degree of professional autonomy. Her paper also shows that when information technology mediates work processes, it creates an information environment, which, while it may facilitate integrated and flexible operations, may also enable a disciplinary matrix of knowledge and power (Orlikowski, 1991).

Further Reading

Books

Although Jackson's (1987) book focuses on conducting fieldwork in folklore, much of his book is relevant to qualitative researchers in business and management.

Websites on the Internet

There are a few useful websites on fieldwork:

- A bibliography related to fieldwork is available at http://coombs.anu.edu.au/Biblio/biblio_fieldwork1.html
- Although it is oriented towards folklore, the following website is a useful introduction to fieldwork: http://www.loc.gov/folklife/fieldwork/

12 *USING DOCUMENTS*

Objectives

By the end of this chapter, you will be able to:

- Understand the purpose of using documents
- Identify various types of documents
- See how to use documents
- Recognize the advantages and disadvantages of using documents

INTRODUCTION

As well as using interviews and fieldwork to gather data, it is also possible to gather data from documents. Documents such as emails, blogs, web pages, corporate records, newspapers, and photographs record what someone said or what happened. They provide some evidence that may allow you to build a richer picture than could be obtained by interviews and fieldwork alone. In fact, sometimes the only empirical data relating to a particular matter are contained in one or more documents. For example, if someone is dead, you cannot interview them, but you might be able to read some of their written records such as a diary. Documents and records are 'any written materials that people leave behind' (Esterberg, 2002: 121).

However, documents can serve as more than just an historical record of someone's thoughts or actions: they can also be seen as actors in some situations (Prior, 2003). For example, a contract between two companies can be enforced in a court of law (even if the original signatories have left both companies); a will has legal force after a person has died (in fact, it only comes into effect after they have died). In both these cases, the document can be thought of as an actor in its own right, independent of the person or persons who wrote it. Of course, in a court of law people might argue about what the 'real intention' of the person was in writing the document, but in the end the judge or jury provides the definitive interpretation of what was meant. Sometimes the decision of a court is seen as going against the original intention of the author. The key point here is that documents can be as significant as speech in social action (Prior, 2003).

Altheide (1996) says that documents are studied to understand culture. He points out that a large part of culture consists of documents. He defines a document as 'any symbolic representation that can be recorded or retrieved for analysis' (Altheide, 1996: 2). Culture is more available to document analysis today because of the information technology revolution (Altheide, 1996).

I define a document as 'anything that can be stored in a digital file on a computer'. This does not mean that it has to be stored there (e.g. a document may exist only in hard copy or on videotape), but in principle it can be. Nowadays, every form of data (text, audio, pictures, or video) can be stored in a digital format.

There are many different types of documents. As well as written materials, there are pictures, diagrams, photographs, videos, television programmes, interactive websites, and software. In this chapter I consider all of these to be various types of documents. Documents can be static or continually in a state of flux, e.g. a blog which might be updated on a daily basis.

Documents have authors and readers. Authors produce documents, whereas readers consume them. As Prior (2003) points out, however, the relationship between producers and consumers is very dynamic. The process of reading a document is not a passive one, but active. He says that 'a reader of any web page, or any screen-based document, can these days easily cut, paste, edit and re-edit text to suit the user's purpose' (Prior, 2003: 16). For example, students often write essays by copying and pasting information from the Internet (hopefully with the appropriate acknowledgement). The way in which the interpretation of a text can be seen as an active process is discussed in more detail in Chapter 14.

Payne and Payne say that documentary techniques are used 'to categorize, investigate, interpret and identify the limitations of physical sources, most commonly written documents, whether in the private or public domain (personal papers, commercial records, or state archives, communications or legislation)' (2004: 60).

TYPES OF DOCUMENTS

One simple way to classify documents is by the type of file on a computer. For example:

- A document that is primarily comprised of text is normally stored as a text or Word document.
- A photograph or image document is normally stored in jpeg format.
- A video is normally stored in DVD format or as a Windows Audio/Media file.
- Music or audio is normally stored in some kind of audio format such as MP3.

Personal, Private, and Public

Payne and Payne suggest that documents can be classified into three main categories: personal, private, and public, 'depending upon *who* wrote them, not the document's ownership or availability to the wider population' (2004: 61).

Personal documents include individuals' letters, diaries, notes, drafts, files, and books. *Private documents* include those that are produced by private organizations for internal purposes, such as minutes of meetings, personnel records, budgets, and memos. *Public documents* include those that are produced for public consumption, such as annual reports, media statements, or articles in newspapers (Payne & Payne, 2004).

Scott says that administrative papers produced by governmental and private agencies are the 'single most important category of documentary sources used in social research' (1990: 59).

Written Documents and Records

Lincoln and Guba (1985) make a distinction between written documents and records. Records attest to some formal transaction, and include marriage certificates, driving licences, bank statements, and so forth. Documents, on the other hand, are prepared for personal rather than official reasons and include diaries, memos, letters, and so forth. In this chapter I regard both written documents and records as simply different types of documents.

Historical Documents

Gottschalk (2006) discusses the various types of documents that are used by historians:

- *Contemporary records* are documents intended to convey instructions regarding a transaction or to aid the memory of the persons involved in the transaction. Contemporary records include court records, business and legal papers, and notebooks and memoranda kept by individuals.
- *Confidential reports* are usually written after the event, and are often intended to create an impression rather than merely to aid memory. Examples of

confidential reports include military and diplomatic dispatches, and professional diaries or journals (e.g. of a doctor).

- *Public reports* are expected to be read by many people by the authors of these reports. Public reports include newspaper reports, memoirs, autobiographies and official histories.
- *Questionnaires* are documents that may have been used to elicit information and opinions.
- *Government documents* include documents such as laws and regulations that may not fit into the first category of contemporary records.
- *Expressions of opinion* include editorials, essays, speeches and pamphlets.
- *Fiction, Song, Poetry and Folklore* provide the historian with an understanding of some of the local color and the environment that helped shaped the author's views.

Photographs, Films, and Videotapes

As well as textual documents, anthropologists have often taken photographs and/or films and videos of the people being studied. Marshall and Rossman (1989) explain that

> this tradition relies on films and photographs to capture the daily life of the group under study. Films provide visual records of passing natural events and are useful as permanent scientific resources. (p. 85)

Hence, if you are writing a case study or ethnography of an organization, a few photographs or even a video can bring your story to life. Ball and Smith (1992) discuss the use of photographs as a type of qualitative data.

In some ways, the qualitative data obtained via photographs and videos can be seen as objective. A photographic image can be seen as an objective record of a subject at a particular moment in time. The camera does not lie (unless the photograph or video has subsequently been edited).

In other ways, however, photographs and videos can be seen as subjective. The photographer decides what to shoot, at what angle, and at what time. It is common knowledge that some people take better photographs than others. Also, with digital cameras and software, it is very easy to 'enhance' images that are not as good as they 'should' be, and delete those that are considered to be unsuitable. Only some images might be included in the final written report. Hence, the qualitative researcher who uses images is actively involved in selecting and editing the visual record. Images can be seen as both objective and subjective (Harper, 2004).

Hesse-Biber and Leavy (2006) suggest a useful distinction between conceptualizing images as 'visual records' or as 'visual diaries'. If you think of a set of photographs as a collection of visual records, these photographs will be imbued with a sense of authority. You will treat them as a record of the social world. However, if you think of these same photographs as a visual diary, you will focus on the medium as much as the content. You will consider the production and editorial process, the person who took the photos, and treat them as if they were memo notes (Hesse-Biber & Leavy, 2006).

As well as taking photographs and videos yourself, you may be able to find films, videos, and/or TV programmes recorded by others that might be relevant to your research topic. In fact, this is very likely if your topic relates to a well-known person or organization that is often featured in the media. The film or video may provide some important insights about a particular event or incident in the past. There is a growing literature on the use of film and photography in sociology and cultural studies (Denzin, 2004), and I suggest that such media could also be very useful for researchers in business and management.

Denzin (2004) points out that:

> A film or a photograph offers an image, or set of images, which are interpretations of the real. The real, or the slice of reality that is captured, can never be reproduced, for what is represented can only occur once. Visual documents are records of events that have occurred in the past (Barthes 1981). (p. 240)

Denzin suggests a set of guidelines for analysing visual documents. These guidelines include 'looking and feeling' the materials, stating the research question, analysing the film, text, or image using 'structured microanalysis' (e.g. doing a scene-by-scene analysis), and a 'search for patterns' (Denzin, 2004).

Electronic Documents

More and more documents are being stored in digital form on a computer, rather than in hard copy. In fact, some documents might only be available in digital form. For example, if you are studying a large organization, much of the communication with customers might be via the organization's website or email. Very few of these emails will be printed out. Also, virtually all organizations nowadays (at least in developed countries) have software that mediates their business processes. For example, an organization might use a customer relationship management (CRM) package. This CRM package usually has the capability of producing all kinds of reports on customers and their relationship with the organization. Likewise, a university's student records management system will have the capability of producing dozens of reports on students and their relationship with the university.

It might be possible for you to get permission to access some of these electronic documents for research purposes. If the organisation is willing to give you a username and password, you might be able to find much useful data such as emails or reports that are produced by the organization's software.

One potential advantage of electronic documents is that they usually contain a timestamp and other details. For example, an email contains the email address of the sender and the recipient, and the date it was received. However, you should be careful not to read too much into timestamps on digital files, as it is relatively easy to change the timestamp if you have special software. Also, the timestamp usually records the date of creation as being the date the file was created on a particular machine. Thus, if the original file was created on a different machine and you copy this same file to a new computer, the date of file creation on the last computer will be the later date that is shown. The timestamp can thus be misleading.

The Internet

Whereas many electronic documents (such as emails) are private and require special permission to access, the Internet contains a wealth of electronic information that is freely available. It is a huge source of documents in electronic form. At the time of writing this book, there are more than 30 billion web pages indexed by various search engines on the Web. These web pages potentially include many important sources of data. Over the last ten years the number of documents on the Internet has grown exponentially.

You can search the Internet for reference materials, government documents, and other data relating to your subject. The Internet can be viewed as one giant document repository like a library or archive.

However, just like other documents, you need to ask basic questions about authorship and credibility. Is this web page reliable? The validity and reliability of many Internet documents are questionable. Another problem with web pages is that they tend to change frequently or disappear altogether. This is why many journals ask authors to record the 'date accessed' in the references section. If you intend to rely on a particular website for qualitative data, I suggest you save the web page to your own computer. If you are using Internet Explorer, choose the 'web page complete' option, as this will also save the graphics and images that accompany the web page. Of course, you should check that there are no special restrictions on copying the page for research purposes and that, if required, you have permission to do so.

HOW TO USE DOCUMENTS

In business and management there are many documentary sources that a qualitative researcher can draw upon. These documents include company annual reports, press releases, minutes of meetings, corporate mission statements, company policies and procedures, websites, and emails. This documentary evidence can be used to supplement the data provided by interviews and fieldwork. Documents often provide much useful background information that might help you in framing your interview questions and planning your fieldwork.

Scott (1990) suggests that four criteria should be used to assess the quality of social research evidence such as documents. These criteria are authenticity, credibility, representativeness, and meaning. He defines them as follows:

1 Authenticity: Is the evidence genuine and of unquestionable origin?
2 Credibility: Is the evidence free from error and distortion?
3 Representativeness: Is the evidence typical of its kind, and, if not, is the extent of its untypicality known?
4 Meaning: Is the evidence clear and comprehensible? (pp. 19–35)

Commenting on these four criteria, Payne and Payne (2004) say that:

'Authenticity' means that the object is what it claims it is: the famous forgery of the 'Hitler Diaries' shows how academic researchers can be misled. 'Credibility' refers to how far the author is to be believed. Was he or she an eye-witness, or learned something at second hand? Did the author set down an accurate, or mistaken, or deliberately self-serving version of events? (p. 63)

'Representativeness' refers to the extent to which a sub sample (e.g. a single letter) can be taken as representative of a wider set of documents. The 'meaning' refers to how the document should be interpreted and understood (Payne & Payne, 2004).

Platt (2005) suggests eight criteria by which a document can be judged as authentic. The authenticity of a document is brought into question when:

1 The document does not appear to make sense or has errors in it.
2 Different versions of the same original document are current.
3 The document contains internal inconsistencies.
4 The document is known to have been transmitted via many copyists.
5 The document is known to have been transmitted by someone with a vested interest in the version given passing as the correct one.
6 The version available is derived from a secondary source suspected of being unreliable.
7 The style or content is in some way inconsistent with that of other instances of the same class.
8 The document fits too neatly into a standard formula or literary form. (pp. 217–18)

Prior suggests that, instead of analysing documents for meaning, documents can be analysed for references. What entities are referenced in the document? He suggests it is useful to look at how the networks of references in a document interlock (Prior, 2003). Analysing text for meaning is discussed in more detail from Chapter 13 on.

If you are planning to conduct archival research as part of your qualitative research project, Hill (1993) says that the first step is to write a literature review. The bibliography you develop can then be used to help direct the search for archival materials (Hill, 1993). You should then develop a 'master name list'. This list 'is the key to locating archival deposits in a name-oriented archival search strategy. Your name list is, in a sense, the cast of characters in an unfolding archival drama. A comprehensive list includes understudies as well as principal actors' (Hill, 1993: 32). This list can include the names of individuals, businesses, and political, social, and professional organizations. It is a good idea to store this list in a spreadsheet or database. You should then check the general catalogue of the archive against your master name list.

Hill suggests that if you are planning to visit an archive that is some distance away, it is important to contact the curator before you make the trip. This can avert any potential problems that you might have in gaining access or finding the relevant materials (Hill, 1993). When you arrive at the archive, the first social interaction usually involves an orientation interview with one of the archivists. This interview must be successfully negotiated in order to gain access to the archival resources: 'Researchers who botch orientation interviews may seriously disable their research projects' (Hill, 1993: 41). On the other hand, if the interview goes well, the archivist might be very helpful in locating materials relevant to your research project.

THE JOY OF DOING ARCHIVAL RESEARCH

… [I]t is a rare treat to visit an archive, to hold in one's hands the priceless and irreplaceable documents of our unfolding human drama. Each new box of archival material presents opportunities for discovery as well as obligations to treat the subjects of your sociobiographical research with candor, theoretical sophistication, and a sense of fair play. Each archival journey is a journey into an unknown realm that rewards its visitors with challenging puzzles and unexpected revelations. (Hill, 1993: 7)

ADVANTAGES AND DISADVANTAGES OF USING DOCUMENTS

Documents are relatively cheap and quick to access (Payne & Payne, 2004). It is usually much easier to obtain data from documents than from interviews or fieldwork. However, in my own case I have tended to use documents as an additional source of data (as a supplement to interviews and fieldwork) rather than on their own. I have found documents to be invaluable for providing important details of events (e.g. the exact date of when a project was approved) and for being able to cross-check findings with other sources. You may also find some documents in an archive that are unique, items that cannot be obtained elsewhere (Hill, 1993).

Documents make things visible and are traceable (Prior, 2003). For example, the documents that report on the Research Assessment Exercise (RAE) in the United Kingdom make the research performance of academic departments, faculties, and universities visible to the government and other interested parties; a document that describes the marketing plan of a company reveals the thinking about the market and the company's place in the market at a particular point in time. If there are many documents on a similar subject, it might be possible to triangulate them and study developments over time.

A disadvantage of using documents is that access can be difficult for some types of documents (e.g. emails, or documents in an archive located far away). Also, it is not always straightforward to assess the authenticity, credibility, representativeness, and meaning of a document, particularly if you do not have access to the original author(s).

EXAMPLES OF USING DOCUMENTS IN BUSINESS AND MANAGEMENT

Using (and Reusing) Email Messages

An interesting example of how documents can be used and reused is provided by the following series of articles.

The story begins with Markus, who conducted case study research at HCP Inc. (a pseudonym), looking at the use of email at work. She obtained her data from interviews, a survey, and documents. The documents were samples of emails that she collected from HCP employees. She was fortunate that a small number of employees, including a senior manager, agreed to give her some of their emails. One of the main purposes of Markus's research was to critique information richness theory. Her findings were published in a working paper and two journal articles (Markus, 1994a; 1994b).

Subsequently, Lee (1994) reanalysed this same email data to show how the process of information richness occurs. A secondary purpose was to demonstrate the value of an interpretive perspective in information systems research (Lee, 1994).

A few years later Ngwenyama and Lee (1997) reanalysed this very same data set once again, this time using the critical social theory of Habermas. Their purpose was to show how the critical perspective adds another dimension to the positivist and interpretive understanding of information richness (Ngwenyama & Lee, 1997).

What is interesting about this series of articles is that, although Markus conducted interviews and a survey, the subsequent articles focused mostly on the meaning of the email messages. All four articles were published in high-quality journals.

Exercises

1 Imagine you are writing a detailed article for an online magazine called 'A Day in My Life'. What documentary evidence could you potentially use? Think of every single document that might provide some documentary evidence of your day, e.g. the newspaper you read, the emails your read/wrote, the websites you visited, the TV shows you watched, and a receipt from an ATM. Can you list every single document?

2 Take a photograph of a street scene in your own city or town. Discuss the extent to which this photograph can be seen as an objective visual record of the social world.

3 Search the Internet for websites that might be a good source of qualitative data. For example, how many documents can you find about a particular well-known company (both official and unofficial)?

4 Find a database in your library that indexes newspaper magazines. See if you can find articles that relate to the same company you researched in the previous question. Are any of the articles not available on the Internet?

5 Use Google Scholar to search for documents relating to your chosen research topic. What kinds of documents appear? Are any documents noticeably absent?

6 Find one or more faculty members at your institution or at a conference who you know conduct qualitative research. Ask them how they have used documents in their research.

Further Reading

Books

One of the most comprehensive books about using documents in qualitative research is entitled *Using Documents in Social Research* by Prior (2003).

PART FIVE

ANALYSING QUALITATIVE DATA

Part V discusses the analysis and interpretation of qualitative data, as illustrated in Figure V.1. Chapter 13 provides an overview of a wide variety of approaches to the analysis and interpretation of qualitative data. The following three chapters then discuss specific qualitative data analysis approaches in more detail. Chapter 14 looks at the use of hermeneutics. Chapter 15 looks at the use of semiotics. Chapter 16 focuses on the use of narrative analysis. All four chapters provide examples of the use of these approaches in business and management.

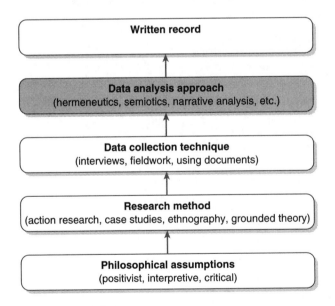

Figure V.1 Qualitative research design

13

ANALYSING QUALITATIVE DATA: AN OVERVIEW

Objectives

By the end of this chapter, you will be able to:

- Understand the purpose of analysing and interpreting qualitative data
- Identify various approaches to analysing and interpreting qualitative data
- Work out which qualitative data analysis approach to use
- Decide whether or not to use qualitative data analysis software

INTRODUCTION

Although a clear distinction between data gathering and data analysis is commonly made in quantitative research, such a distinction is problematic for many qualitative researchers. For example, from a hermeneutic perspective it is assumed that the researcher's presuppositions will affect the gathering of the data. The questions posed to informants will largely determine the answers that you get. The analysis will affect the data and the data will affect the analysis in significant ways. Therefore it is somewhat simplistic to think of the data analysis phase as distinctly separate from the data gathering phase. Often there is some iterative activity between the various phases in a qualitative research project (Myers, 1997c). Nevertheless, I think that it is useful to think of the data analysis phase as logically following the data gathering stage. Most of the analysis and interpretation of the data tends to occur towards the end of a research project. Hence, this is why Part V follows a discussion of some of the qualitative techniques for data collection that were discussed in Part IV.

One of the reasons for focusing on the analysis and interpretation of qualitative data is that a qualitative researcher almost always ends up with a huge amount of data. The researcher has to figure out what he or she is going to do with all of it. For example, if you conduct a one-hour interview with someone, you may end up with approximately 15 pages of text or 7,000 words. You only need to interview ten people, and you are already up to 70,000 words! If you consider that you will most probably gather additional data besides those obtained from interviews, it is obvious that you cannot possibly include all of your data in a thesis or book (in fact, your readers probably do not want to read all of it anyway). Hence, you need to reduce the data somehow or edit the data into some kind of manageable form. Qualitative data analysis approaches enable you to do that. They help you to focus on some of the most important aspects of your data.

Another reason for focusing on qualitative data analysis is to transform your data into something that is meaningful to you and your intended audience. It is not enough simply to reduce the quantity of data; rather, the whole point is to come up with some insights that help you and others to understand or explain the subject at hand. This requires you to interpret your data in an interesting way. Again, this is where qualitative data analysis approaches can help. They can help you to answer questions such as: What is the meaning of my data? What are the main themes in my data? How do my data contribute to knowledge in my field?

There are many different ways to analyse qualitative data. Given the tremendous variety of approaches, this chapter provides only an overview of some of the ones that are most commonly used in business and management. However, following this overview, three approaches to analysing qualitative data are discussed in more detail in subsequent chapters. Hermeneutics is discussed in Chapter 14, semiotics in Chapter 15, and approaches which focus on narrative in Chapter 16. It could be argued that grounded theory is also a mode of analysis, but since grounded theory has been discussed earlier, a separate chapter will not be devoted to it in Part V. However, some general principles that grounded theorists use (e.g. with respect to coding) will be discussed in this chapter, since some of the principles can be applied to other qualitative data analysis approaches besides grounded theory.

Although I am discussing each qualitative data analysis approach separately in this and the following chapters, it can be very fruitful to combine some of these approaches. For example, it is possible to combine hermeneutics with narrative analysis, just as it is possible to combine some forms of narrative analysis with discourse analysis or the analysis of metaphor. The two main things to watch out for are to make sure that the data you have gathered support the use of the particular data analysis approaches and that the approaches are used in a reasonably consistent manner. However, it is also perfectly acceptable to use just one approach to qualitative data analysis. Obviously it is much simpler to do that.

APPROACHES TO ANALYSING QUALITATIVE DATA

As I have just mentioned, there are many different ways to analyse and interpret qualitative data. I will now review some of the most common ones that are used in business and management.

Coding

One of the simplest ways to analyse qualitative data is to do some kind of coding on the data. A code can be a word that is used to describe or summarize a sentence, a paragraph, or even a whole piece of text such as an interview.

Miles and Huberman say that: 'Codes are tags or labels for assigning units of meaning to the descriptive or inferential information compiled during a study. Codes are attached to "chunks" of varying size – words, phrases, sentences, or whole paragraphs, connected or unconnected to a specific setting' (1994: 56).

As soon as you start coding a piece of text, you have already started to analyse it. Coding is analysis. You are assigning a label to a chunk of textual data and classifying that chunk into a certain category. Coding helps you to reduce the size of your data (at least in your mind). Codes are useful for retrieving and organizing the data, and they speed up the analysis (Miles & Huberman, 1994).

Ryan and Bernard (2000) suggest that there are six fundamental tasks associated with coding. These tasks are sampling, identifying themes, building codebooks, marking texts, constructing models (relationships among codes), and testing these models against empirical data. In more detail:

1 **Sampling** identifies the texts that are to be analyzed, and the basic units of analysis within these texts.
2 **Identifying themes** usually involves the researcher inducing themes from the text itself. However, themes can also be derived from the literature.
3 **Building codebooks** involves organizing lists of codes (often in hierarchies) and their definitions.
4 **Marking texts** involves the assigning of codes to units of text.
5 **Constructing models** involves identifying how the themes, concepts, beliefs and behaviors are linked to each other.
6 **Testing models** involves testing the model developed in step 5 on a different or wider set of data.

There are various types of codes: descriptive codes (open codes), interpretive codes (axial or selective codes), theoretical codes, pattern codes, etc. As some of these codes were discussed earlier in Chapter 9, I will not discuss them here.

Memos

As well as coding, memos are a useful way of starting to analyse your data. Memos are in effect your own commentary on what was happening or what you were doing during your research project. They state what you were thinking, feeling, and/or doing at a certain time.

Esterberg (2002) says there are two main types of memos: procedural memos and analytic memos. Procedural memos focus on the research process. They summarize what you did and how you did it. They help you to keep track of what you have done. Analytic memos focus more on the subject matter. They focus on the data and contain hunches and ideas about what the data mean (Esterberg, 2002). They are the first step in developing concepts and themes that arise from your data.

Analytic Induction

Another way to analyse qualitative data is to use analytic induction. Analytic induction is a way to develop causal explanations of a phenomenon from one or more cases. Ryan and Bernard (2000) describe the sequence of steps that are used as follows:

> First, define a phenomenon that requires explanation and propose an explanation. Next, examine a case to see if the explanation fits. If it does, then examine another case. An explanation is accepted until a new case falsifies it. When a case is found that doesn't fit, then, under the rules of analytic induction, the alternatives are to change the explanation (so that you can include the new case) or redefine the phenomenon (so that you can exclude the nuisance case). Ideally the process continues until a universal explanation for all known cases of a phenomenon is attained. (p. 787)

Markus's article is a good example of analytic induction in business and management (Markus, 1983). Markus tested three theories of resistance to management information systems with data from an in-depth case study. The first theory holds that resistance is caused by people – resistance is people determined. The second theory holds that resistance is caused by the technology – resistance is systems determined. The third theory holds that resistance is caused by the interaction of the people with the system. The case study data illustrate the superiority of the interaction theory (Markus, 1983).

Series of Events

Another way to analyse qualitative data is to list a series of events. An event listing is a series of events organized by chronological time periods.

Table 13.1   Series of events (adapted from Lee & Myers, 2004)

Date	Events
1990	SEKTOR group of companies formed with Billy Wilton as chief executive
1991–3	CamCo, MaxCo, and Xenon managed as independent business units All business units are seen as production arms of SEKTOR
1993	Stark formed from the merger of CamCo, MaxCo, and Xenon David Callon becomes general manager of Stark Movement to develop a single corporate identity begins
1993–mid 1998	Stark seen as the marketing arm of SEKTOR group
1994	Strategic Information Technology Project starts
1995	ERP project starts
1998	ERP system goes live
1998	Gene Romm becomes general manager of Stark A clearer separation of businesses is espoused, i.e. disintegration
1999–present	Stark seen as a production arm of SEKTOR

The events can possibly be sorted into categories. Some events occur before others and are connected. The events can be described in narrative form and/or summarized in a table or flow chart (Miles & Huberman, 1994).

Table 13.1 is an example of a series of events listed in tabular form. The table appears in an article that discusses company strategy and its relationship to the implementation of enterprise resource planning (ERP) systems. The table summarizes some of the major events that occurred in a particular company over a ten-year period (events that were related to changes in senior managers and strategy). As can be seen, the events are listed in chronological order. Each of the rows summarizes what happened. A more detailed narrative of the events is included in the article (Lee & Myers, 2004).

Critical Incidents

The critical incident approach involves asking people to discuss events or incidents that are deemed by the researcher to be extremely important and pertinent to the research (Miles & Huberman, 1994). It is, in effect, a shorter form of the 'series of events' approach. The critical incident approach 'provides a systematic means for gathering the significances others attach to events, analyzing the emerging patterns, and laying out tentative conclusions for the reader's consideration' (Kain, 2004: 85). Often, these incidents are then analysed together, to see if there are commonalities between them.

Although the critical incident technique has strong positivist roots, it can be used with interpretive research as well (Kain, 2004).

Events can also be states. For example, a manager might become alarmed at the downturn in sales in a particular region. This might be deemed a critical incident by the researcher.

Hermeneutics

Another way to analyse qualitative data is to use hermeneutics. Hermeneutics can be treated as both an underlying philosophy and a specific approach to qualitative data analysis (Bleicher, 1980). The following discussion is concerned with using hermeneutics as a specific approach to qualitative data analysis.

Hermeneutics suggests a way of understanding textual data. It is primarily concerned with the meaning of a text or text-analogue (an example of a text-analogue is an organization, which the researcher comes to understand through text or pictures). The basic question in hermeneutics is: what is the meaning of this text (Radnitzky, 1970: 20)?

Taylor (1976) says that:

> Interpretation, in the sense relevant to hermeneutics, is an attempt to make clear, to make sense of an object of study. This object must, therefore, be a text, or a text-analogue, which in some way is confused, incomplete, cloudy, seemingly contradictory – in one way or another, unclear. The interpretation aims to bring to light an underlying coherence or sense. (p. 153)

One of the key concepts in hermeneutics is the idea of the hermeneutic circle. The hermeneutic circle refers to the dialectic between the understanding of the text as a whole and the interpretation of its parts, in which descriptions are guided by anticipated explanations (Gadamer, 1976a). It follows from this that we have an expectation of meaning from the context of what has gone before. The movement of understanding is constantly from the whole to the part and back to the whole. Gadamer says that: 'It is a circular relationship ... The anticipation of meaning in which the whole is envisaged becomes explicit understanding in that the parts, that are determined by the whole, themselves also determine this whole' (1976a: 117).

Ricoeur suggests that: 'Interpretation ... is the work of thought which consists in deciphering the hidden meaning in the apparent meaning, in unfolding the levels of meaning implied in the literal meaning' (1974: xiv).

If hermeneutic analysis were to be used in business and management, the object of the interpretive effort could become one of attempting to make sense of a company as a text-analogue. In a company, the different stakeholders can have confused, incomplete, cloudy, and contradictory views on many issues. The aim of the hermeneutic analysis could be one of trying to make sense of the whole and the relationship between the people and the company. The use of hermeneutics is discussed in more detail in Chapter 14.

HERMENEUTICS AND EMAIL COMMUNICATIONS

In the field of information systems, Lee (1994) uses hermeneutics to critique information richness theory (IRT). IRT postulates that electronic mail is a lean medium that does not readily support the level of communication richness associated with, for instance, a face-to-face meeting. According to IRT, email filters out important cues such as body language and tone of voice and, unlike a face-to-face meeting, is not conducive to immediate feedback. IRT considers the property of leanness to be inherent to the medium of electronic mail.

Contrary to IRT, Lee shows how richness occurs in email communications. In examining actual email exchanged among managers in a corporation, his study interprets how email users themselves understand and experience it. Using various hermeneutic concepts, he finds that richness or leanness is not an inherent property of email as a medium, but an emergent property of the interaction of the medium with its organizational context. He shows that a complex world of social constructions may be evoked through email communications in a way which is not unlike what happens in face-to-face meetings (Lee, 1994).

Semiotics

Semiotics is primarily concerned with the analysis of signs and symbols and their meaning. A sign or symbol is something that can stand for something else. According to Eco, 'semiotics is concerned with everything that can be taken as a sign' (1976: 7). This broad definition means that words, images, and objects can all be studied as signs, as long as they have been recorded in some way and can be studied (e.g. in writing or on video).

There are various kinds of semiotics, although there are two main semiotic traditions. The European tradition is based on the work of Saussure, whereas the American tradition is largely based on the work of Peirce. Saussure was concerned with the role of signs as part of social life, whereas Peirce was more interested in a more abstract 'formal doctrine of signs'.

Chandler (2008) says that:

Contemporary semioticians study signs not in isolation but as part of semiotic 'sign systems' (such as a medium or genre). They study how meanings are made: as such, being concerned not only with communication but also with the construction and maintenance of reality.

In business and management, the greatest use of semiotics has been in marketing, consumer research, and information systems. This is because of the pervasiveness of signs in marketing communications (e.g. brand names, logos, and advertising) and the importance of 'information' in information systems.

The use of semiotics is discussed in more detail in Chapter 15.

Content Analysis

Payne and Payne say that content analysis 'seeks to demonstrate the meaning of written or visual sources (like newspapers and advertisements) by systematically allocating their content to pre-determined, detailed categories, and then both quantifying and interpreting the outcomes' (2004: 51).

Krippendorf defines content analysis as 'a research technique for making replicable and valid references from data to their contexts' (1980). The researcher searches for structures and patterned regularities in the text and makes inferences on the basis of these regularities.

To do this, the researcher first of all develops a set of categories of words and phrases. These codes are then applied to units of text. Once the texts have been coded, various statistical techniques can be applied. Content analysis is thus, in effect, a quantitative method of analysing the content of qualitative data (documents, pictures, and videos).

McNabb (2002) comments that:

> The main advantage of content analysis is that it provides the researcher with a structured method for quantifying the contents of a qualitative or interpretive text, and does so in a simple, clear, and easily repeatable format. Its main disadvantage is that it contains a built-in bias of isolating bits of information from their context. Thus, the contextual meaning is often lost or, at the least, made problematic. (p. 414)

Content analysis is thus most useful when the meaning of the text is relatively straightforward and obvious (McNabb, 2002). It is useful for looking at frequencies of words and their change in frequency over time. It can be used for analysing historical trends, e.g. mention of the Internet in marketing magazines over the last ten years. It can be used to analyse interview texts, e.g. counting the use of brand names.

Conversation Analysis

Conversation analysis looks at the use of language by people as a type of action, or as a skilled accomplishment by competent actors. A key concept within conversation analysis is the idea of the *speaking turn*. The principle of turn-taking in speech is claimed to be a universal feature of all conversations.

Unlike written documents, verbal conversations tend to be informal, semi-structured, and ungrammatical. Often the topic can change in an instant, leaving the previous topic of conversation hanging or unfinished. Conversation analysis is useful for analysing the change in meanings that can occur during verbal communications.

Hence, unlike content analysis which tends to assume that the meaning of words is relatively straightforward, conversation analysis does not presume the existence of fixed meanings in words and idioms. Rather, it assumes that the meanings are shaped in the context of the exchange. To understand and explain these meanings, the researcher has to immerse him- or herself in the verbal interactions (Klein & Truex, 1995) that have been previously tape recorded.

Discourse Analysis

Discourse analysis looks at the way texts are constructed and is concerned with the social contexts within which the text is embedded. The word 'discourse' refers to communication that goes back and forth, like an argument or debate. All language can be treated as a social interaction (there is always a speaker/writer and listener/reader), but discourse analysis focuses mostly on language in use – the use of naturally occurring language in speech and/or written text. Hence, discourse analysis is concerned with actual instances of language as used in communication.

Johnstone (2002) says that

> the basic question a discourse analyst asks is: Why is this text the way it is? Why is it not another way? Why these particular words in this particular order? (p. 8)

Although there are many different kinds of discourse analysis, many researchers using discourse analysis tend to focus on 'language games'. A language game refers to a well-defined unit of interaction consisting of a sequence of verbal moves in which turns of phrases, the use of metaphor, and allegory all play an important part. Discourse analysis encourages multiple readings and interpretations of a text (Klein & Truex, 1995).

Gill (2000) says there are three broad traditions of discourse analysis. The first is known as critical linguistics, social semiotics, or critical language studies. The second is influenced by speech–act theory, ethnomethodology, and conversation analysis. The third tradition is associated with post-structuralism, perhaps the most well known being the work of Michel Foucault (Gill, 2000).

Narrative Analysis

Narrative is defined by the *Concise Oxford English Dictionary* as 'a spoken or written account of connected events; a story' (Soanes & Stevenson, 2004). Traditionally, a narrative requires a plot, as well as some coherence. It has a linear structure, with a beginning, middle, and end. Narrative analysis is a qualitative approach to the interpretation and analysis of qualitative data.

There are many kinds of narrative analysis. In an oral narrative, for instance, the narrative is a record of events that are seen as significant by one person (the narrator). Other narratives describe significant events in the life of an organization. Harvard case studies fit into this category, as they have a plot with a more or less obvious ending. Business students are expected to figure out the moral of the story. At the other extreme are post-modern 'ante-narratives'. Ante-narrative analysis tends to reject 'grand narratives' as single voiced, instead looking at the fragments of multiple stories. Boje (2001) provides an excellent discussion of the many different kinds of post-modern narrative analysis approaches and their application to qualitative research in organizations and management.

Metaphorical Analysis

A metaphor is the application of a name or descriptive term or phrase to an object or action to which it is not literally applicable (e.g. a window in Windows Vista). Metaphors do not appear in isolation, but are part of larger meaningful structures.

Metaphorical analysis 'allows a systematic reflection of the metaphors in which, and through which, we perceive, speak, think, and act' (Schmitt, 2005: 369).

Schmitt says that the first step of metaphorical analysis is to identify the metaphors contained in the text. A metaphor can be determined when:

a. A word or phrase, strictly-speaking, can be understood beyond the literal meaning in context of what is being said; and
b. The literal meaning stems from an area of physical or cultural experience (source area)
c. which, however, is – in this context – transferred to a second, often abstract, area (target area). (Schmitt, 2005: 384)

The second step involves sorting the metaphorical idioms and clustering them under a smaller number of concepts.

Koller (2004) discusses the use of metaphorical analysis to study business media such as the *Financial Times* and *Business Week*. She looked at metaphor frequency in four sample texts, then looked at the metaphor scenario (the scenario within which the metaphor was used). This was followed by describing metaphoric chains within the texts. Metaphoric chains elaborate and extend the use of a metaphor (Koller, 2004).

WHICH QUALITATIVE DATA ANALYSIS APPROACH?

For the novice qualitative researcher, the sheer number of alternative approaches to qualitative data analysis might seem bewildering. All of them are concerned with qualitative data such as documents, pictures, or video, but each approach has a slightly different focus. Some approaches are quite similar, whereas others are completely different and might even have underlying assumptions which are opposed.

My personal view is that there is no such thing as one approach that is better than all the others. Rather, each approach has its advantages and disadvantages. Hence, in choosing a particular way to analyse your data, I suggest some of your considerations should be as follows:

1   Do you find the approach interesting?
2   Is the approach reasonably consistent with your own philosophical assumptions about knowledge and reality?
3   Is the approach reasonably consistent with the research method you employed?
4   Have you gathered the right quantity and quality of data for the particular qualitative data analysis method?
5   Do you have a supervisor or some other faculty member who can provide advice and guidance on the use of your preferred approach?

The first consideration is perhaps the most important of all – do you find your proposed approach to qualitative data analysis interesting? If you find a particular approach boring, then it is unlikely that you will do a good job of qualitative data analysis. You need to choose an approach that you find intellectually stimulating.

The second consideration suggests that if you are a positivist researcher, then something like content analysis or analytic induction might be consistent with your own philosophical assumptions. If you are an interpretive researcher, then something like hermeneutics, semiotics, or narrative analysis might be more appropriate. A critical researcher might choose discourse analysis or some form of ante-narrative.

The third consideration asks you to check that your approach to qualitative data analysis is consistent with your research method. For example, if you used grounded theory, then it might be best to continue to use some kind of coding, rather than try to use something like hermeneutics or discourse analysis.

The fourth consideration looks at the data you have gathered. If you have transcripts of tape-recorded conversations, then conversation analysis might be a good choice. On the other hand, if you do not have tapes of any conversations, then obviously conversation analysis is out of the question.

The fifth consideration is very important if you are writing up a thesis for a research Masters or PhD. You need good advice on the appropriate use of a particular approach. By appropriate, I mean using it in the way in which it is normally used within your own discipline. In the final analysis, your examiners will assess your thesis based on their own experience of acceptable use within a particular tradition. Advice on what qualifies as appropriate or acceptable in your discipline is what an experienced supervisor should be able to give, such that you navigate the examination process successfully. The worst outcome is one where your examiners are unqualified to examine your work, i.e. they do not have the skills or the experience in the approach you have used. In this case you run the risk of failure. It is a bit late to complain about the unfairness of the examination process after it has taken place; hence, it is much better to ensure you have the appropriate guidance early on.

USE OF QUALITATIVE DATA ANALYSIS SOFTWARE

These days, most qualitative researchers use quite a few computer software applications to help them with their research. This usually includes, at a minimum, Microsoft Word (or some other word processing software) to write up their notes and their transcriptions of interviews, and to help in the writing and editing of a thesis, papers, and/or books. Additionally, many people use a bibliographic software package such as EndNote or ProCite. If you are writing a thesis or many papers, this kind of software can save you a lot of time in managing your references (e.g. by automatically reformatting them for a different journal style).

As well as word processing and bibliographic software, a majority of qualitative researchers probably also use email, a search engine on the Internet (such as Google), and their own internal university systems for library access. In my own case, although I still receive the print version of many journals (as a member of an association or as an editorial board member), I find that I rarely consult the hard copy any more. I find it so much easier and quicker to access the electronic version of an article in a journal in one of the bibliographic databases (such as ABI/Inform) that are available in my own university library. One advantage of these online databases is that I am able to access them from home or when I am overseas.

Qualitative data analysis (QDA) software, however, is a different type of software to the ones mentioned above. Sometimes known as Computer-Assisted Qualitative Data Analysis Software (CAQDAS), this software can be used to help with the analysis of qualitative data. Weitzman and Miles (1995) say that QDA software can help the qualitative researcher in the following ways:

- Making notes in the field, writing up or transcribing field notes
- Editing: correcting, extending, or revising field notes
- Memoing: writing reflective commentaries on some aspect of the data
- Coding: attaching keywords or tags to segments of text to permit later retrieval
- Storage: keeping text in an organized database
- Search and retrieval: locating relevant segments of texts
- Data 'linking': forming categories, clusters, or networks of information
- Content analysis: counting frequencies, sequence, or locations of words and phrases
- Data display: placing selected or reduced data in a condensed organized format
- Conclusion-drawing and verification: helping interpretation of data and testing findings
- Theory-building: developing systematic explanations of findings; testing hypotheses
- Graphic mapping: creating diagrams that depict findings or theories
- Preparing interim and final reports

Although almost all QDA software packages allow you to code, search, and retrieve, there are significant differences between them. Some will allow you to import documents from Microsoft Office, whereas others will allow you to import plain text documents only. Some will allow you to work with multimedia documents such as videos, photos, or music, whereas others will allow you to work with textual documents only.

Of the approximately 15 software packages that are available, the two most popular are NVivo and Atlas/ti. NVivo is the latest version of the software from QSR International, software which was previously known as NUD*IST (Nonnumerical Unstructured Data, providing ways of managing ideas by Indexing, Searching and Theorizing) or N6. Many universities have site licences for at least one of these products. Barry (1998) provides a useful comparison of both products; however, her review is now somewhat dated as both products have improved considerably over the past decade.

Should You Use QDA Software?

If you are doing qualitative research in business and management, should you use QDA software? My advice is as follows.

If you are using a research method and QDA approach that require you to code, search, and retrieve text, such as grounded theory or content analysis, then I strongly recommend that you use a good QDA software package. Such a package will make the process so much quicker and easier.

On the other hand, if you are using a research method and a QDA approach that is more holistic, such as hermeneutics and narrative analysis, then you may prefer not to use QDA software. This is because a software package cannot mechanize the kind of analysis that characterizes these approaches. Qualitative researchers using such approaches rely mostly on their own judgement and intuition when they are analysing their data. However, even in this case, I believe that you might find QDA software useful. This is because you do not have to use coding with the software if you do not wish to code. Instead, you can use the software to annotate text and/or create memos linked to specific sections of text. Alternatively, you can use the coding capability of the software, but think of it as marking, tagging, indexing, or labelling instead (Ereaut, 2002). In other words, you can use it for your own purposes and to suit your own style of research if you so choose.

As a general rule, therefore, I recommend that almost all qualitative researchers should consider using QDA software. However, if you use the software, you should remember that it is only a tool. You should also remember that it can be a temptation to become too detailed in your analysis simply because the software allows you to do so. I have found this to be especially the case with more inexperienced researchers. The danger is that you will become too bogged down in the detail (e.g. coding) and not see the big picture. However, if you have a clear idea beforehand of what kind of analysis you plan to do, then you should be able to avoid this trap and use the software appropriately.

EXAMPLES OF ANALYSING QUALITATIVE DATA

Narrative Analysis in Accounting

Davie (2005) examines the role of accounting in the financial restructuring of the Fijian timber industry. She tells the story of a recently corporatized state-owned enterprise in Fiji, namely Fiji Pine Limited (FPL).

The research method used was that of ethnography. Her data were collected via observation (in ethnic Fijian villages), attending meetings, interviews, and archival records. Her ethnographic research was oriented towards studying accounting's role in institutionalized patterns of discrimination in affirmative-action initiatives.

Davie's main topic is the attempt to give preference to indigenous Fijians in the Fijian timber industry. The financial restructuring of the pine industry was part of the affirmative-action policy of the Fijian government.

Her story reveals how accounting–finance expertise enabled a highly sensitive and controversial political issue of indigenous preferencing to be hidden under a veneer of acceptable calculations. She says her research shows how accounting can become aligned with racially discriminatory development policies (in this case, favouring the indigenous Fijians). Her conclusion is that accounting is not in itself racist, but it can become racist through the context in which it is practised (Davie, 2005).

Exercises

1   The following is a simple coding exercise:

   • First, choose an article from a newspaper (about one page long) or a transcript of an interview (if you have one).
   • Second, develop an initial understanding of the content of the text.
   • Third, try breaking the text down into meaningful segments. Create some codes to summarize and label the content (perhaps one for each sentence).
   • Fourth, write some brief memos about the content. What is the text about?
   • Lastly, summarize what you have learnt from the text. What insights have you gained?

2   If you conducted an interview earlier (e.g. as one of the exercises for Chapter 10), analyse the text using one or more of the qualitative data analysis approaches mentioned in this chapter.

Further Reading

Books

Johnstone (2002) provides a good overview of discourse analysis, as does Boje (2001) of narrative analysis.

Although the book by Weitzman and Miles (1995) is now quite old, it is still one of the best in terms of providing criteria for evaluating qualitative data analysis software. However, while it is useful in terms of suggesting what to look for, I would not actually use its analysis of the various software packages, as the software has changed significantly over the past decade.

Websites on the Internet

There are quite a few useful websites on qualitative data analysis:

- 'Semiotics for Beginners' by Daniel Chandler provides a very good overview of semiotics concepts at http://www.aber.ac.uk/media/Documents/S4B/sem01.html
- Stef Slembrouck's site 'What is meant by Discourse Analysis?' is a very useful overview at http://bank.ugent.be/da/da.htm
- Narrative Psychology is an excellent resource on narrative and related areas at http://www.narrativepsych.com
- Christine Barry's comparison of the two most popular qualitative data analysis software packages is useful, even though it is now somewhat dated: http://www.socresonline.org.uk/3/3/4.html

14 HERMENEUTICS

Objectives

By the end of this chapter, you will be able to:

- Understand the purpose of using hermeneutics
- Appreciate some of the fundamental concepts of hermeneutics
- Distinguish between various approaches to using hermeneutics
- Be more confident in using hermeneutics
- Recognize the advantages and disadvantages of using hermeneutics
- See how hermeneutics has been used in business and management

INTRODUCTION

As we saw in the previous chapter, hermeneutics is one approach to analysing and interpreting qualitative data. This chapter discusses hermeneutics in more depth so that you can appreciate some of the fundamental hermeneutic concepts and become more confident in using hermeneutics in your own research work.

Hermeneutics focuses primarily on the *meaning* of qualitative data, especially textual data. In a qualitative study such as a case study or ethnography, the researcher gathers much textual data. Case study notes, interviews, documents, and field notes record the views of the actors in an organization and describe certain events, and so on. Once this material is gathered, the researcher then has the task of ordering, interpreting, and explaining it in order to make some sense of it.

Hermeneutics provides a set of concepts to help qualitative researchers analyse their data; these concepts can help a researcher to interpret and understand the meaning of a text or multiple texts. The hermeneutic concepts are particularly useful in situations where there are contradictory interpretations of organizational issues and events (e.g. why a certain system was a failure). Hermeneutics is an approach that lends itself to in-depth analyses of social and organizational situations in management and business.

The main purpose of hermeneutics is human understanding: understanding what people say and do, and why. The hermeneutic effort consists of an attempt to make clear, or to make sense of, an object of study.

Hermeneutic philosophy was originally concerned with the interpretation of the Bible and other sacred texts. In the twentieth century, however, hermeneutics was taken up by social philosophers and applied not just to written texts, but to the interpretation of speech and actions (Myers, 2004). Social philosophers such as Gadamer, Habermas, and Ricoeur looked at how the interpretive techniques of hermeneutics could be applied in the social sciences (Mueller-Vollmer, 1988; Palmer, 1969).

Hermeneutic philosophy has also been used by sociologists and cultural anthropologists (Agar, 1986; Geertz, 1973). In this case, culture is treated like a text that needs to be interpreted and understood (Frost, Moore, Louis, Lundberg, & Martin, 1985). The qualitative researcher seeks to discover the meaning of actions or statements in their social and organizational contexts (Bryman, 1989; Myers, 2004).

As an approach to meaning analysis, hermeneutics has been used to analyse qualitative data in various business disciplines, such as information systems and marketing (Arnold & Fischer, 1994; Lee, 1994; Myers, 2004). In information systems research, for example, the subject of organizational discourse about information technology has become an important theme (Wynn, Whitley, Myers, & De Gross, 2002). Hermeneutics has been used to help us understand how information is interpreted and how information systems are used (Boland, 1991). Hermeneutics has also been used to help us understand the information systems development process (Boland & Day, 1989) and the impact of information technology in social and organizational contexts (Lee, 1994; Myers, 1994). In marketing, hermeneutics has been used in consumer research to study the meaning of advertising for consumers (Ritson & Elliott, 1999).

> The purpose of using hermeneutics is to aid human understanding: it helps the qualitative researcher in business and management to understand what people say and do, and why.

Hermeneutics Defined

Hermeneutics can be treated as both an underlying philosophy and a specific mode of analysis (Bleicher, 1980). As a philosophical approach to human understanding, it provides the philosophical grounding for interpretivism (Klein & Myers, 1999; Myers, 1997b). As a mode of analysis, it is an approach to qualitative data analysis. This chapter is concerned primarily with using hermeneutics as an approach to analysing and interpreting qualitative data. Used in this way, it helps a qualitative researcher to understand and interpret the meaning of a text or text-analogue.

Taylor (1976) says that:

> Interpretation, in the sense relevant to hermeneutics, is an attempt to make clear, to make sense of an object of study. This object must, therefore, be a text, or a text-analogue, which in some way is confused, incomplete, cloudy, seemingly contradictory – in one way or another, unclear. The interpretation aims to bring to light an underlying coherence or sense. (p. 153)

The concept of 'text-analogue' refers to anything that can be treated as a text, such as an organization or a culture. Texts include not just written documents, but conversations and even non-verbal communications such as gestures or facial expressions (Diesing, 1991). The hermeneutic task consists in understanding what a particular text means.

For example, let us assume the following scenario. Say that a marketing researcher, Sally, decides to conduct case study research related to marketing strategy in a company. Sally gathers as much data as possible related to the company's marketing strategy. These data include public documents such as the annual report, published statements in newspapers by the CEO, and internal company documents. Once she starts interviewing people, Sally finds that the story is not as clear as the public documents imply. She finds that the marketing director has a different view of the company's marketing strategy than the chief financial officer. The more she talks to people, the more versions of the marketing strategy she gets. Eventually, after doing more in-depth research, Sally comes to the realization that the official marketing strategy as published in the annual report and other official company documents bears little relation to what the company actually does. For instance, the company says customers are its first priority, but then customers have an average wait time of 12 minutes for their calls to be answered by the calls centre.

In this scenario, the organization can be treated as a text that is confused, incomplete, cloudy, seemingly contradictory – in one way or another, unclear. (Taylor, 1976: 153) At the conclusion of the data gathering phase of the research, Sally ends up with hundreds of pages of text (including diagrams, computer data, audiotapes of interviews, etc.). In a sense, there might be hundreds, if not thousands, of subtexts (such as interviews with particular people). Now Sally needs to organize, sort, and edit all this text so that she can write her thesis. Hermeneutics helps a researcher to interpret the text such that it makes sense. It helps the researcher to produce a story that is believable.

HERMENEUTIC CONCEPTS

Hermeneutics provides a set of concepts that help a researcher to understand a text. These concepts will now be described.

Historicity

One fundamental concept in hermeneutic philosophy is that of historicity. Wachterhauser (1986) describes the concept of historicity as follows:

> 'Historicity' does not refer to the incontestable but obvious fact that we live out our lives in time. It refers instead to the thesis that who we are is through and through historical. This concept refers to the claim that the relation between being human and finding ourselves in particular historical circumstances is not accidental but rather essential or 'ontological'. This means that what we are cannot be reduced to a noumenal, ahistorical core such as a transcendental ego or, more broadly, a human nature that is the same in all historical circumstances. Rather, who we are is a function of the historical circumstances and community that we find ourselves in, the historical language we speak, the historically evolving habits and practice we appropriate, the temporally conditioned choices we make … In short, hermeneutics defends the ontological claim that human beings are their history. (p. 7)

This implies that our understanding of ourselves and others in business organizations occurs in an historical context where our 'historically informed present informs our interpretation of any topic or subject' (Myers, 2004). Understanding a phenomenon means being able to talk about it with others in a community (Wachterhauser, 1986).

To illustrate the applicability of this concept, let us return to our scenario of Sally doing case study research on marketing strategy. She finds that, for the past 12 months, both the revenues and profits of the company have been down. She also finds that the chief financial officer appears to have much more influence over the CEO than the marketing director. Two to three years ago, however, when both revenues and profits were growing, it appears that the marketing director had more influence.

Now we see that the current mismatch of the strategy with action appears to be a result of historical circumstances. Perhaps the strategy, as described in official company documents, was developed a few years ago; perhaps the strategy correctly described senior management's intention at that time. However, with the downturn, the chief financial officer has insisted on cost cutting and some redundancies to keep the company in good financial health. That is his job.

The Hermeneutic Circle

Another fundamental concept in hermeneutic philosophy is that of the hermeneutic circle. The idea of a hermeneutic circle refers to the dialectic between the understanding of the text as a whole and the interpretation of its parts, in which descriptions are guided by anticipated explanations. As Gadamer (1976a) explains:

> It is a circular relationship … The anticipation of meaning in which the whole is envisaged becomes explicit understanding in that the parts, that are determined by the whole, themselves also determine this whole. (p. 117)

To explain the concept of the hermeneutic circle, Klein and Myers (1999) relate Gadamer's example of how we are to translate the meaning of a sentence into a foreign language:

> As a case in question, consider the sentence 'they are playing football'. In order to understand the individual parts of the sentence (i.e. whether football is a round ball, an egg-shaped ball or no ball at all), we must attempt to understand the meaning of the sentence as a whole. The process of interpretation moves from a precursory understanding of the parts to the whole and from a global understanding of the whole context back to an improved understanding of each part, i.e. the meanings of the words. The sentence as a whole in turn is a part of some larger context. If from this context it is clear that nobody is engaged in sport at all, then we can conclude that the meaning of 'they are playing football' must be metaphorical. To apply the metaphor, one needs to interpret 'football' as an issue which is contested which in turn involves a new understanding of the meaning of the term 'playing' as involving something abstract which is being 'thrown or kicked around'. Also, 'playing' no longer means physical movement on a grassy field. (p. 71)

Thus the movement of understanding is constantly from the whole to the part and back to the whole.

The idea of the hermeneutic circle can be applied not just to texts, but to any text-analogue.

To illustrate this concept, let us return to Sally doing her case study research on an organization. As I have said, the organization itself can be treated as a kind of text. Sally starts by gaining some general knowledge about the organization (the whole). This might involve reading some annual reports, newspaper reports, and any other publicly available information (the parts). After doing this, Sally then might interview specific people within the organization about certain subjects or events. As more interviews are conducted and as more information is gathered, she understands more about the organization as a whole and how the various parts fit together. She will gain a better understanding of how everything fits together and why things are the way they are. The movement of understanding 'is constantly from the whole to the part and back to the whole'.

However, as we have seen, her research might also reveal some apparent absurdities or contradictions. The company's marketing strategy says one thing, but the actions of the organization suggest something else. As more people from different parts and functions of the organization are interviewed, some contradictions and differences of opinion emerge. There may be differences of opinion as to why a certain event happened (e.g. why the advertising firm in charge of the advertising campaign was fired). In this case, the hermeneutic process should continue until the apparent absurdities, contradictions, and oppositions in the organization no longer appear strange, but make sense. From the perspective of a qualitative researcher, the fieldwork is not complete until all the apparent contradictions are resolved – at least in the researcher's mind (Myers, 2004).

We can see that the concept of the hermeneutic circle suggests that we have an expectation of meaning from the context of what has gone before. Hermeneutics suggests that we come to understand a complex whole from preconceptions about the meanings of its parts and their interrelationships.

Ricoeur defines interpretation as 'the work of thought which consists in deciphering the hidden meaning in the apparent meaning, in unfolding the levels of meaning implied in the literal meaning' (1974: 13).

This task of unfolding the levels of meaning is at the heart of hermeneutics. The goal of interpretation is 'to produce a reading of the text that fits all important details into a consistent, coherent message, one that fits coherently into the context' (Diesing, 1991: 110).

Prejudice

Another concept that is essential to hermeneutics is that of 'prejudice'. Hermeneutics suggests that 'prejudice', pre-judgement, or prior knowledge plays an important part in our understanding. The basic idea is that our attempt to understand a text always involves some prior knowledge or expectation of what the text is about. In fact we cannot even begin to understand a text unless we have some understanding of the language in which it is written. Understanding a language involves, at a minimum, prior knowledge of the vocabulary, rules of grammar, and social conventions with regard to the appropriateness of what should or should not be said. Thus prior knowledge is a prerequisite for understanding, even though most of this knowledge might be tacit knowledge and taken for granted (Myers, 2004).

In positivist social science, however, 'prejudice' or pre-judgement is seen as a source of bias and therefore a hindrance to true knowledge; objectivity, according to positivism, is best attained if a social scientist adopts a value-free position and does not let biases interfere with his or her analysis. By contrast, hermeneutics suggests that understanding always involves interpretation; interpretation means using one's own preconceptions so that the meaning of the object can become clear to us (Gadamer, 1975: 358). Understanding is thus not merely a reproductive process, but a productive process, and interpretations will always keep changing (Myers, 2004).

Hermeneutics thus suggests that prejudice or foreknowledge is the necessary starting point of our understanding. The hermeneutic maxim is: 'no knowledge without foreknowledge' (Diesing, 1991: 108). The critical task of hermeneutics then becomes one of distinguishing between 'true prejudices, by which we understand, from the false ones by which we misunderstand' (Gadamer, 1976a: 124). Of course, the suspension of our prejudices is necessary if we are to begin to understand a text or text-analogue. But as Gadamer points out, this does not mean that we simply set aside our prejudices. Rather, it means that we, as researchers, must become aware of our own historicality (Gadamer, 1976a: 125). By this he means that we need to become aware of how our own views and biases are to a large extent determined by our own culture and personal history. Our own ideas and personal experience (education, family situation, job, etc.) have a significant impact on how we view the world. Of course, in many scientific experiments it is considered important to know how the research instrument is 'calibrated'. What hermeneutics emphasizes is that in almost all kinds of social research, the research instrument is the researcher. Therefore it is important to know how the researcher approached the research (Myers, 2004).

This awareness of the dialogue between the text and the interpreter has been brought to the fore in contemporary hermeneutics. The earlier hermeneutic philosophers such as Dilthey ignored this dialogical relationship between the text and the interpreter and attempted to understand the objective meaning of a text in its own right.

Let us return again to the story of Sally's case study research. Sally, as a marketing researcher, believes that a company's marketing strategy should be taken seriously. She is disappointed that the company seems to have abandoned its marketing strategy, even though she can understand the reasons for doing so. She tries to be objective in writing up the case, but in her own mind she wishes that the marketing director had more influence with the CEO once again. She thinks it is a bit unfair that he is being blamed for what is, after all, a downturn in the market across the board.

Autonomization and Distanciation

Two further concepts that are important in hermeneutics are those of autonomization and distanciation (Myers, 2004). Ricoeur (1981) makes an important distinction between verbal speech and written text. He says that the author's meaning, once it is inscribed in a text, takes on a life of its own. This process of autonomization takes place whenever speech is inscribed in a text: the text takes on a fixed, finite, and external representation. This means that the text now has an autonomous, 'objective' existence independent of the author. Once something is published or in the public domain, it is virtually impossible to take it back. A good example of this is when a politician says something in an interview with a reporter. Many times a politician will 'regret' something that was said or apologize for it, but after the statement is published, it is impossible to take it back. Many politicians have been forced to resign because of a statement that has taken on a life of its own.

Closely related to the concept of autonomization is that of distanciation (Lee, 1994). Distanciation refers to the inevitable distance that occurs in time and space between the text and its original author on the one hand, and the readers of the text (the audience) on the other. A fundamental characteristic of a text is that it is communication 'in and through distance' (Ricoeur, 1991: 76). Since the text takes on a life of its own, it becomes dissociated from the original author, the originally intended audience, and even its original meaning. Although not all hermeneutic philosophers are agreed on this point, Ricoeur suggests that the goal of hermeneutics is not to get 'behind' the text, i.e. to seek to reconstruct the mind of the author or original readers. Ricoeur says that we can never really do this.

For example, we can never really understand what Plato was thinking when he wrote one of his classic books of philosophy. This is impossible given the distance in time and space between Plato and us. No matter how good an imagination we have, we cannot simply abandon our own prejudices, biases, culture, and personal history (since many of these things are taken for granted by us and they are part of our being). Rather, the hermeneutic task is to make Plato's writings our own. The 'text is the medium through which we understand ourselves' (Ricoeur, 1991: 87).

However, if we are doing qualitative research today, then this insight of Ricoeur's should be tempered with the knowledge that we can sometimes go back and interview the original author of a document. It is technically feasible to try to figure out what someone was thinking at the time. Nevertheless, I believe Ricoeur's main point is still valid: a text, even if the author is still alive, takes on a life of its own.

To return to Sally and her case study research. It has been six months since she did the empirical part of her research. She is now writing the final draft of her thesis. She finds that she is becoming much more sympathetic to the chief financial officer than she was before. She now realizes that the cost-cutting measures recommended by him were indeed for the good of the company as a whole. A recent article in the business section of the local newspaper has praised the company for reacting quickly to the downturn, whereas the company's competitors are now in a much worse financial position. Sally decides to call up the chief financial officer to see if she can have one last interview. Unfortunately, she finds that he has left the company. Sally calls the personal assistant of the chief financial officer at his new company. The personal assistant, however, says that he is far too busy to be interviewed. Sally tries to convince her otherwise, but the personal assistant is simply not interested in Sally's research with her boss's previous company. Why should she care? Another interview is just not possible.

In Sally's case, she has to make do with the transcript of the original interview with the chief financial officer. The author is no longer available for a further interview.

Appropriation and Engagement

Another two concepts are those of appropriation and engagement. Hermeneutics suggests that we only come to understand the meaning of a text if we appropriate the meaning of the text for ourselves, i.e. we make it our own. This act of appropriation is essential for understanding to take place (Myers, 2004). Gadamer suggests that meaning does not reside in 'the subjective feelings of the interpreter' nor in 'the intentions of the author'. Rather, meaning emerges from the engagement of the reader and the text. As a reader engages with the text, both the reader and text (or the meaning of the text) are changed. This process of critical engagement with the text is crucial.

Now that Sally has finished her thesis, she feels that she has a much better understanding of the dilemmas of the various people in the company that she studied. She can see why certain people reacted the way they did. Also, she now has a much better understanding of marketing strategy and how that strategy can get derailed. Her supervisor says the story of the derailing of the company's marketing strategy is interesting and needs to be told to a wider audience, so they both start working on a paper for submission to a peer-reviewed journal.

TYPES OF HERMENEUTICS

There are different types of hermeneutics. The early hermeneutic philosophers such as Dilthey advocated a 'pure hermeneutics' which stressed empathic understanding and the understanding of human action from the 'inside'. This form of hermeneutics is the most objectivist form of hermeneutics: it sees the text or object to be investigated as 'out there' and amenable to being investigated in a more or less objective manner by the scientist (Bleicher, 1982: 52).

Bleicher (1982) says that Dilthey failed to take account of the double hermeneutic. Giddens (1976) describes the double hermeneutic as follows:

> Sociology, unlike natural science, stands in a subject–subject relation to its 'field of study', not a subject–object relation; it deals with a pre-interpreted world; the construction of social theory thus involves a double hermeneutic that has no parallel elsewhere. (p. 146)

The double hermeneutic says that the qualitative researcher does not stand, as it were, outside of the subject matter looking in. He or she does not study natural phenomena such as rocks or forests from the outside. Rather, the only way a qualitative researcher can study people is 'from the inside'. That is, he or she must already speak the same language as the people being studied (or, at the very least, be able to understand an interpretation or translation of what has been said). The double hermeneutic recognizes that social researchers are 'subjects' and are just as much interpreters of social situations as the people being studied (Myers, 2004).

Radnitzky points out that the pure hermeneutics advocated by philosophers such as Dilthey is uncritical in that it takes statements or ideologies at face value (Radnitzky, 1970: 20ff.). He cites Gadamer as saying that 'we don't have to imagine oneself in the place of some other person; rather, we have to understand what these thoughts or the sentences expressing them are about' (Radnitzky, 1970: 27).

In contrast to pure hermeneutics, post-modern hermeneutic philosophers argue that there is no such a thing as an objective or 'true' meaning of a text. 'Facts' are what a cultural, conversational community agrees they are (Madison, 1990: 191). Post-modernist hermeneutic philosophers say that a text always goes beyond the author, and every reading is a different reading. This form of hermeneutics is the most subjectivist.

Somewhere between these two positions is critical hermeneutics (Myers, 2004). Critical hermeneutics has emerged following the debates between Habermas and Gadamer (Gadamer, 1976b; Kogler, 1996; Ricoeur, 1976;

Thompson, 1981). Critical hermeneutic philosophers recognize that the interpretive act is one which can never be closed as there is always a possible alternative interpretation (Taylor, 1976). In critical hermeneutics the interpreter constructs the context as another form of text, which can then, of itself, be critically analysed. In a sense, the hermeneutic interpreter is simply creating another text upon a text, and this recursive creation is potentially infinite. Every meaning is constructed, even through the very constructive act of seeking to deconstruct, and the process whereby that textual interpretation occurs is self-critically reflected upon (Ricoeur, 1974).

Critical hermeneutics is thus aware of the double hermeneutic and acknowledges the reflective critique of the interpretation applied by the researcher. This awareness of the dialectic between the text and the interpreter has been brought to the fore in contemporary hermeneutics. Classical or 'pure' hermeneutics ignored this dialectic in the attempt to understand a text in terms of itself.

However, critical hermeneutic philosophers disagree with some post-modern versions of hermeneutics that assume that all interpretations are equally valid (which is itself a normative statement). Some interpretations are better than others. If there are no grounds for judging between alternative explanations, then David Irving's view that the systematic extermination of Jews in German concentration camp gas chambers did not occur is as equally valid as the generally accepted historical view of the Holocaust. Critical hermeneutic philosophers reject this position and suggest that we can judge between alternative explanations, even though that judgement may not always be correct and may change over time. The fact that we sometimes get it wrong does not mean that we should suspend our judgement altogether.

Critical hermeneutic philosophers also suggest that there are socio-economic and political constraints within which human communication takes place. In this form of hermeneutics there is thus an attempt to mediate 'hermeneutically-grounded self-understanding' and 'the objective context in which it is formed' (Bleicher, 1982: 150).

A slightly different form of hermeneutics, closely related to that of critical hermeneutics, is that of 'depth hermeneutics'. Depth hermeneutics assumes that the surface meaning of the 'text' hides, but also expresses, a deeper meaning: 'It assumes a continuing contradiction between the author's conscious and unconscious mind, a false consciousness, which appears in the text' (Diesing, 1991: 130). This form of hermeneutics is a hermeneutics of suspicion (Klein & Myers, 1999). Ricoeur argues that it is possible in certain circumstances to see consciousness as 'false' consciousness. He illustrates the operation of the principle of suspicion with examples of critical analysis from Marx and Freud (Ricoeur, 1976).

USING HERMENEUTICS: AN EXAMPLE

To illustrate some of the practicalities of using hermeneutics, I will draw on an example from my own research work in the field of information systems (Myers, 1994). This particular study used critical hermeneutics and was concerned with the failed implementation of a centralized payroll system for the New Zealand Education Department. Although the system did achieve some measure of success, in the end the centralized payroll system was abandoned.

I was attracted to studying this particular project for several reasons. First, the project received a substantial amount of publicity within New Zealand. The problems with the implementation of this new system were broadcast on national radio and television and featured on the front page of *The New Zealand Herald*. As this new system affected every teacher in a public school in the country, there was wide public interest in it. Second, one of my main research interests at that time was the implementation of information systems. The case fitted perfectly within the scope of this interest. Third, since I had used critical hermeneutics in my earlier research work, I was very interested to see if critical hermeneutics could be applied to this area of information systems research. My hunch was that it would apply very well, since there appeared to be many different stakeholders. For all these reasons, therefore, this case seemed a very good choice.

Unlike ethnographic research, which tends to be very open-ended, I decided to use the interpretive case study method, mostly because it takes much less time. I focused on just one question: why did the system fail? The empirical part of the study was actually the shortest I have ever done in my career, but paradoxically one of the most interesting. The case study material was collected from interviews, documents, and newspaper and magazine reports.

Once I had gathered all the data, the next step was to write a narrative history of the project. This was fairly straightforward, since I simply recounted the major events over time. This was then followed by the case analysis. From a hermeneutic perspective, the case was interesting because of the sharply divergent and sometimes contradictory views of the main protagonists. The project was characterized by conflicting interpretations among the participants about what happened, who was to blame, and how successful the project was. For example, while the system received very bad publicity in the media and was seen as a failure by teachers, 'the Director of Management Services proclaimed some 4 months after implementation that the system was successful in that it was now on target to meet its main financial goal of saving the government millions of dollars in interest payments' (Myers, 1994: 196). Despite this apparent 'success', I discussed the continued opposition of the teachers' union to the payroll system and the government's decision to scrap it just a few months later.

In the first instance, my aim in the analysis section was to show how each person's view 'made sense' when considered from their point of view. My analysis juxtaposed some of the conflicting interpretations and my analysis of them, showing how it was possible for two or more people to hold contradictory views of the same phenomenon or event. For example, the payroll system itself was seen as 'one of the means by which the government intended to restructure educational administration in New Zealand' (Myers, 1994: 197). The opposition of the teachers' union and others to the system was explained (at least in part) by noting that the system became in effect a symbol of the government's resolve to restructure educational administration in New Zealand. Many of them opposed this government initiative. In the final analysis I argued that the disaster itself 'made sense' given the social and historical context within New Zealand at the time. The analysis revealed the various interests of the parties and what they were trying to achieve. I found that the apparent paradox (i.e. the government deciding to scrap the system despite the fact that it was working correctly) could only be explained by looking at the broader social and historical context.

In addition to the case analysis, the article also attempted to make a contribution to implementation theory in information systems. The article argued that most existing models of information systems implementation were somewhat narrow and mechanistic, and that the implementation of the New Zealand Education Department's payroll system could only be understood in terms of its wider social and historical context. I argued that 'success' is a matter of interpretation.

The above example draws attention to a few practical points about using hermeneutics in business and management research (Myers, 2004). First, it is more interesting to use hermeneutics where there are disagreements or contradictory interpretations of the same phenomenon or event. This gives the researcher something to interpret and explain. Second, prejudice, as used in the hermeneutic sense, is something to build upon rather than be avoided. My previous background and experience, along with my current research interests, were the starting point for this particular research project. In a hermeneutic study there is no need to appeal to a false objectivity. In fact this particular research project fitted with my previous experiences, prior knowledge, and interests. However, this is not to say that I had already made up mind as to why the system failed. This was an open question and required further empirical research. Third, it is not necessary to discuss every single hermeneutic concept in every paper or journal article. This is because conference papers and journal articles are, by definition, quite short. In this particular article I focused on just one hermeneutic concept, that of the hermeneutic circle. I believe it is much better to focus on those issues that seem particularly pertinent to the case at hand, rather than try to cover everything. Having said this, however, I think it is important for researchers seeking to use hermeneutics to be familiar with the most important concepts, even if they are not discussed in every paper. Otherwise, there is a danger that hermeneutics will be used inappropriately and simplistically. Fourth, I think it is important to generalize from the case study or the field study to theory (Klein & Myers, 1999). Hermeneutics is something that enables one to do that and in fact almost requires it. This is because a hermeneutic researcher usually starts out with some kind of theoretical framework that he or she wishes to explore within the context of a company or situation.

CRITIQUE OF HERMENEUTICS

The main advantage of using hermeneutics in analysing and interpreting qualitative data is that it enables a much deeper understanding of people in business and organizational settings. It requires a researcher to look at an organization through the eyes of the various stakeholders and from many different perspectives. Hermeneutics allows the qualitative researcher to portray the complexity of organizations and look at them from many angles, e.g. from a social, cultural, and political perspective.

Another advantage of using hermeneutics is that hermeneutics is well grounded in philosophy and the social sciences more generally. This means that it is relatively easy to justify the use of hermeneutics to those who are not so familiar with it.

One disadvantage of hermeneutics is that it focuses the researcher almost entirely on text rather than lived experience. However, this can be seen as a good thing if you are looking towards writing up and publishing your research findings. From the perspective of writing up, the sooner you transform your experiences into text the better.

Another potential disadvantage of hermeneutics is that it can be difficult to know when to conclude a study. Since the hermeneutic interpreter is simply creating another text upon a text, and this recursive creation is potentially infinite, when does the interpretive process stop? There is no easy answer to this question. For qualitative researchers in business and management, however, I suggest that the hermeneutic analysis can stop when you (and your supervisor, if applicable) believe that you have satisfactorily explained most, if not all, of the 'puzzles' or apparent contradictions in the story. When the text – which was perhaps confused and unclear before – becomes clear (at least to you), then you can start writing it up.

EXAMPLES OF USING HERMENEUTICS

Richness in Email Communications

Lee (1994) uses hermeneutics to critique information richness theory. Information richness theory classifies communications media by their capacity to process rich information. According to this theory, richness varies according to the medium's capacity for immediate feedback, the number of cues and channels utilized, personalization, and language variety. The theory postulates that face-to-face communication is the richest medium, whereas a document (such as an email message) is a lean medium. Richness or leanness is conceptualized as an invariant, objective property of the medium itself (Lee, 1994).

After providing an excellent explanation of the differences between interpretivism and positivism, Lee then draws on the hermeneutic theory of Ricoeur (1981) to show that richness or leanness is not an inherent property of the email medium, but an emergent property of the interaction of the email medium within its organizational context.

Instead of using his own qualitative data, Lee uses data from a previously published study by Lynne Markus. He uses transcripts of some actual email messages exchanged among managers from within a corporation to illustrate how richness occurs. These transcripts are related to a particular event in the company that turned out to be politically sensitive and managerially troublesome.

By analysing a series of email exchanges related to this one event, Lee shows that email messages are rich if one takes into account the wider social and political context within which the email communications take place. He also points out that managers who receive email are not passive recipients of data, but active producers of meaning. Lee's hermeneutic analysis reveals a complex world of social and political interactions that are embedded in, and an integral part of, email communications within the company (Lee, 1994).

The Social Uses of Advertising

Ritson and Elliott (1999) say that consumer research in marketing has generally failed to address the socio-cultural settings that contextualize all consumption activity. In the specific case of advertising theory, they say that researchers have tended to ignore the social dimensions of advertising. Hence, this study focuses on the social uses of advertising.

The authors used ethnographic research to study the meaning of advertising in the socially contextualized lives of adolescents. They decided to study adolescents because this group has been shown to be particularly active in the social use of a variety of different forms of popular media. They are also 'advertising literate', in the sense that they have an ability to use advertising meanings for the purposes of social interaction.

One of the authors collected data from six sites (i.e. schools) over a period of six months. Qualitative data collection techniques included observation, fieldwork, and group interviews. All the interviews were tape recorded and transcribed to produce over 500 pages of interview data.

Although only the first author was involved in data collection, both authors analysed the textual data (the transcripts of interviews, field notes, and so forth). The authors used a hermeneutic, iterative approach in their data analysis. They found that the differences between the two interpretations proved to be highly productive. This dialogue between the two researchers helped them to re-analyse the data and produce stronger and more interesting results. One of their conclusions was that adolescents are able to appropriate advertising texts for themselves, independently from the product that the advertisements were promoting.

Exercises

1 Find an issue in the newspaper about which there is considerable disagreement and various opposing viewpoints. Using only the text at your disposal, apply two or three hermeneutic concepts to interpret the text. Are you able to understand the meaning of the text from more than one perspective?

2 Brainstorm to come up with a list of three or four possible research topics. Now come up with one or two research questions per topic.

3 Can you think how some of these topics could be studied using hermeneutics? What kinds of data could you use?

4 Conduct a brief literature search using Google Scholar or some other bibliographic database and see if you can find articles using hermeneutics in your chosen field. What kinds of topics appear?

Further Reading

Books

If you want to learn more about hermeneutics, I suggest you look at one or more of the general introductions. Palmer's (1969) collection of readings on hermeneutics, entitled *Hermeneutics: Interpretation Theory in Schleiermacher, Dilthey, Heidegger, and Gadamer*, is excellent. *The Hermeneutic Reader* edited by Mueller-Vollmer (1988) is another first-rate collection. Both books include selected works by prominent hermeneutic scholars.

From there, you might want to look at Gadamer's (1975) book *Truth and Method*, which is regarded as a classic in the field. Gadamer's main concern is the veracity of interpretation. Given that we cannot escape our pre-understandings and context, how can we avoid being purely relativistic? Gadamer's solution is to suggest that our prejudices and biases can be made subject to critical scrutiny.

Bernstein's (1983) book *Beyond Objectivism and Relativism* represents an important landmark in social philosophy. He shows that there is an important hermeneutical dimension to all science (including the natural sciences). Bernstein's work has had a significant influence on Thomas Kuhn (Kuhn, 1996).

A good introduction to critical hermeneutics is the book by Thompson (1981) entitled *Critical Hermeneutics: A Study in the Thought of Paul Ricoeur and Jurgen Habermas*. Thompson also edited and translated a collection of essays by Ricoeur (1991). This collection presents a comprehensive view of Ricoeur's critical hermeneutics, and looks at the consequences of his hermeneutic philosophy for the social sciences. Ricoeur is best known for his proposal of a 'hermeneutics of suspicion'. He argues that it is possible in certain circumstances to see consciousness as 'false' consciousness.

Articles

Klein and Myers (1999), in an article entitled 'A set of principles for conducting and evaluating interpretive field studies in information systems', suggest a set of principles for the conduct and evaluation of interpretive research in information systems. As these principles are derived primarily from anthropology, phenomenology, and hermeneutics, I believe they are equally relevant to other business disciplines besides information systems.

Websites on the Internet

There are quite a few useful websites about hermeneutics:

- The Wikipedia encyclopedia entry on hermeneutics provides a good introduction at http://en.wikipedia.org/wiki/Hermeneutic
- The International Institute of Hermeneutics is at http://www.chass.utoronto.ca/iih/
- The ISWorld Section on Qualitative Research contains many useful references at http://www.qual.auckland.ac.nz/

15

SEMIOTICS

Objectives

By the end of this chapter, you will be able to:

- Appreciate the potential value of using semiotics
- Understand some important semiotic concepts
- Recognize the advantages and disadvantages of using semiotics
- Know how to use semiotics
- See how semiotics has been used in business and management

INTRODUCTION

As we saw in Chapter 13, semiotics is one approach to analysing and interpreting qualitative data. This chapter discusses semiotics in more depth so that you can appreciate the potential value of using semiotics and understand some of the most important semiotic concepts.

Semiotics is primarily concerned with the analysis of signs and symbols and their meaning. Signs and symbols can be studied not only in language (both written and spoken forms), but also in rituals, culture, images, and art – in fact, anything that can be 'read' as text.

Early in the twentieth century Ferdinand de Saussure, a French professor of linguistics, said that all communication between people was made by means of signs. Since Saussure, semiotic scholars have applied his theory of language to anything which can be considered to be a sign or symbol. Hence, as well as language, semiotics can be applied to images, videos, objects, myth, and culture. For example, a flag (a piece of cloth with a specific design) can represent a country such as the United States, as can one or more words (e.g. the United States or Uncle Sam). Just as words in a language have rules that govern their usage, so do other kinds of signs and symbols. There are various rules and social conventions that govern the usage of a flag. For example, a flag flying at half mast may signify that an important person, such as a president or prime minister, has died.

Semiotic researchers do not study signs in isolation. Rather, they study the conventions governing the use of signs and sign systems. They try to understand how signs and symbols are related to each other. It is usually considered important for the researcher to study the meaning of signs and symbols within their social, cultural, and historical context (McNabb, 2002). As Hackley (2003) describes:

> The meaning of signs is arbitrary. In principle, anything could stand for anything else. It is the cultural context that frames the interpretation of signs and imbues signs with localized meanings. (p. 162)

This means that a sign can mean one thing in one particular cultural context, but mean something quite different in another. For example, looking at someone directly during an interview is considered normal and polite in most Western cultures. In most Polynesian cultures, however, it is considered rude to look directly into the face of someone who is of higher status than you yourself. Hence, Polynesians consider it normal and polite to look away and not to stare at the other person during an interview. Unfortunately, this very same behaviour is often misinterpreted by Western interviewers as a sign of rude or 'shifty' behaviour. Hence, the meaning of a sign (in this case a gesture, or body position) varies depending upon the cultural context.

Signs can also change their meaning over time. Hackley compared advertisements for beer in the United Kingdom in the 1960s and 1990s and found that the representations of men and women changed considerably over that period. Given the change in social mores and culture, Hackley says that the representations of men and women in the advertisements of the 1960s 'would be unthinkable today' (Hackley, 2003).

There are various kinds of semiotics, although there are two main semiotic traditions. The European tradition is based on the linguistic work of Saussure, whereas the North American tradition is largely based on the work of Peirce. Saussure was concerned with the role of signs as part of social life, whereas Peirce was interested in a more abstract 'formal doctrine of signs'.

Chandler (2008) says that:

> Contemporary semioticians study signs not in isolation but as part of semiotic 'sign systems' (such as a medium or genre). They study how meanings are made: as such, being concerned not only with communication but also with the construction and maintenance of reality.

Semiotics has been used to analyse qualitative data in many disciplines, such as literary criticism (Scholes, 1982) and sociology. Perhaps one of the most well-known proponents of semiotics was the French anthropologist, Claude Lévi-Strauss, who applied Saussure's theory to the analysis of cultural systems (Lévi-Strauss, 1996). Lévi-Strauss argued that surface cultural phenomena, such as myths and rituals, actually reflect deep, underlying cultural structures. These deep structures are embedded in human thought, and are universal; hence, the subdiscipline 'structural anthropology' of which Lévi-Strauss was the foremost exponent. One of the key ideas of structural anthropology is that individual concepts or beliefs cannot be understood in isolation; rather, they must be understood in terms of an entire cultural system.

Lévi-Strauss discussed the nature of myth and the role of myth in human thought. He argued that, although each myth appears to be unique, myths throughout the world are actually very similar. Myths always consist of elements that oppose or contradict each other and other elements that 'mediate', or resolve, these oppositions. He claimed that if mythical thought obeys universal laws, then all human thought must obey universal laws as well. He suggested that all cultures reflected (and were structured by) these deep oppositions in the human mind, such as the oppositions between good/evil, sacred/profane, clean/dirty, and so forth (Desai, 2002).

In business and management, semiotics has been used especially in information systems, management, marketing, and organizational studies. Marketing researchers have used semiotics in research on advertising, brand image, and marketing communications (Hackley, 2003). Desai (2002) says that semiotics and Lévi-Strauss's ideas in particular have proved to be very useful for understanding consumer cultures and 'brand myths', which in many cases appear to be structured by cultural oppositions. In information systems, researchers have looked at the meaning of information in organizational contexts and how this relates to the design and development of information systems (Holmqvist, Andersen, Klein, & Posner, 1996; Liebenau & Backhouse, 1990). In management, semiotics has been used to study organizational communication and organizational culture (Barley, 1983). Semiotics is potentially a very useful qualitative data analysis approach in any study that seeks 'insights into the constructed, arbitrary and culturally mediated character of human understanding' (Hackley, 2003: 171).

Semiotics Defined

There are multiple definitions of semiotics; however, all of them are concerned in some way with the analysis of the meaning of signs. According to Eco, 'semiotics is concerned with everything that can be taken as a sign'

(1976: 7). This broad definition means that words, images, actions, and objects can all be studied as signs, as long as they have been recorded in some way and can be studied (e.g. in writing or on video).

Nöth (1990) refers to semiotics as the 'science of meaning'. Morris (1985) defines it as follows:

> Semiotic(s) has for its goal a general theory of signs in all their forms and mani-festations, whether in animals or men, whether normal or pathological, whether linguistic or nonlinguistic, whether personal or social. Semiotic(s) is thus an interdisciplinary enterprise.

SEMIOTIC CONCEPTS

Semiotics provides a set of concepts that help a researcher to understand a sign or a symbol. Some of these concepts will now be described.

Signifier and Signified

Saussure thought that the process of the interpretation of signs involved a rela-tionship between two things: the *signifier* and the *signified*. A sign must have a signifier and a signified, and both are needed for communication to take place. The *signifier* is a sign or symbol that can stand for something else. By definition, all words are signifiers since they always stand for something else (e.g. a thought, a feeling, or a thing). A signifier is used by the person wanting to communicate. The *signified* is what the sign or symbol represents – what it is interpreted to mean by the receiver of the communication. Obviously, for the receiver of the message to understand correctly the meaning of the sign or symbol used by the sender, they both need to use the same sign system. Hence, Saussure emphasized the importance of sign systems and the role of signs in social life.

Sign, Object, and Interpretant

Peirce thought that the process of the interpretation of signs involved a rela-tionship between three things, rather than two: the *sign*, the *object*, and the *interpretant*. The interpretant (usually a person) fulfils the office of an inter-preter; that is, it refers to the interpretation placed on the sign. Hence, there is the sign, the object it refers to, and the interpretation of the sign. Peirce's view explicitly recognizes that the same sign can have different meanings depending upon the context.

Icon, Index, and Symbol

As well as proposing a process for the interpretation of signs, Peirce suggested a relatively simple classification scheme. He classified signs into three basic types: icons, indices, and symbols.

An *icon* is a sign that signifies its meaning by qualities of its own; it is like the thing it represents. For example, the icon of a trash can on Apple and Windows computers looks like the thing it represents.

A sign can also act as an *index*:

> An indexical sign points to or indicates something else. For example, a wavy line on a road might 'point to' bends in the road a few hundred yards ahead. A picture of a silhouette of a man on a door might 'point to' or indicate that a men's bathroom is right here behind this door. (Hackley, 2003: 167)

A *symbol* is something that stands for, or is symbolic of, something else. For example, a black T-shirt with a silver fern emblazoned across the front symbolizes the All Blacks (the national rugby team of New Zealand). When Saatchi & Saatchi were commissioned by the New Zealand Rugby Football Union to develop a marketing plan, they formally identified a 'constellation' of ten brand values for the All Blacks. The three core values were 'excellence', 'respect', and 'humility'. The extended values were 'power', 'masculinity', 'commitment', 'teamwork', 'New Zealand', 'tradition', and 'inspirational'.

Symbols can be very powerful. As one journalist commented: 'Is there anyone who has ever laced up a pair of rugby boots in New Zealand and not privately dreamed of wearing the black jersey?' (Brown, 2003). Of course, it is a relatively simple matter to (literally) put on a black jersey, but Brown is referring to the more powerful meaning of actually becoming an All Black and representing the country in a test match.

Encoding and Decoding

Central to semiotics is the idea of messages and a code. The only way that messages can be sent from one person to another is via the use of a code.

Encoding is the process of transforming any thought or communication into a message. Decoding is the process of reading the message and understanding what it means. Sebeok (1994) says that:

> Encoding and decoding imply a code, a set of unambiguous rules whereby messages are convertible from one representation to another; the code is what the two parties in the message exchanged are supposed to have, in fact or by assumption, totally or in part, in common. (p. 9)

An obvious example of this is language. If we take this particular book, only someone who understands English can understand the meaning of this book. By definition, they must be able to read the Latin alphabet on which English is based. The road or highway code is another good example. Only someone who can read the road signs correctly is allowed to obtain a driver's licence. Hence, an important task for researchers using semiotics is to decode the meanings implied in signs and symbols. Eco (1984) points out that there are many different kinds of codes.

Pragmatic, Semantic, and Syntactic

Semiotic researchers often make a distinction between various levels of the meaning of signs. Three of these levels are the pragmatic, semantic, and syntactic levels.

The *pragmatic* level refers to the cultural context within which communication takes place. The pragmatic understanding of a sign is what the people involved at the time expect and assume the sign to mean in a particular situation. For example, if I were to say to an academic colleague, 'I am teaching tomorrow', she would immediately assume that I am talking about teaching a class at university. The meaning of my statement is 'obvious'. The idea that I might be referring to teaching something else such as tennis would not even occur to her. This 'taken-for-granted' meaning is the pragmatic level.

The *semantic* level refers to the precise meaning of the signs. What does the sign refer to? As words and signs can have many different meanings, the semiotic researcher has to figure out which interpretation is correct in any given context.

The *syntactic* level refers to the rules governing the use of the signs. In effect, this is the logic or grammar that specifies how the words or signs should be used. For example, there are published rules governing how flags should be displayed, and published rules about the placement of road signs.

Syntagmatic Analysis

Syntagmatic analysis involves studying the structure of a text and the relationships between its parts. Chandler (2008) says that:

> Structuralist semioticians seek to identify elementary constituent segments within the text – its syntagms. The study of syntagmatic relations reveals the conventions or 'rules of combination' underlying the production and interpretation of texts (such as the grammar of a language). The use of one syntagmatic structure rather than another within a text influences meaning.

Chandler says that there are essentially three syntagmatic relationships. The first is a sequential relationship, as found in film and television narrative sequences. The second is a spatial relationship, as found in posters and photographs (where signs and symbols are juxtaposed). The third is a conceptual relationship, such as in an argument. He points out that many texts contain more than one type of syntagmatic structure, though one may be dominant (Chandler, 2008).

Paradigmatic Analysis

Whereas syntagmatic analysis studies the 'surface structure' of a text, Chandler says that paradigmatic analysis seeks to identify the various paradigms which underlie the content of texts. A paradigm 'is a set of associated signifiers or signifieds which are all members of some defining category, but in which each is significantly different' (Chandler, 2008).

For example, the words 'black' and 'white' belong to the same category (colour), but are opposites. A paradigmatic analysis involves studying 'the oppositions and contrasts between the signifiers that belong to the same set from which those used in the text were drawn' (Chandler, 2008):

> Paradigmatic analysis involves comparing and contrasting each of the signifiers present in the text with absent signifiers which in similar circumstances might have been chosen, and considering the significance of the choices made. It can be applied at any semiotic level, from the choice of a particular word, image or sound to the level of the choice of style, genre or medium. The use of one signifier rather than another from the same paradigm is based on factors such as technical constraints, code (e.g. genre), convention, connotation, style, rhetorical purpose and the limitations of the individual's own repertoire. The analysis of paradigmatic relations helps to define the 'value' of specific items in a text.

Polysemy

Texts and signs can have multiple meanings. For example, the two words 'red light' can refer to a light at an intersection (the light itself being a sign for 'stop'), or they can refer to a part of the city (the 'red light' district). The same two words (or signs) can have different meanings. Which meaning is meant in a particular sentence or situation depends upon the context.

Of course, while the author or the sender of a message might try to control or influence the way the audience interprets it, there is always the possibility that the receiver will interpret the message differently. This is almost guaranteed if there are multiple audiences.

Barthes suggests that all images are polysemous. Images imply a 'floating chain' of signifieds, the reader being able to choose some and ignore others (Barthes, 1985).

Scott says that meaning is not static and that the meaning of texts and signs is continually shifting. Previous perceptions of linear processes of fixed meanings are now challenged by post-modern cultural enquiry which sees meaning as a 'network of associations' (Scott, 1994).

HOW TO USE SEMIOTICS

The qualitative researcher using semiotics has to study the signs and symbols that are used in a particular domain and identify the conventions of their use. He or she has to decode the meanings conveyed by the signs. The idea is to uncover the rules that govern human behaviour.

In marketing, semiotics can be used to study signs and symbols in advertising and consumer research. There is an increasing awareness in marketing that the interpretation of advertising is shaped by cultural values and the symbolic meanings of words and rituals. Consumer theory argues that consumption is not merely an economic activity, it is also a cultural activity with a multiplicity of meanings (Desai, 2002).

You only need to walk down a city street or turn on the TV to realize that we are bombarded with brand names, logos, video clips, or music. At the supermarket a certain kind of music might be playing to get us into the mood for shopping, or a salesperson might try to entice us to taste a particular product. The advertising, product design, the packaging of the products, the pricing, and the placement of the products in a certain position can all be read as signs. The purpose of these signs is to communicate a certain message to the 'target' audience with the net result being buying behaviour (or so the advertisers hope). Marketing researchers are probably interested in the following questions: Have the signs communicated the right message to the right people? What impression has been conveyed by the use of the signs? How effective have the signs been?

Of course, there are many other research questions that can be considered. For example, Floch (1988) used structural semiotics to analyse major store design alternatives regarding store layout and interior architecture. Arnold, Kozinets, and Handelman (2001) used institutional semiotics to reveal the myriad of meanings in a Wal-Mart advertising flyer. Beyond the promise of deep savings on a wide range of products, the flyer reflected a rich blend of family, community, and national norms. The world's largest retailer projected an image in the flyer of a neighbourly, small-town shopkeeper, thereby legitimating itself among its consumer constituency (Arnold et al., 2001).

Table 15.1 An approach to semiotic analysis (Hackley, 2003)

Questions to ask:	What does X signify to me? Why does X signify this to me? What might X signify for others? Why might X signify this for others?
Possible sources of X:	
Objects (visual semiosis)	For example, clothes, hairstyles, make-up styles, the ways objects are used by people, use in press ads of printed copy, typeface, use of logo/pictorial symbolic image, the spatial interrelationships of objects
Gesture (bodily semiosis)	For example, body types, facial types, expressive gestures, facial expressions, posture, gaze, juxtaposition of bodies, juxtaposition of bodies with products
Speech (verbal semiosis)	For example, use of idiomatic expressions, regional or national accent or dialect, use of metaphor/metonymy, tone and volume of speech, pace delivery, use of voiceover, use of humour, emphasis on particular words/phonemes

Hackley suggests that doing semiotics entails the deconstruction of meaning in given contexts: that which is everyday and taken for granted 'must be made strange and unfamiliar' (2003). This is because we take our own culture and subjective understanding for granted. His approach to semiotic analysis is summarized in Table 15.1, using the semiotic analysis of advertising as an example. His approach involves deconstructing an advertisement as a 'string of signs'.

Hence, semiotics can be used to study the way consumers interpret marketing communications. More broadly, semiotics can be used to study consumption and anti-consumption. As Hackley points out: 'Your ownership of branded goods can signify much about you, such as your social status, the groups to which you claim membership and your aspirations and fantasies about yourself' (2003: 165).

Eco (1976) points out that there are many potential semiotic research applications. The researcher can focus on cultural codes, mass communications, rhetoric, visual communication and written languages, amongst other things.

CRITIQUE OF SEMIOTICS

Semiotics is potentially a very powerful way of analysing and interpreting qualitative data in business and organizational settings. It enables and indeed encourages the qualitative researcher to use any type of data, whether those data are in the form of text, images, or music. It requires the researcher to step outside of the everyday and common-sense way in which we see the world, and to decode the meaning of signs and symbols.

Another advantage of semiotics is that it is well grounded in linguistics and structural anthropology. This means that it is relatively easy to justify the use of semiotics.

Perhaps the main disadvantage of semiotics is the tendency to focus solely on the structures of meaning (e.g. binary oppositions), and to treat people as somewhat passive. Since semiotics emphasizes the importance of interpreting the meaning of signs and symbols within a particular social and cultural system, it has a tendency to become formalistic and can ignore the way in which people actively create meaning.

Another disadvantage of using semiotics is that it relies almost entirely on the insights of the researcher. Considerable creativity is required to produce a good semiotic analysis of qualitative data. This may suit some qualitative researchers but not others.

EXAMPLES OF USING SEMIOTICS

Using Semiotics to Study Occupational and Organizational Cultures

Barley (1983) shows how semiotics provides one avenue for conceptualizing and analysing occupational and organizational cultures. Barley studied a funeral home for three months, during which he observed and conducted multiple interviews in a metropolitan neighbourhood of an eastern city in the United States. His purpose was to understand how a funeral director understands funeral work.

His first task was to uncover the basic units of semiotic analysis: signs that have relevance for funeral directors. Hence he familiarized himself with the work of the funeral home and after several weeks of interviews, analysed the transcripts to discover domains of objects, events, and action into which the funeral directors seemed to segment the flow of their work. Once he had identified the domains (56 in total), he then conducted more interviews to elicit the categories and subcategories of each domain. His goal was to map each domain in terms of a structural and attribute analysis.

Barley found that the typical case of a funeral director consists of a series of events: removing the body, making arrangements with the family, embalming and preparing the body, holding a wake, holding a funeral, and, finally, interment. He analysed the system of codes that funeral directors use to make funeral scenes appear more 'natural' or 'normal'.

In his article, Barley discusses three codes: the 'code of posed features' (whereby the body is made to look as if it were sleeping), the 'code of furnishings' (to make people feel comfortable and at home during the funeral), and the code of removals (to make the death room appear normal).

Barley's article thus illustrates the use of semiotics to map the systems of meaning employed by people in a particular occupation or organization. He was able to discover codes underlying the meaning of several domains of action and communication, showing how they are consistently structured. The discovery of such cultural codes, using structural analysis, represents 'tightly formulated rules for producing actions and interpretations deemed appropriate by members of the culture' (Barley, 1983: 410). He argues that semiotics offers a set of concepts and methods of analysis 'for directly confronting the nature of culture as a system of meaning and encourages the creation of theory and analysis congruent with the nature of the beast itself' (Barley, 1983: 411).

Why Consumers Value Special Possessions

Why do consumers value special possessions? Grayson and Shulman (2000) point out that special possessions can represent personally relevant events, people, places, and values:

> A retiree treasures a book his wife gave him on their wedding day. A college student saves the ticket stub from a recent concert. A restaurant owner frames the first dollar his business ever earned. A university professor keeps a bottle of champagne given in thanks by a graduating student. An attorney could not bear to lose the necklace she bought for herself when she was promoted to partner. (p. 17)

Grayson and Shulman used semiotics to understand the representation processes that support these meanings. Specifically, they used the semiotic concept of indexicality to extend understanding of how meanings are embedded in irreplaceable special possessions.

They found that special possessions establish a semiotic linkage, enabling consumers to verify self-selected moments from their personal history. As they explain:

> Our research suggests that irreplaceable special possessions are indices because they have a factual, spatial connection with the special events and people they represent. Given Peirce's assertions regarding the nature of indices, we further posit that the indexicality of irreplaceable possessions allows them to serve a factual or evidentiary function for their owners. Just as in a court of law, where physical evidence often verifies a past event by virtue of its physical and factual relationship with the crime, irreplaceable special possessions serve as evidence for their owners. They verify important moments of personal history. (Grayson & Shulman, 2000: 19)

Their research shows the value of semiotic frameworks as applied to research on possession ownership and also sheds light on the value of authenticity to consumers (Grayson & Shulman, 2000).

A Semiotic Analysis of Corporate Language

Fiol (1989) used semiotics to analyse CEOs' letters to shareholders in an attempt to explain differences in the propensity of organizations to enter into joint ventures. She analysed the narrative structures of these letters using semiotic concepts. The central proposition of her study is that 'joint-venturing firms are likely to exhibit weak boundaries separating the company from external environments and strong boundaries among organizational subunits. Conversely, non-joint-venturing firms are likely to exhibit strong boundaries separating the company from external environments and weak boundaries among organizational subunits' (Fiol, 1989: 278).

She points out that letters to shareholders not only communicate facts about the firm, but also communicate implicit beliefs about the organization and its relationship to the surrounding world. Fiol says that CEOs' letters to shareholders are like folk tales in that they tell many stories that have a set of recurring structures that reflect underlying values. All such letters have a similar object: to convey a positive image to shareholders.

She performed a semiotic analysis on CEOs' letters to shareholders in ten chemical companies' annual reports. All ten firms had similar product lines, markets, and sizes. Her analysis only partially supported her central proposition, reflecting the unstable nature of the environmental context. However, she found that all the letters displayed simple belief patterns that may underlie the seemingly complex relationships between organizations and their environments.

Exercises

1 With Table 15.1 as a guide, use semiotic analysis to deconstruct the meaning of a particular advertisement.
2 Using the same advertisement, analyse it by asking the following questions: What is the purpose of the advertisement (the pragmatic level)? What is the meaning of the words and signs used (semantic level)? What are the rules governing the use of the signs and symbols (syntactic level)?

(Cont'd)

---

3   Conduct a brief literature search using Google Scholar or some other bibliographic database and see if you can find articles using semiotics in your chosen field. What kinds of topics appear?

4   Browsing the websites on the Internet listed below, identify some of the current writers using semiotics. What kinds of topics appear? Can you work out how these topics might have relevance to business and management?

Further Reading

Books

A useful introduction to semiotics is the book by Sebeok (1994). He suggests six species (or types) of signs: signal, symptom, icon, index, symbol, and name. *The Savage Mind* (Lévi-Strauss, 1996) is a classic text showing how semiotics has been used in structural anthropology. For those studying information systems, the collected set of readings in Holmqvist et al. (1996) is a good introduction to the use of semiotics in that field.

Articles

The *Journal of Consumer Research* in marketing has published many articles on semiotics over the past 20 years or so. For example, Mick (1986) provides a reasonably comprehensive overview of semiotics and its applications and implications for consumer research. He points out that the world of consumers is full of signs and symbols.

Websites on the Internet

The following websites on semiotics are very useful:

- Daniel Chandler has an excellent site entitled 'Semiotics for Beginners' at http://www.aber.ac.uk/media/Documents/S4B/sem01.html
- Martin Ryder provides an excellent index to semiotic resources on the Internet. His index is divided into three categories: topics in semiotics, seminar authors, and active writers: http://carbon.cudenver.edu/~mryder/itc_data/semiotics.html
- The Open Semiotics Resource Center is at http://www.semioticon.com/

16 *NARRATIVE ANALYSIS*

Objectives

By the end of this chapter, you will be able to:

- Understand the purpose of using narrative analysis
- Appreciate the different types of narrative analysis
- Identify the advantages and disadvantages of using narrative analysis
- Be more confident in using narrative analysis
- See how narrative analysis has been used in business and management

INTRODUCTION

Narrative analysis, like discourse analysis or semiotics, is a specific approach to the analysis of qualitative data. In this chapter I will review how narratives can be structured and the various kinds of narrative analysis.

Narrative is defined by the *Concise Oxford English Dictionary* as 'a spoken or written account of connected events; a story' (Soanes & Stevenson, 2004). Traditionally, a narrative requires a plot, as well as some coherence. It has some sort of ordered sequence, often in linear form, with a beginning, middle, and end. Narratives also usually have a theme and a main point, or a moral, to the story. It has been suggested that narrative is an important way through which human experience is made meaningful (Polkinghorne, 1988).

In the social sciences, the word 'narrative' has often been used to describe the empirical materials that the researcher has gathered. In this sense, a narrative refers to the life history of a person who has been interviewed, a story about a significant aspect of their life, or a specific event. A personal narrative might refer to their diaries, journals, or letters (Chase, 2005). Narrative analysis thus 'examines the informant's story and analyzes how it is put together, the linguistic and cultural resources it draws on, and how it persuades a listener of authenticity' (Riessman, 1993: 2).

However, a narrative can also refer to an organizational narrative. Czarniawska (1998) says that organizational narratives are 'the main mode of knowing and communicating in organizations' and that their 'construction and reproduction must be documented' and their contents interpreted. Narrative analysis can open up organizational texts for negotiation 'and thus enter into a dialogical relationship with organizational practice' (Czarniawska, 1998: 17).

A narrative can also be a story created by the researcher. This kind of narrative is an edited reconstruction of events or aspects that are seen as relevant to the subject or theory being discussed.

In every case, a narrative always has a sequence (Riessman, 1993). Narrative is a distinct way of making sense of the world. The use of the word 'narrative' emphasizes the voice of the person telling the story and focuses on the uniqueness of the story. As Chase (2005) describes:

> Narrative is retrospective meaning making – the shaping and ordering of past experience. Narrative is a way of understanding one's own and others' actions, or organizing events and objects into a meaningful whole, and of connecting and seeing the consequences of actions and events over time … Unlike a chronology, which also reports events over time, a narrative communicates the narrator's point of view, including why the narrative is worth telling in the first place. (p. 656)

McKenna makes a similar point when he says that narratives are 'ways of developing identities, representing experience, and of giving meaning to lives in the past, present and anticipated future' (2007: 146).

Narrative analysis has been used in many disciplines including anthropology, information systems, management, marketing, psychology, and sociology. The data gathering phase of qualitative research is often written up in narrative form. In information systems the focus has mostly been on understanding language, communication, and meaning among systems developers and organizational members. In marketing, researchers have looked at consumers' narratives and how consumers construct narratives about themselves and the world. In management, narrative is a common way of presenting data about organizations and organizational actors. Management and organizational researchers have considered how stories symbolize aspects of organizational culture or the role of story-telling in organizational sense-making.

APPROACHES TO NARRATIVE ANALYSIS

There are many different approaches to narrative analysis; however, some approaches are preferred in some disciplines more than others. Many narratives describe the life history of one person. The narrative is a record of events that are seen as significant by the narrator. Other narratives describe significant events in the life of an organization. Ante-narrative analysis, on the other hand, tends to reject 'grand narratives' as single voiced, instead looking at the fragments of multiple stories. Some of these kinds of narrative analysis and the sorts of distinctions that are made will now be discussed.

Writing Versus Reading

From the perspective of doing qualitative research in business and management, a useful distinction can be made between writing and reading with respect to the use of narrative analysis.

Writing a narrative means that you have decided to use narrative analysis as a way of organizing and presenting your data. Writing a narrative involves the use of one or more narrative structures to tell a story. The key task is to collate all the various materials you have collected (interviews, field notes, documents, etc.), and to tell the story in a coherent manner.

As many of my own research projects have been concerned with the development and implementation of a particular information system over time, I have often used narrative analysis in this way. I have written a narrative as a way of organizing and presenting the data in a coherent way. The narrative is in effect a compilation of data from interviews, documents, and so forth, telling the story of what happened and when during an information systems project.

Reading a narrative means that you have decided to use narrative analysis to interpret the meaning of a pre-existing narrative account. For example, you may want to analyse a previously published narrative or a personal life story as told by one of your interviewees. In this sense 'narrative' mostly refers to part, or all, of your qualitative data.

Top Down Versus Bottom Up

One way to classify narrative approaches is to distinguish between top-down and bottom-up approaches. A *top-down* approach analyses the narrative text 'according to a set of culturally established rules of grammar and exposition' (McNabb, 2002: 418). This approach is often used in education. Teaching cases in business and management usually follow this approach, as they tend to be written according to a formula. Positivist case studies also tend to use this approach.

Bottom-up approaches 'use elements in the text to build a structure for analyzing the whole' (McNabb, 2002: 418). Instead of using a formula – and fitting qualitative data into that formula – this approach leads to greater variety in narrative structures. This approach is the one that is followed most often in ethnographic research and interpretive types of studies.

Realist, Constructivist, and Critical

Realist narratives assume a one-to-one correspondence between the narrative and events that are described. Realist narratives are often portrayed as common-sense, descriptive accounts of reality, and are sometimes written in an authoritative tone. If the narrative comes from one or more individual cases (people or organizations), the narratives are often described as being representative of the population as a whole.

Constructivist narratives assume that the narrator constructs events through narrative, as opposed to simply describing them. Constructivist (or interpretive) narratives are usually portrayed as subjective, partial views of reality. Instead of arguing for the representative nature of the narrative, constructivist narratives tend to emphasize their uniqueness. For example, Riessman (1993) says that narrative analysis gives prominence to human agency and imagination, hence it is well suited to studies of subjectivity and identity.

Critical narratives assume that the telling or publishing of narratives can be a force for change. Narratives can be used for emancipation. They can also be used to elicit previously silenced narratives, narratives that those in power resist hearing (Chase, 2005). For example, feminist narratives might give voice to previously silenced groups of women (Riessman, 1993).

Genres

The concept of genres refers to the idea that narratives can be written in different styles. Narratives written according to a certain genre will have distinctive stylistic features, content, and structure. A genre is a convention for telling the story in a certain kind of way.

For example, a narrative can take the form of an adventure story, a fairytale, a romance, a farce, a tragedy, or a comedy. Riessman (1993) says that narrative genres include stories (which have protagonists, inciting conditions, and culminating events), habitual narratives (when events happen over and over), hypothetical narratives (which depict events that did not happen), and topic-centred narratives (snapshots of past events that are linked thematically).

Voice

Chase (2005) suggests a typology of three voices or narrative strategies that can be employed by qualitative researchers.

The first narrative strategy is where the researcher develops an *authoritative voice* in his or her writing. By writing in an authoritative voice, the researcher separates his or her voice from the voice of the narrator, and interprets the narrator's story in the light of the researcher's own cultural, institutional, or organizational discourse. Although in this style of writing the researcher can be accused of privileging his or her own voice, Chase (2005) says that this is not necessarily the case, as a researcher may also present extensive quotations from a narrator's story.

The second narrative strategy is where the researcher develops a *supportive* voice. This strategy pushes the narrator's voice to the fore. Although this strategy runs the risk of romanticizing the narrator's voice, Chase (2005) says that it can help to create a self-reflective and respectful distance between the researcher's and narrator's voices.

The third strategy is where there is a complex interaction between the researcher's and narrator's voices. Chase (2005) says this strategy is common in narrative ethnographies and auto-ethnographies, where the researcher makes him- or herself vulnerable. Although this strategy is sometimes criticized for being self-indulgent, Chase says that at least we can understand how the researcher interpreted the narrator's stories.

Post-modern Narrative and Ante-narrative Approaches

Boje (2001) provides an interesting discussion of the many different kinds of post-modern narrative analysis and their application to qualitative research in organizations and management. He uses the term 'ante-narrative' to describe narratives that are quite different from the usual single-voiced, third-person narrative found in management and organization studies; rather, these ante-narratives are fragmented, non-linear, incoherent, collective, unplotted, and pre-narrative speculation. He suggests that both narrative and ante-narrative analysis can be fruitfully used in research on organizations (Boje, 2001).

Boje also says that the term 'ante-narrative' has two meanings. The first interprets 'ante' as meaning 'before'; hence, ante-narrative is something that is told before the narrative is finalized. In organizations stories are often fragmented, non-linear, and incoherent. Narrative analysts transform these ante-narrative folk stories into less messy narratives and in so doing they 'create an account that is fictively rational, free of tangled contingency' (Boje, 2001: 2). Hence, narrative comes after ante-narrative, in which coherence is imposed on otherwise fragmented experiences.

The second meaning of 'ante-narrative' is to use it in the sense of a bet – as in, 'up the ante'. In this sense, ante-narrative is a somewhat speculative appreciation or interpretation of an experience. Narrative analysts impose order onto the story and provide a moral and agreed plot. Hence, while ante-narrative is speculative, narrative imposes a coherent story line.

Boje (2001) says that ante-narrative is not the same as 'anti-narrative'. In fact, he suggests that both narrative and ante-narrative analysis can be combined in organization studies.

Boje describes eight ante-narrative analysis approaches, all of which are able to deal with 'the prevalence of fragmented and polyphonic storytelling in complex organizations' (2001). These alternative ante-narrative approaches are as follows:

1 **Deconstruction**
2 **Grand narrative**
3 **Microstoria**
4 **Story network**
5 **Intertextuality**
6 **Causality**
7 **Plot**
8 **Theme.**

In *deconstruction*, the narrative is not fixed, but moves and flows with the networks of embedded meaning. Deconstruction challenges linearity, sequence, voice, and plot.

Although post-modernists are suspicious of *grand narratives*, Boje says that not everyone wants them banished. In fact, the grand narratives of modernity are still very powerful, and hence these should be studied along with the ante-narrating of little stories.

Microstoria are 'little people's' stories that do not fit into the 'great man' accounts that are fashionable in organization studies.

Story network analysis is where the narrative analyst traces the names of 'little people' and their social relations (family and economic) to other people. The organization is seen as a story-telling system in which the stories become nodes or links in the narrative analysis.

Intertextuality involves a dialogic conversation among writers and readers of texts. Boje says that intertextuality is all the dialoguing that goes on between and within narratives.

Causality analysis studies the non-linear ante-narrative pathways of story reconstruction before the retrospective sense-making of narrative – it looks at the acts of storytelling that construct and reconstruct reality.

Plot analysis raises questions regarding authorship – who gets to author the narrative and produce a plot?

Theme analysis questions the usual taxonomic classification of narratives into themes and opens up the hierarchy of classification to see what gets left out.

Boje (2001) says that all these eight ante-narrative analysis approaches are post-modern alternatives to more traditional narrative analysis.

HOW TO USE NARRATIVE ANALYSIS

If you are planning to collect narratives during interviews (and hence narratives will be your main source of data), then you need to work at *inviting* stories from your informants. As Chase (2005) points out, some interviewees might not take up the part of narrator unless you specifically ask them to do so. One of the key tasks of the researcher is to try to work out beforehand what is 'storyworthy' in the narrator's social setting (Chase, 2005).

You also need to provide a facilitating context for the research interview, and ask open-ended questions that 'open up topics and allow respondents to construct answers, in collaboration with listeners, in the way that they find meaningful' (Riessman, 1993: 54).

If you are planning to write a narrative of an organization, then the typical form in management and organization studies is to write it up as a case study. Case studies usually use chronology as the main organizing device (Czarniawska, 1998). An essential requirement is that the story should be interesting.

One relatively simple model that can be used to analyse an existing narrative is the Labov/Cortazzi model (McNabb, 2002). This model suggests that there are six elements to every narrative. The six elements are abstract, orientation, complication, evaluation, result and conclusion. The questions that are derived from these elements can be used to interrogate various types of documents (e.g. interview transcripts or newspapers). However, the model can also be used to help you create a narrative from your own documents.

Another model that can be used to analyse narrative is Burke's dramatism (Riessman, 1993). This model suggests that there are five elements to every narrative. These elements are act, scene, agent, agency, and purpose. The five elements concern 'what was done (act), when or where it was done (scene), who did it (agent), how he or she did it (agency), and why (purpose)' (Burke, quoted in Riessman, 1993: 19).

CRITIQUE OF NARRATIVE ANALYSIS

For qualitative researchers in business and management, perhaps the most useful way of using narrative analysis is in the creation or critique of organizational narratives. Narrative analysis is potentially an excellent way in which we can enter into a dialogue with managers and business people in organizations (Czarniawska, 1998). All of us (both academics and practitioners) can relate to stories. It is one way of making our research more relevant to practice.

However, because of its depth, narrative analysis is not particularly useful if you are planning to interview large numbers of people. It can be very time consuming to collect life histories of people, and even more time consuming to analyse them.

Nevertheless, narrative analysis can be very powerful. It is an in-depth approach to analysing qualitative data, enabling us to study personal experience and meaning in management and organizational settings. Narrative analysis helps us to see 'how events have been constructed by active subjects' (Riessman, 1993: 70).

EXAMPLES OF USING NARRATIVE AND METAPHOR

A Narrative Analysis of Strategic Discourse

Barry and Elmes (1997) analyse management strategy as a form of narrative. They say that 'strategy must rank as one of the most prominent, influential, and costly stories told in organizations' (Barry & Elmes, 1997: 430). They argue that narrative analysis is appropriate for capturing the diversity and complexity present in strategic discourse.

They point out that narrative analysis can be applied both to strategizing and to strategies. In the former, strategy can be examined as a narrative process in organizations, one in which stories about directionality are contested. In the latter, formal published strategies can be examined as narrative artefacts.

Barry and Elmes (1997) posit that strategy can be considered a form of fiction. By fiction, they do not mean to imply that strategy is false, but rather that it is something that is created:

> As authors of fiction, strategists are subject to the same basic challenge facing other fictionalist writers: how to develop an engaging, compelling account, one that readers can willingly buy into and implement. Any story the strategist tells

is but one of many competing alternatives woven from a vast array of possible characterizations, plot lines, and themes. (p. 433)

Barry and Elmes discuss the various narrative devices that strategists use to make their strategic discourse appear both credible and novel. For example, strategies are often described in the third person, giving the impression that the strategy represents an unbiased, rational point of view. Strategies can also take an epic form, with the hero/company portrayed as confronting a number of enemies and/or obstacles: 'If everyone in the company were to pull together, the company should emerge victorious with increased market share, profits, and job security' (Barry & Elmes, 1997: 437).

They conclude their article by making suggestions with regard to how strategic narratives may change within the 'virtual' organization of the future (Barry & Elmes, 1997).

Consumers' Identity Narratives

How consumers use products to construct their identity has become an important theme in marketing research. Research in marketing has shown that people use consumption to maintain their sense of identity through time and define themselves in relation to other people.

Ahuvia (2005) looks at the role that possessions and activities play in the construction of a coherent identity narrative. In particular, he focuses on possessions and activities that consumers love. Consumers will often say they love a purchased possession or activity (e.g. 'I love snowboarding' or 'I love my new car'), which can often indicate something about themselves and their relationship to other people.

Ahuvia's data were obtained from in-depth interviews and follow-up phone interviews with ten consumers. However, the stories of only two consumers were discussed in the article (due to space limitations). He says that the two cases selected were representative of the interviews as a whole and provided good illustrations of the major findings. He asked his informants what, if anything, they loved and then discussed these loved items.

From the interview data, Ahuvia constructed a 'life narrative' for each person, summarizing their life story. For each person, he then discussed what each one loved and the resulting identity conflicts. For example, he found that Pam was an investment banker but actually loved composing music:

Pam experiences a conflict between Pam the composer, a risky choice but one she sees as an expression of her inner self, versus Pam the businesswoman, a practical choice supported by her family. Within this identity conflict, Pam's loved objects all played a partisan role, serving to buttress her artistic persona and distance her from the businesswoman persona. (Ahuvia, 2005: 174)

He found that love objects served as mementos of key events or relationships in the life narrative, helping to resolve identity conflicts, and tended to be tightly embedded in a rich symbolic network of associations. His interviews with consumers revealed three different strategies that they used to create a coherent self-narrative: these were labelled 'demarcating', 'compromising', and 'synthesizing' solutions.

Demarcating is where a loved object serves to demarcate and reinforce a boundary with respect to one's identity: 'In Pam's identity conflict between creating a life as a composer and pressures to pursue a less risky career in business, all the objects she claims to truly love demarcate and reinforce the boundary between her desired composer identity and rejected business-woman identity' (Ahuvia, 2005: 181).

Compromising and synthesizing solutions are used by consumers when all alternatives possess desirable aspects: 'In a compromise solution, consumers give up what they see as some of the attractive features of each identity position to stake out a middle ground between them' (Ahuvia, 2005: 181). Ahuvia says that, while compromising is very common in everyday shopping, it is rare in object love. However, products can provide consumers with synthesizing solutions to identity conflicts.

Ahuvia's article thus shows that, while consumers purchase hundreds of products, some of them play a special role in consumers' understandings of who they are as people. The article reveals how consumers use loved objects and activities to construct a coherent self-narrative in the face of identity conflicts (Ahuvia, 2005).

Narratives of Information Systems Development Projects

Davidson (1997) analyses three project history narratives that she collected during a field study of an information systems development project. She was interested in how project participants communicated their knowledge, assumptions, and expectations to negotiate a shared understanding of information systems requirements.

She says that creating and maintaining accounts of action and events in the information systems development projects 'were critical sensemaking processes that shaped participants' interpretation of IT requirements and influenced their decisions about the design and implementation of IT artifacts' (Davidson, 1997: 125).

In her interviews with informants, she found that they often told stories about major events and episodes in a particular IT project, identified key actors, and attributed goals and motives to these actors. Each individual seemed to have his or her own unique perspective on the project.

She systematically analysed the project history narratives using eight categories, which are as follows:

1   Narrator's abstract
2   Narrator's perspective
3   Orientation/contextual descriptions
4   Actors
5   Problematic situation
6   Goal/problem solution
7   Actions and events
8   Outcomes.

She concluded by saying that narrative analysis is very useful for studying the development and implementation of IT. Information systems development 'is often characterized by ill-defined problems or vague goals, conflict and power struggles, and disruptions that result from pervasive organizational change' (Davidson, 1997: 142). Narrative analysis can inform our understanding of these activities.

Exercises

1   Using Davidson's (1997) 8 categories as a guide, analyse a published case study in business and management. Can you answer the questions for all six elements?
2   Search your weekend newspaper for stories. Analyse one of the more in-depth stories using Davidson's (1997) 8 categories as a guide. Are there other aspects of the story that you consider to be important?
3   Conduct a brief literature search using Google Scholar or some other bibliographic database and see if you can find articles that use narrative analysis in your chosen field. What kinds of topics appear?
4   Can you think of some additional topics in your own field that could be studied using narrative analysis? What kinds of data could you use?

Further Reading

Books

I think the book by Boje (2001) is particularly useful for qualitative researchers in business and management. The books by Polkinghorne (1988) and Czarniawska (1998) are also interesting.

Websites on the Internet

There are quite a few useful websites on qualitative research:

- Narrative Psychology is an excellent resource on narrative and related areas at http://narrativepsych.com
- The International Society for the Study of Narrative sponsors the International Conference on Narrative each year. See http://narrative.georgetown.edu/
- Narrative Inquiry is a forum for theoretical, empirical, and methodological work on narrative. See http://www.clarku.edu/faculty/mbamberg/narrative INQ/

PART SIX

WRITING UP AND PUBLISHING

Part VI discusses the issues associated with writing up and publishing qualitative research, as illustrated in Figure VI.1. Chapter 17 discusses the process of writing up, while Chapter 18 discusses the process of getting published. Both chapters contain many practical suggestions for writing up and getting published in business and management.

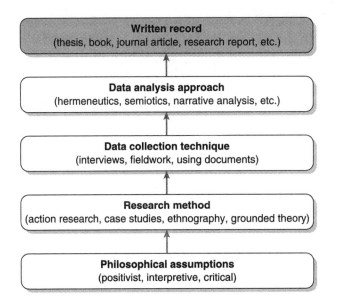

Figure VI.1 Qualitative research design

17 — WRITING UP

Objectives

By the end of this chapter, you will be able to:

- Understand the purpose of writing up
- Develop a writing plan
- Appreciate different writing styles and genres
- Avoid making some common mistakes
- Work out ways in which you can improve your own writing

INTRODUCTION

In qualitative research the process of writing up the research is just as important as doing the research itself. Within the social sciences today, there is probably as much emphasis on the writing up of qualitative research as there is on the doing of qualitative research itself (Atkinson, 1990; Clifford & Marcus, 1986; Van Maanen, 1988).

One reason for this emphasis on writing is that the qualitative researcher, by definition, is someone who 'writes about people'. As Grills (1998b) explains:

> in the writing, we make decisions about the story we will tell – how the tale will be made theoretically interesting, what questions we will engage with our work, and what aspects of our research will be presented and what will be set aside. Through this process, lived research and the experiences that accompany it are represented and mediated by text. (p. 199)

In a sense, then, the qualitative researcher is a story-teller (Grills, 1998b). It is easy to underestimate the importance of writing up and the time it takes actually to do it.

You might be tempted to think that you are basically done when you have finished all your empirical research and completed your analysis of the data. However, this is a big mistake. The write-up does not happen automatically and in fact some people take just as long to write up as they did to conduct the empirical part of their research. Also, there are many different ways to write up your research, and hence many choices to be made. The writing-up phase requires planning, considerable thought, and effort.

In some ways, I think the writing-up phase is actually the most important of all. Of course, doing qualitative research is a tremendous personal learning experience and that in itself is of much value. You get to learn a lot about other people and yourself. However, the only way that most people can learn about your work is through the finished article, thesis, or book. Of course, if you present your findings at a research seminar or in a presentation of some sort, then I agree that some people will learn about your work without having to read it; they will hear you talk about it instead. But the fact remains that only those who attend the seminar will learn about it. However, if you write up your research work and have it published, then potentially hundreds, if not thousands, of people can learn about your research findings. Your research, instead of being just a personal learning experience, enables other people to learn from what you did. Your research becomes a contribution to the research literature in a particular discipline. This published contribution is something which others can build upon.

The corollary is also the case. Let us assume that you complete a very interesting and innovative research project, and come up with some original findings. If you do not write up these findings and have them published, then no one else within the same field will know about them. In fact, someone else may have to conduct the same or a similar research project all over again, simply because you did not let people in your discipline know about what you achieved.

In the natural sciences there are many instances of scientists in different parts of the world claiming to have made a particular ground-breaking discovery first. This illustrates the importance with which most scientists view authorship. The best way for scientists to ensure that they are credited with a particular discovery is to have the work documented in published form, and normally this is in a peer-reviewed journal article.

This chapter, therefore, discusses the process of writing up. It considers the writing process per se. It is hard to overemphasize the importance of good writing. The following chapter focuses on the process of getting published.

APPROACHES TO WRITING UP

There are many different ways to write up qualitative research. There is a considerable variety of possible outputs: for example, dissertations, theses, reports, books, conference papers, journal articles, blogs, websites, newspaper and magazine articles. There are also many different writing styles and genres. Depending upon your chosen field and institution, some writing styles, genres, and outputs may be more acceptable or valued than others.

A Writing Plan

Regardless of the type of output (e.g. thesis, book, or journal article), I have found that it is always worthwhile to have a writing plan. One possible writing plan is to use the template provided in Table 17.1. This template lists eight items that should be considered at the start of a research project. I suggest that you attempt to fill out this template as soon as possible.

Table 17.1 A writing template

Eight questions	Description
1 Title?	What is the title of the thesis, article, or book I am writing?
2 Purpose?	What is the purpose of the article or book I am writing?
3 Authors?	Who are the authors of the work, and what is their intended contribution?
4 Audience?	Who is the intended audience for the work?
5 Method?	What research method am I planning to use?
6 Publication outlet?	Which journal, conference, or book publisher will I submit the work to?
7 Theoretical contribution?	What is my proposed theoretical contribution?
8 Practical contribution?	What is the practical relevance of my work (if any)?

Of course, the description for each of these items might change as your research project progresses, but the sooner you are able to come up with a concise description of each item, the better. In fact, I suggest producing a draft of the template in Table 17.1 before you even begin the empirical research. This is because it helps to focus your mind on the end product (the written output) and goes some way towards preventing your getting bogged down in collecting data. Collecting qualitative data is very interesting, and I find it one of the most enjoyable aspects of doing qualitative research. I enjoy meeting people and learning about the challenges they face. However, you can never collect enough data. There is always someone else you should interview, or one more piece of documentary evidence that you think you need. It is perfectly possible to spend years collecting data such that you never actually get around to producing the write-up.

Actually, I had a PhD student who fell into this trap. He was doing ethnographic research in one of the largest companies in New Zealand (one of the Global 500 companies). He would 'finish' his fieldwork, but then find out later that there was some exciting new development that had just occurred in the company. He would insist that he had no choice but to go back into the company and conduct just a few more interviews. The problem for my PhD student was that this happened more than once. Approximately one year later I started to lose patience and declared that his fieldwork was complete. I advised him to start writing up his PhD thesis right away based upon the (partial) data that he had by then collected. Of course, he was perfectly free to go back and collect more data after the PhD thesis was completed. However, it was time for me, as supervisor, to crack the whip. It was time for him to stop collecting data, and to start writing.

I am pleased to say that he was awarded his PhD without too much difficulty and more than one article has now been published from his doctoral research. As it turned out, he ended up including only a fraction of his empirical data in the completed thesis. In fact, he has enough data, even within the pages of the thesis, to provide the basis for numerous articles.

Hence, the purpose of having a template such as the one illustrated in Table 17.1 is to help you to stay focused on the ultimate goal. Your ultimate goal should be to write up your research in a research output of some sort (e.g. a thesis or conference paper), and then publish it (if appropriate). The questions included in the template are designed to help you stay focused. Lack of focus is one of the biggest risks in doing qualitative research.

1   Title?   I find that if I have a title in mind from the start, this helps me to focus on all the other questions which follow. Of course, I might revise the title later, but a title that captures the purpose and contribution of the work is tremendously helpful.

2   Purpose?   I suggest you try to explain the purpose of the article or book in *one* sentence. If you cannot clearly describe the purpose of your research in a succinct manner, the most likely reason is that you yourself are not entirely clear what it is all about.

3   Authors?   This question is not appropriate if you are the sole author of the work (e.g. a thesis); however, if there are multiple authors, it is very important to discuss who they are going to be from the beginning. I have seen

many people argue about the order in which the authors' names should appear on a journal article, when this issue should have been sorted out (or at least discussed) right from the start. Of course, the order might change if one author ends up doing more work than anticipated, but it is a good idea to discuss this early on so that the issue is out in the open.

4   Audience?   I suggest you actually write down the names of specific people that you think might be the potential audience. If you are writing a PhD thesis, then think of potential examiners besides your own supervisor. If you are writing a book, think of the target market (e.g. undergraduate or post-graduate students, researchers, etc.). If you are thinking of writing a journal article, then think of who might be a good reviewer for your paper. If you are unable to come up with anyone, then one suggestion is to take a look at some of the authors that you are citing in the bibliography. I find it is very helpful to have specific people in mind when writing up my work, because I will then write for this audience. The finished work will have a much greater chance of being appropriate and of interest to this target audience.

5   Method?   It is important that you have good support for whichever research method you are planning to use in your own institution. This includes having a good supervisor, i.e. a person who is 'qualified' and has the experience and expertise to do the job. It also includes having the right research training before you start the work, e.g. perhaps being able to take one or more courses on qualitative research. It is not impossible, but certainly very difficult, to use a research method well without appropriate advice and guidance from within your own institution.

6   Publication Outlet?   This question asks you to think about the most appropriate publication outlet for your research work. If you are considering writing up your work as a journal article, conference paper, or book at some stage, then I suggest you start thinking about writing for that particular outlet from the start. This will affect the sort of topic you choose, your research method, and the style of your research. It will also affect your intended audience. For example, if you are considering writing a journal article, you should consider the people who are currently involved in the journal (the senior and associate editors, recent authors, and so forth), and see what kind of research they are doing and what kind of research is currently being published. This is because research is a social process (as well as a rational one). As someone with substantial editorial experience, I can tell you that it is not a winning strategy to submit a paper to a journal when you have hardly even looked at the type of papers that it publishes. Editors get frustrated when a paper is submitted by an author who has obviously no real understanding of

the style or standard of research of the publication outlet in question. If, after looking at the particular publication outlet in detail, you are still unsure about the fit of your proposed research within the aims and scope of the journal, conference, or publisher, then ask someone who has some experience with that particular outlet for some advice.

7 Theoretical Contribution? This question is important because it is a requirement of most of the top journals in business and management for research articles to make a good contribution to theory. Of course, if you are writing for a conference or a second- or third-tier journal, this may not be so important. However, I still think it is a good idea to try to describe your proposed theoretical contribution in just one paragraph. This may be very general at the start of your research project, but at least this question will help you to focus on how you think your work will contribute to the wider discipline. The theoretical contribution will most likely emerge from your literature review. The literature review places your own research project in context.

8 Practical Contribution? It is a good idea to try to describe your practical contribution in one paragraph. Depending on the particular business discipline, this question may not be essential if you are planning to write up your research solely for a top academic journal, but I think it is still a useful exercise. Of course, this practical relevance might change your answers to some of the earlier questions (e.g. potential audience).

I am sure there are other additional questions that could be considered to help you write up your research; however, I believe the eight questions in Table 17.1 succinctly summarize the most relevant questions for qualitative researchers in business and management.

Writing Styles and Genres

As I mentioned earlier, there are many different writing styles and genres that can be used to write up qualitative research (Harvey & Myers, 1995; Myers, 1999). I will briefly review some of these here.

Van Maanen (1988) discusses three styles of writing that can be used to write up ethnography: these are the realist, confessional, and impressionist styles. I believe these styles are equally relevant for some other kinds of qualitative research, such as action research or case study research.

The realist style of writing is perhaps the most positivistic style of writing. This genre is one where there is an extremely detailed description of cultural traditions, beliefs, and practices. This style of writing gives preference to 'typical forms', those cultural practices or forms that supposedly typify the culture being described. The realist style also gives precedence to the native's perspective. The story is told almost exclusively through the eyes of the natives, virtually ignoring the role of the researcher in the writing of the story. The article or book reads as if it were an extremely objective, authoritative, and politically neutral account.

A classic literary device used in this style of writing (in ethnographic research at least) is the 'ethnographic present'. The ethnographic present is a literary device that gives the impression that things have always been the same, e.g. the author might say that 'Every year the natives get together to celebrate the start of spring' or 'The software development team uses mobile phones to communicate with users overseas.' But this literary device is a-historical, since it neglects to mention when these activities started. The writer using this device also fails to acknowledge that these practices may change at some point in the future. Cultural traditions and practices can change over time.

The confessional style of writing is almost just the opposite. The confessional tale adopts a highly personalized and self-absorbed style. The emphasis is not at all on the natives' perspective, but rather on the field worker's experience. This writing style emphasizes the authority of the researcher and his or her account of what happened (Van Maanen, 1988). An example of the confessional style in business and management is Schultze's account of her ethnographic work about knowledge management (Schultze, 2000).

A weakness of the confessional style is that the quality of confessionals varies dramatically. Some authors are able to write extremely interesting confessional tales, whereas others can be quite boring. The authors of confessional tales are sometimes accused of 'navel gazing', of writing 'vanity' tales and of being self-indulgent. This is because the authors of confessional tales can become so concerned with themselves that this overshadows the account of the culture or organization being studied. A good confessional tale, however, can be very interesting indeed, particularly if it reads like an adventure story.

The impressionist style focuses on the recall of experiences and impressions from the field. The author attempts to capture a scene in a moment of time, and presents the doing of fieldwork in a novelistic way. There tends to be a deliberate selection of the atypical in the written account, which again is the opposite of the realist style of writing. The impressionist writer avoids interpreting or analysing the story too much, since the impressionist's mission is to deny the all-embracing answer. In effect, the impressionist invites the readers to make their own sense of the tale (Van Maanen, 1988).

A weakness of the impressionist style is that very few people are able to use it successfully. It requires the researcher to be an excellent writer, something akin to being a novelist. Unfortunately, not everyone can write in this style.

As well as the three styles of writing discussed by Van Maanen (the realist, confessional, and impressionist styles), other styles include the narrative, literary, and jointly told styles. I will briefly discuss each of these in turn.

The narrative style tends to see the case study or ethnography as the writing of history. Both the researcher and the subject matter are situated historically, and the researcher pays attention to the chronological nature of events. For example, much of the research in the field of information systems is concerned with information systems projects and information systems development. A researcher studying a particular project might document some of the significant events that occurred over the life of the project, e.g. when the consultants were hired, or when the system went live. The advantage of the narrative style is that it is often easy for the reader to see how things progressed the way they did, i.e. how one significant event led to another. The writing of a good narrative, however, requires the author to make sure that only relevant details of events are included. The narrator has to make good decisions with regard to what to include and what to exclude. An example of the narrative style is the article by Larsen and Myers (1999), which narrates the story of a business process re-engineering project in a bank.

The literary style uses fiction-writing techniques to tell the story. The author uses dramatic plots, narration, and so forth to tell us about the research findings. A good feature of the literary style is that the research findings are often very interesting to read. A weakness, however, is that such research accounts tend to be emotionally charged and this can distort the reality they seek to portray (Van Maanen, 1988).

The jointly told style is where the research report or article is co-authored by the researcher and a 'native'. This style could be very appropriate in research that is concerned with international and cross-cultural issues in business and management. The advantage of this particular style is that it tells the story from both points of view – from the researchers and the subjects of the research (although the native may also be a researcher). A potential weakness of this style, however, is that there is a tendency for such research reports to be less critical than other styles of writing. This is perhaps to be expected, given that one of the authors is from the research site. Another potential weakness of this style is that the researchers may not give much thought to the question of which native is selected to be the co-author. Obviously, if the 'native' is the CEO of a manufacturing company, he or she will have quite a different perspective to that of a factory worker in the same company.

Some Practical Suggestions

Start Writing as Soon as Possible   If you are doing qualitative research, you should start writing as soon as possible. Many people think that they would like to get their ideas straight first, and then start writing. The idea is that you leave the writing up until the end when you have got 'the story' figured out.

However, as Wolcott (1990) points out, this is a big mistake. The problem with qualitative research is that you obtain so much data, and you have so many ideas to distil, that it is very difficult, if not impossible, to get your ideas straight first without writing them down.

Wolcott (1990) makes the point that 'writing is thinking'. As you start to write things down, this in itself forces you to clarify what you are thinking. The more you write, the more you clarify your own thoughts. Writing actually helps a researcher to think straight and to figure out what the story should be. Writing it down actually brings some structure and form to your own ideas.

Of course, you might not have the correct form or the correct structure when you write the first draft, but you can always revise it later. The key thing is that by having your thoughts on paper or on a computer screen in front of you, it actually helps you to think. Hence, the motto of every qualitative researcher should be to start writing as soon as possible.

To help you do this, it is a very good idea to draft an extended table of contents as early as possible. If you are writing a journal article or book chapter, it is very helpful to write an outline of the article with the major headings. If you are writing a thesis or a book, the table of contents should include all the major chapters and as many headings and subheadings as you can think of. Once you have done this, you might find you can write some chapters already. For example, you might be able to write the first draft of the literature review; if you are doing case study research, you might be able to write the chapter that provides an overview of the entire organization. The key thing is to start writing early. Once you have written one or two chapters of a thesis, the whole project does not seem as daunting as it did earlier.

Write a Good 'Story'   I find that many students make the mistake of thinking that they have to write in a certain scientific (read 'boring') style. They seem to think that by using a certain technique (e.g. writing in the passive voice, or in the third person) this will make the research seem more objective. However, this is a mistake. In my view, every qualitative researcher should attempt to write a good story. This story should be interesting and compelling for the audience; it should grab their attention and make them want to read your article or thesis from start to finish.

A few years ago I had a conversation with one of the senior editors of *Management Science*. This particular journal is a first-tier journal that publishes mostly quantitative research. We were talking about the 'publishing game' and he pointed out to me that every single article in *Management Science* needs to tell a good story. Without a good story, the article will not be published. However, most stories in this particular journal are told with numbers, rather than text. The story needs to be sufficiently compelling that the reviewers and editors can agree that the manuscript is a new contribution to knowledge.

Data Selection   Since qualitative researchers usually accumulate much data, a common 'problem' is deciding what to include or exclude from the written document. It is easy to think that 'everything' is important, especially when you are in the middle of a qualitative study. However, if you try to include everything in a thesis or article, you will quickly overwhelm your readers with too much detail. The net result is that the finished product is actually quite boring for your readers, and they will skim through it quickly and be glad when they get to the end. In fact, the chances are that they will not read it at all! Hence, it is important to spend some time editing the thesis or article such that the story can be told within the word limit set by the editor or your supervisor. It is a mistake to think that longer is better.

On the other hand, it is important in many situations to provide a 'thick' rather than a 'thin' description of your findings. Providing a certain amount of detail allows for the readers to 'audit' your findings. That is, they are able to see for themselves how you came to your conclusions.

I also recommend that, even in relatively short conference papers or journal articles, you include at least some direct quotations from interviews. Reporting verbatim what one of your informants said gives a certain amount of credibility to your article. Providing some primary data such as this gives some face validity to your findings. It proves that you did indeed talk to some of the people in the organization. Including direct quotes from interviews also brings your story to life, and as long as they are selected carefully, such quotations can help to make the story more interesting.

Get the Details Right First Time   Although you can always revise your first draft later, there are a few things you should always get right first time. If you get these things correct from the start, you will save yourself so much time later.

The first thing is the spelling of proper names like people's names, place names, and so forth. These names should be spelt consistently throughout a document. If you are writing a thesis of 100 pages or more, there is nothing more frustrating than finding out that people's names are spelt inconsistently and incorrectly throughout. So get the spelling right first time.

Another thing is direct quotations from your sources. Quotations should be completely accurate, word for word, with the exact reference and page number (if the quotation is from a book or article). Again, there is nothing more frustrating than when you find right at the last minute that you do not have that vital page number. Then you have to go back to the library and, even worse, you might find that the book you need is not available because someone else has borrowed it. All you need is a page number, but it can be frustrating trying to find it again later. Something very simple can take you an inordinate amount of time to fix later, when it would have been so much easier to get it right from the start.

Bibliographic Database and Reference Management Software   I also recommend that everyone use a bibliographic database and reference management software program such as EndNote or ProCite. If you are planning to be an academic, or you are writing something substantial like a thesis, then you should definitely consider using bibliographic database software.

One of the main benefits of using this kind of software is that you only need to enter a reference once. As long as you get the reference details right first time, then you do not need to enter them ever again. The software will format the reference in the reference style of your choice, such as for the *Academy of Management Journal*, the *Journal of Marketing*, or in APA format. Many of these reference styles are provided with the software as a matter of course.

I find this software very useful, particularly as I use some references over and over again in different papers. Also, if you are revising a previous version of a paper for a journal, then it is a very simple matter to change the reference style. Just a few clicks of the mouse and the format of the entire bibliography is changed. What used to take me a few hours in the old days, now takes me no time at all. So I strongly recommend that you start using this kind of software as soon as possible in your research career. Fortunately many research universities will have a site licence for one of these software programs.

Exercises

1   Find a qualitative research article or book that you think is well written and interesting. What makes it such a good article or book?
2   Using the writing template of Table 17.1, analyse the article or book you identified in the previous question.

(Cont'd)

3   Now apply Table 17.1 to your own work, perhaps an essay or a conference paper. Write at least one sentence for each of the eight questions.

4   If you are writing a thesis or book, draft an extended table of contents for the entire work, including sub-headings in the proposed chapters.

5   Encourage a faculty member within your own institution to organize a writing workshop for PhD students and interested faculty members. This workshop can be held over the space of 2–3 days, and its the purpose is for everyone actually to write while they are there. Of course, the writing might be interspersed with presentations about writing by those who are recognised as good writers.

Further Reading

Books

For writing up qualitative research in general, I highly recommend Wolcott's (1990) book, entitled *Writing Up Qualitative Research*. This book has many practical suggestions.

Another useful book is called *Doing and Writing Qualitative Research* (Holliday, 2002). This book tackles the practical problems that writers face when they attempt to transform the rich data they have gathered from their research into the written word.

18

GETTING PUBLISHED

Objectives

By the end of this chapter, you will be able to:

- Understand the purpose of getting published
- Appreciate the differences between publication outlets
- Avoid making some common mistakes
- Improve your chances of getting published

INTRODUCTION

When I was first starting out as an academic researcher, a well-published researcher in my field gave me some excellent advice. She said to me, 'research is not finished until it is published'. I have used this as a motto in my own research work ever since.

I suggest this should be a motto for everyone doing qualitative research. If you have the attitude that a research project is not finished until you have published something from it – whether it is a journal article, a book, or just a conference paper – then you will keep working until that is achieved. You will not rest until you have succeeded in having at least one publication accepted.

I have found this motto to be very motivational in my own research career. It ensures that you finish a research project before you get sidetracked with too many other things. Towards the end of a long research project most of us have a tendency to get bored with it or to become tired. It might seem much more interesting to drop it altogether and move on to something else. But if you have the motto that 'research is not finished until it is published', then you will keep going until that objective is achieved.

There are many reasons for publishing your research findings. One of the most important is so that others might learn from your research work, and, hopefully, use it as a basis for their own future research work.

Let us imagine the following scenario. Assume that you have conducted a research project for your doctorate. During the course of your research project, you have learnt many things. The process of doing your doctoral research has been an excellent personal learning experience. You have also come up with some original findings. These findings provide an answer to one part of a jigsaw puzzle that has bothered scholars in your field for some time.

However, if you do not publish your findings, then no one else will know about them. As far as other scholars in your chosen field are concerned, that one part of the jigsaw puzzle remains unsolved (simply because they do not know that your solution exists). Hence, when another PhD student in some other part of the world conducts a literature review on the same topic, he or she will not find your research findings (which have remained unpublished). This PhD student thus has to solve that part of the jigsaw puzzle all over again. And when this student eventually reveals the solution in a publication, he or she is the one who will gain the credit for this new discovery, not you.

Hence, if you want your research project to be more than just a personal learning experience, you should try to publish something from it. Having a publication enables other researchers to learn about your findings. It means that your research becomes a contribution to the body of knowledge in a particular field, and also becomes available for others to build upon. Of course, there is in addition some personal satisfaction in seeing your own work in print.

Besides the important goal of contributing to a field, and the personal satisfaction of publishing, there are other reasons for trying to get your work published. In most research universities today, an important criterion in determining promotion and tenure is a person's research and publications record. The more 'well published' you can become, the more chance you have of being promoted and gaining tenure. Of course, it is not so much the total number of publications that count, but the quality of the outlets in which your work appears.

Publication Outlets

There is a variety of publication outlets for qualitative researchers in business and management. These outlets include magazines for business practitioners, peer-reviewed journal articles for academics, papers published in conference proceedings, and books or chapters in edited books. These days many publication outlets are available on the Internet as well as on paper.

These various publication outlets each have their advantages and disadvantages. One of the advantages of presenting a paper at an academic conference is that you can get some feedback on your research work. Another is that you get to see what other researchers in your chosen area of research are working on. One of the advantages of writing an article for a magazine for business practitioners is that it demonstrates the relevance of your work to practice. It might also improve your consulting practice.

In some fields, such as anthropology or history, a book is regarded as the defining publication for a researcher. Realistically, a book is the only place where an author can convey the richness of the data. For academics in business and management, however, the most important publication outlet is the peer-reviewed academic journal. Although all publication outlets have their pros and cons – and they should not be seen as mutually exclusive – as a general rule journal articles are regarded much more highly than any other kind of publication outlet in business schools.

Therefore, if you intend to have a career in academia and in a business and management discipline, it is important to know how to get published in peer-reviewed journals. Having one or more articles in these academic journals is often a prerequisite for a successful academic career. Hence, the main purpose of this chapter is to help you succeed in the publishing game. I hope that you can become a 'well-published' qualitative researcher, one whose research work is often cited by others.

The Peer Review Process

As I have just said, researchers in business and management are expected to publish their work in journal articles. The reason for this is that manuscripts submitted to academic journals are subject to a peer review process, which gives some assurance of quality. Business school deans and others on the promotions and tenure committee believe that the peer review process is more rigorous in academic journals than elsewhere. In the more highly ranked academic journals in particular, the peer review process is very tough. Many good research articles are rejected and only the best survive. Hence it is important to understand the peer review process. Let me explain how it works.

Essentially, the peer review process is a form of quality assurance that is used in every academic discipline. The general idea is that one's research work is subject to review by one's peers i.e. other 'qualified' researchers who are able to judge the quality of the work. If the findings are judged to be significant and robust by one's peers, then the manuscript will be accepted and published as a new contribution to knowledge. However, if the findings are judged to be insignificant and not robust, then a manuscript will be rejected. As you can see, the peer review process, by definition, is a social process. Peer review involves having your work evaluated by others.

In order to explain the peer review process more fully, I will use as an example the process at *MIS Quarterly*. I am familiar with this process since I was a senior editor at *MIS Quarterly* for five years, and, before that, an associate editor for three. I also have experience as an author of articles published in the journal.

MIS Quarterly is the top research journal in information systems and is included in the *Financial Times* list of the top 40 academic journals in business. In 2006 *MIS Quarterly* had the highest impact-factor rating of any academic journal in both information systems and computer science, with an ISI Web of Knowledge impact factor of 4.978 (briefly, the impact factor is viewed by many as a proxy for the importance of a journal in a field; it looks at the average number of times published articles are cited by others up to two years after publication; hence, the higher the impact factor, the more impact the journal is assumed to have on a field).

The first step of the review process at *MIS Quarterly* involves the screening of a manuscript by a senior editor. When one or more authors submit a manuscript to the journal for consideration, they are able to nominate one or more senior editors whom they would like to handle their manuscript (based on what they consider to be the appropriateness of the expertise and research interests of the senior editor). If a senior editor agrees that the manuscript is of interest to him or her, then the manuscript is assigned to that senior editor. The senior editor then screens the manuscript based on its appropriateness and suitability for the journal. Many manuscripts are rejected at this point and returned to the authors. This could be for many reasons. For example, the manuscript might not fit the mission and scope of the journal. By definition, any article submitted to *MIS Quarterly* should be concerned with some aspect of information systems, but if the manuscript is only tangentially related to this subject, then it will be rejected. Another reason could be that the manuscript does not fit the style of the journal. All articles in *MIS Quarterly* have a certain style and are expected to be of a certain standard. No matter what the reason, if a manuscript is rejected during the screening process, it is because it is judged by the senior editor as having virtually no chance of surviving the peer review process. Given their extensive experience with the review process and the expected standard of articles published in the journal, the senior editors (SEs) all have full authority to accept or reject papers. In my view it is much better for all concerned (authors, reviewers, and editors) if those manuscripts that are clearly unsuitable are weeded out sooner rather than later, even though authors of rejected papers might not always appreciate this at the time. A good number of papers are rejected at this point.

The second step of the review process involves the screening of the manuscript by an associate editor. Again, authors are able to nominate one or more associate editors (AEs) that they consider to have the required expertise and research interest for their particular manuscript (although there is no guarantee that the author's suggestions will be followed, since AEs can choose whether or not they wish to handle papers assigned to them). Some papers may also be weeded out at this point, based on the experience and advice of the AE.

The third step of the review process involves sending the paper out for review. Normally, three reviewers are asked to review the paper and to evaluate its suitability for publication in *MIS Quarterly*. One reviewer might be an expert in the methodology, another might be an expert in the subject area, and the third might be one of the reviewers suggested by the authors. At least one or more of these reviewers is likely to have published in *MIS Quarterly* or another journal of similar quality. They will be selected by the SE and AE based on their expertise (i.e. their previous publication record). The main thing that the reviewers look for is whether the paper is an original research contribution (or a potential contribution) to the field of information systems. As with the nomination of the SE and AE, authors can nominate potential reviewers for their paper. Of course, authors should not nominate a reviewer who may have a potential conflict of interest. A conflict of interest includes things like being a co-author, a colleague at the same institution, or a current or former student. Avoidance of a conflict of interest is vital in order to ensure the integrity of the review process.

The fourth step of the review process involves the AE looking at all three reviews, writing a report, and making a recommendation to the SE.

The fifth step involves the SE making the decision. This decision is final, and is based on the report of the AE, the three reviews, and the SE's own assessment of the paper. Unfortunately, as is the case with most top journals, the vast majority of papers are rejected at this point, given the rigorous nature of the review process. Some, however, are considered to have sufficient potential such as to warrant a 'revise and resubmit' decision. This means that the authors are invited to revise their paper, based on the feedback they have been given, and to resubmit the paper at a later date. In my experience, very few papers are accepted at this stage (in fact, none during my tenure as an SE).

When the authors have finished revising the paper, they then resubmit it to the journal. The review process then starts all over again, beginning at the first step. If, during the fifth step, the SE decides that the authors have successfully addressed the criticisms of the paper raised during the first review cycle, then the SE might accept the paper for publication. Alternatively the paper might be rejected, or the authors invited to revise the paper once again (although three review cycles is very unusual and in some journals is frowned upon altogether).

There are a few important features of the review process that help to ensure the quality of the published articles. First, the reviewers at *MIS Quarterly* are likely to be experts in some particular aspect of the paper (e.g. the topic or methodology). In other words, they themselves will have published their work in *MIS Quarterly* or other first-tier journals. They will be leading researchers in the field.

Second, the peer review process is double-blind. This means that the authors do not know who the reviewers are, and the reviewers do not know who the authors are. The idea of having double-blind review is to try to ensure that the paper is reviewed in an objective manner. It is assumed that if the reviewers knew who the authors were, then well-known authors might have a higher chance of success than those who are not so well known. Hence, the double-blind system tries to make sure that reviewers are not influenced by the names of the authors.

Third, AEs and SEs are appointed to these roles based on merit. The SEs vote on who should be appointed as AEs. Their vote is based on their experience with those nominated to this role. This experience includes the quality of the reviews the person has provided for *MIS Quarterly* in the past, and their publications record. SEs also get to vote on which AEs should be appointed as SEs.

In summary, the peer review process at *MIS Quarterly* and other academic journals is a quality control mechanism, ensuring that only the best articles are published. Of course, not all journals have the same quality standards. There is a big difference between those in the first tier, such as *Academy of Management Journal, Accounting, Organisations and Society*, or *Journal of Marketing,* and those in the third or fourth tier. However, almost all academic journals, no matter which tier they are in, have some kind of peer review system in place. It is this system that sets apart academic journals from most other types of publications. The peer review system is the reason why academic journal articles are regarded as the most important publication outlet for academics in business and management.

COMMON MISTAKES AND PITFALLS

In my experience there are some common mistakes and pitfalls that people make in trying to get their research work published in academic journals. I will discuss these common mistakes and pitfalls, and then suggest how they might be overcome.

Getting Your Paper Rejected

The first thing you should realize is that everyone gets their papers rejected at some time or another. This is especially the case if you are trying to get your research published in a top journal. In fact, the more you submit your papers to journals, the more times you are likely to experience rejection. If you do not like the idea of having your papers rejected, then the best way to avoid this is not to submit anything at all!

My experience, as an author, reviewer, and editor, has shown me that even the best and most published researchers have their papers rejected. Many of my papers have been rejected over the years. But one significant difference between a well-published researcher and someone else is that a top researcher will quickly revise the paper and submit it to a different journal. These researchers do not spend too much time wallowing in their sorrows, complaining about the unfairness of the reviewers.

I distinctly remember my first experience of rejection. I submitted what I thought was an excellent paper to a top journal in information systems. I was extremely disappointed therefore (this is putting it mildly) when I received the review packet which stated that my paper had been rejected. The reviewers and the editor did not appear to appreciate what I was trying to do. In quite a few places they seemed to misunderstand my research work. Being very disillusioned by the whole experience, I put this particular paper in my filing cabinet, where it sat for almost one full year (I still used a filing cabinet in the early 1990s).

Looking back now, I realize how inexperienced and immature I was at that time. I made a few fundamental mistakes. The first mistake was to leave the paper in the filing cabinet for a year. As it turned out, the next time I submitted it to a journal the paper was accepted with minor revisions. Why did I wait one full year to revise it? A second mistake was to assume that because the reviewers did not understand my paper, the fault lay with them. But in reality, the main reason for their misunderstanding the paper was that I did not explain it well enough. In other words, the fault lay with me. That was a hard lesson to learn. I had failed to appreciate that the peer review process is a social process.

Although I still do not enjoy receiving a rejection letter, I am now much more used to it. After waiting a day or two for the emotional disappointment to pass, I read the reviews and the editor's report in as objective a manner as I can. Usually, I find that I agree with most of their criticisms (particularly if the reviewers are 'qualified' and experienced qualitative researchers). In fact, I find that the sooner I am able to take their comments on board, and the sooner I am able to understand their points of view, the sooner I am able to revise the paper. And the sooner it is revised, the sooner I am able to resubmit it to another journal.

Why Are Papers Rejected?

Of course, it would be nice if we could avoid getting our papers rejected in the first place. However, for most of us rejection is just a fact of academic life. So I will now consider the most common reasons why manuscripts are rejected. After considering these reasons for rejection, I will then suggest ways in which you can avoid these common problems.

The following analysis is based on my own experience as an associate and senior editor of *MIS Quarterly*. As I said earlier, I was an associate editor for three years and a senior editor for five. During this time I handled qualitative research manuscripts only.

In my experience, although there were many reasons for rejection, I found there were two main reasons that cropped up again and again. These were:

1 The lack of a contribution to knowledge.
2 The 'story' is not convincing.

I will discuss each of these reasons in turn.

The Lack of a Contribution to Knowledge

The first main reason for rejection is the perceived lack of a contribution to knowledge. Reviewers might react this way if they believe that the paper is unfocused. Being unfocused means that the reviewers are unsure as to what the main point of the paper is. Often there might be many points in the paper.

Reviewers may also believe that the literature review is inadequate. In other words, the authors may not have done a good enough job of reviewing the literature relevant to the topic. The literature review may not be sufficiently up-to-date, or certain key articles may be missing.

Reviewers may also think that the manuscript is not sufficiently new or original. Perhaps the manuscript does not contradict conventional wisdom. The top journals always want to publish an article that is new or original, rather than something that simply repeats or confirms what has been published earlier. In fact, some business journals explicitly state in their guidelines for authors that they will not accept replication studies. Of course, it is important for such studies to be published if progress is to be made in a particular discipline; however, these can often be published elsewhere.

This last objection is a particularly difficult one to overcome. It is relatively easy to convince your students that what you are telling them is new knowledge, but not so easy to convince your academic colleagues that your research findings are original. It is, of course, even more difficult to convince the editors and reviewers of a journal that what you have discovered is new. This is especially the case if the journal is in the first tier, and the editor and reviewers are well known international scholars. Well-published international scholars are likely to say that they have heard it all before.

The Story Is Not Convincing

The second main reason for rejection is that the story is not convincing or plausible. Although you might think that this criterion only applies to qualitative research, a senior editor of *Management Science* once told me that all articles submitted to this journal need to have a good story as well. As you may know, *Management Science* is a first-tier journal that publishes mostly quantitative research. But in this particular case, the story is told with numbers.

Reviewers might think that the story is not convincing if they believe there is a lack of depth to the story. This could be because the evidence comes from a limited range of sources, or because important data about the organization and the people are missing. Alternatively, it could be because the reviewers are not sure what the researcher has done or how he or she did it. If the paper is based on ethnographic research, then the reviewers might be disappointed that there is no 'thick description'.

Possible Solutions

To address the first problem (the lack of a contribution to knowledge), a good starting point is to complete the following sentence: 'the purpose of this paper is ... '. Every journal article should have just one main point. Of course, theses and books might have many points. Each chapter might have its own main point. But in a 20-page journal article, you do not have the space to argue for multiple points. Hence, your journal article should have one main point, and you must be able to summarize this point succinctly. If you find this too difficult, and you find yourself waffling on for a few sentences, then it probably means that you are not clear enough about the purpose of the paper. If you are not clear about the purpose of the paper, then I can guarantee that the reviewers of your paper will not be either!

I have found that one way to address this first problem is to have a paper in mind right from the start of the research project. Normally you would think that the writing-up phase is the very last thing you should consider (especially since this chapter on publishing is in the second-to-last part of the book). However, these days, I tend to think of a possible publication outlet at the start. For example, if I am discussing a potential research project with a colleague, I immediately start to think about which journal I have in mind, and which scholars might be interested in it. I think of possible reviewers for the paper and put myself in their shoes: would they find this particular article interesting? Is this particular point (the main one I am about to make in the article) something that they would consider to be a new contribution to knowledge? If the answer is 'yes' (although it might pay to check with one or two people if you are not really sure), then I believe the project is worth doing. If the answer is 'no', then I do not believe the project is worth doing. If the point of the paper simply repeats something that these scholars already know, and if they find it boring, then I consider it would be a better use of my time to choose a different project altogether. If the answer is 'maybe', then some further thinking and investigation are required before I reach a definite answer.

Another way to address this problem is to ensure that your literature review is complete and up-to-date. Unfortunately, this problem is more difficult than it seems; it is in fact something of a 'wicked' problem. Let me explain. If your literature review includes a recently published article from a top journal, then it is likely that that article is already three or four years old. This is the length of time that it would have taken for the authors to work on the paper and navigate the review process, and for the publisher to make it available. The authors, meanwhile, have already moved on to a new research problem. The article that has just been published reflects what they were thinking four years ago, but now they are working on new things.

This means that if you base your research project only on the most up-to-date research literature that is available, you are already at a disadvantage. All the top researchers in your field are working on new problems, while you continue to work on problems that were important yesterday. How is it possible to solve this 'wicked' problem? How is it possible to get ahead of the game, such that you are working on new problems?

One way is to become a reviewer for journals and conferences. If you become a reviewer, then you get to see articles long before they are published. You get to see what other researchers are working on now. I have met many people who say that if you become a regular reviewer, this takes important time away from your own research. It is true that while you are reviewing someone else's work you are not working on your own. However, there is a certain counter-intuitive logic that operates here. If you review other people's research articles, then you actually get better at writing your own. You start to see what the common problems are in writing up research articles for publication. You also start to see what other people are working on now, long before publication. Hence, I strongly recommend that all scholars should try to become involved in the peer review process. As the process is a social process by nature, getting involved as a reviewer can help you to understand what the requirements are for a paper to be accepted.

Another way to try to solve this problem is to attend academic conferences where excellent qualitative research is presented. At the conference, I suggest you ask other researchers what they are working on. Social networking is all part of the socialization process in a particular academic field.

To some extent, those who are actively involved in an academic discipline (as authors, reviewers, editors, or conference chairs and so forth) can be seen as being part of a scientific community or social club (Kuhn, 1996; Whitley, 1984). Although all social clubs have their problems, normally one of the easiest and best ways to succeed in a particular endeavour is to join the club. Hence, becoming a reviewer, and attending and presenting at academic conferences, are all important steps in becoming socialized into the club. It helps you to understand what the rules are and what it takes to become a successful researcher.

With respect to the second problem (the story is not convincing), there are a few essential things that you can do. First, you should ensure that a significant mass of data is collected. This is especially important for an in-depth case study or ethnography. Second, it is a good idea to include verbatim comments from interviews. Quotes from interviews give some face validity to your article, and give the article more credibility. They show that you have indeed talked to some of the key people, and that you gathered some interesting data (as long as the quotes are interesting, of course). Third, make sure that you clearly describe your research method. If you conducted a case study, for example, you should also mention how many interviews you conducted, and with whom; you should also mention all your other data sources, and how long it took you to do the research. All these details will help others to evaluate your research work and how you went about it. Fourth, I suggest that you specify how your research should be evaluated. This is especially important if you are using a new qualitative method or a new method of qualitative data analysis. If the particular approach you have taken is new in your field, then you run the risk of your reviewers not knowing how to evaluate your work appropriately. However, if you can point to the use of the method in another related field, then this might be very helpful. The reviewers then have some basis on which to evaluate your own article.

PRACTICAL TIPS

I will finish this chapter by giving some practical tips on getting your own qualitative research work published in an academic journal article.

A common problem that many qualitative researchers in business and management face is the one of trying to write up their results within the space constraints of a 20-page journal article. Most qualitative research methods lead to the gathering of a significant mass of data and qualitative researchers often find it difficult to fit everything into 20 pages. Another problem is the expectation that singular findings will be presented in each paper. As I said earlier, each journal article should have just one main 'point'. Often a qualitative doctoral thesis such as an ethnographic study will have many points.

As I mentioned earlier, one practical solution is to treat each paper as a part of the whole. That is, you have to devise a way to carve up the work so that parts of it can be published separately. Then the issue becomes which part of the story is going to be told in one particular paper. A qualitative researcher has to come to terms with the fact that it is impossible to tell the 'whole story' in any one paper, so he or she has to accept that only one part of it can be told at any one time. One advantage of such a strategy is that there is potential for a qualitative researcher to publish many papers from just the one research project. Usually it is possible to tell the same story from different angles.

A good example of someone who adopted this strategy is Wanda Orlikowski, a qualitative researcher in the field of information systems at MIT. Orlikowski succeeded in having many papers published based on the one period of ethnographic fieldwork she did for her PhD at NYU.

I suggest that qualitative researchers constantly seek to improve their manuscript before submitting it to a conference or journal. This can be done by asking colleagues to comment on the working paper version.

Another approach is to ask a more senior colleague (i.e. someone who has successfully published their own work) to join you as a co-author. For example, your own supervisor may be willing to become a co-author. In my own case,

I learnt so much about the process of getting published in top journals from one of my own co-authors, Heinz Klein. Heinz was the first international scholar that I started to collaborate with. Without Heinz as a co-author, I doubt if I would ever have been able to publish my work in *MIS Quarterly*, let alone win the Best Paper Award. The collaboration itself has produced far more than we could ever have done by ourselves.

Hence, I highly recommend writing with another colleague, particularly where this involves a collaboration of equals. A slightly trickier situation is where there is a power differential between the co-authors, e.g. between a supervisor and student. In this case, I recommend the following.

First, any collaboration should be of a purely voluntary nature. I believe it is unethical for supervisors to force students into co-authoring with them. If you as a student have conducted the research, then I believe you are the right-ful owner of the findings (even if the supervisor guided you along the way). Hence, it should be your free choice as to whether you publish the findings yourself or publish them with someone else as a co-author. Having said that, however, I believe that, realistically, very few of us are able to succeed in get-ting our work published in good journals by ourselves, particularly when we are first starting out as researchers. For that reason I always suggest to my own students that I am happy to be a second author on their first paper, if they would like me to be. However, the choice is completely up to them.

Second, I believe it is advisable to discuss and agree upon a proposed pub-lishing plan with your co-author(s) right at the start. As I mentioned in the previous chapter, you should discuss authorship and questions such as: Who will be the first author? Which publication outlet will we target? Who will take overall responsibility for the various sections of the article? Who will be responsible for shepherding the article through the review process? I think it is much better for everyone to agree on these matters at the start, rather than leave them until later. If you assume things, this is simply a recipe for argu-ments and some unhappiness later on. It is so much better to make the arrangements explicit from the start, and then no one is surprised later. In my own case, I like to remain on very good terms with all my co-authors, whether students or colleagues. Publishing should be fun, not a nightmare!

Third, I believe that if someone agrees to be a co-author, then they should actually contribute something! Unfortunately, I have come across situations in which someone's name is on a paper, even though it appears that they did not do any work. I know some academics feel under pressure to publish something either to survive ('publish or perish') or to gain promotion. However, I cannot accept this as an excuse. If they cannot actually write something, then maybe they are just not suited to being an academic. In any case, I believe it is unethical to have someone's name on a paper when they have not contributed anything to the work. If someone's name appears on a paper as an author, then that person should have actually authored something. Otherwise, the list of authors' names is misleading.

If you are starting out as a new researcher, another good idea is to send your paper to a conference first. As a general rule, it is easier to get a paper accepted for a conference than for a journal. Then you might be able to use the feedback you received from the conference to improve the manuscript. Many conferences allow authors to resubmit a revised version of a paper published in the conference proceedings to a journal (in fact some conferences explicitly recommend the best papers to a journal). Also, many journals are happy to accept revised versions of papers presented at conferences. As long as the journal version is sufficiently different from the conference paper, journal editors will usually have no objection to this. As a qualitative researcher, I have found that the journal version is usually two to three times longer in any case. Often papers accepted for conference proceedings have a very strict word limit. Having said this, however, I am aware that there are differences between editors in their attitude to this kind of publication strategy; hence, I recommend that you check with the appropriate people beforehand, to make sure that this approach is acceptable to them.

Once you have completed the research project and written it up in article form, the next issue to consider is where you plan to send your manuscript. My general advice is to send your article to an 'appropriate' journal. By appropriate, I mean that the subject matter and style of the article fit the particular journal in question. Also, your research work should be of a similar standard to what is normally published there. In my own case, I tend not to submit much of my work to the top journal in my field (*MIS Quarterly*). This is because I do not believe it is appropriate for that outlet. If you submit an article to a top journal when it is not really suitable, one problem you face is that it can spend a long time in the review process, only to be rejected at the end. If you keep sending it to top journals, and keep getting rejected, the research project on which the project is based starts to age. If you keep going along this track, you will find that the manuscript in question has passed its use-by date, and it becomes difficult to publish at all. At the other extreme, you do not want to send a ground-breaking article to a little known journal with a very low impact factor. If it is truly ground-breaking, then you want as many people to know about it as possible. The more highly ranked journals tend to have a higher readership. Also, you will gain more recognition by publishing in a top-tier outlet. Hence, it is important to send your manuscript to an 'appropriate' journal. Taking into consideration the subject, style, and quality of your article, do not aim too high or too low.

When you submit an article to a journal, often the journal will invite you to recommend suitable editors or reviewers. If this option is available to you, I strongly recommend you take advantage of it. Even if the editor only selects one of your suggested people, the fact that you have recommended some people at least gives the editor some idea of who might be 'qualified' to review your work. These suggestions will be appreciated. If you do not suggest anyone, then you face the real prospect of your work being evaluated by reviewers who do not have the required expertise in the topic and/or qualitative method you have used.

Lastly, if your paper ends up being rejected, remember to refine, revise, and resubmit once again. If it is rejected yet again, do the same thing: refine, revise, and resubmit to a different journal. I must admit that there was one paper some years ago that I submitted and resubmitted almost half-a-dozen times. In the end I gave up, and decided that this particular paper was not worth the effort. Fortunately, this experience has been the only one in my entire career. I hope that you will persevere, and that you are successful in your publishing career.

Exercises

1 Conduct a brief literature search using Google Scholar or some other bibliographic database and see if you can find articles that rank the journals in your field. What are the top journals? Why are they ranked as the top journals (consider the criteria that are used)?

2 Choose one of the top journals in your field that has a reputation for publishing qualitative research (e.g. *Academy of Management Review*, *Accounting, Organizations and Society*, *Journal of Consumer Research*, *MIS Quarterly*, etc.). How many qualitative research articles were published over the past year or so? Of these, what research methods did they use? What approach to data analysis did they use?

3 Find one or more faculty members at your institution or at a conference who you know publish qualitative research. Ask them what advice they would give for a successful publishing career.

4 If you are a PhD student or faculty member, ask someone you know who is an editor or programme committee member of a conference if you can review one or more papers for them. After you have completed the review, ask for some feedback about the quality of your review.

5 If you have written a thesis, can you think of a potential article from each of the chapters? Compose a title, abstract, and outline for each article. Can you think of possible publication outlets?

6 Submit your article to a conference or journal. You may wish to consider asking a more senior person (i.e. someone who has successfully published their own work) to join you as a co-author. If your first article is rejected, try again.

Further Reading

 Books

A good book for writing up and publishing qualitative research is the book by Wolcott (1990). A more general book about publishing one's research in journal articles is the book by Henson (1999). Silverman (2005) includes a chapter on getting published.

PART SEVEN

CONCLUSION

Part VII is the last part of this book. Chapter 19 summarizes some of the key points, while the Glossary provides brief definitions of many of the most important concepts in qualitative research.

19

QUALITATIVE RESEARCH IN PERSPECTIVE

A fundamental theme of the book has been that qualitative research, along with quantitative research, can make a contribution to knowledge in business and management. Both approaches are needed, although this book has only discussed the former. It has been designed to be relevant for students in almost all business disciplines.

I have tried to write a reasonably comprehensive book, one that covers a variety of research methods and approaches. The specific methods and approaches I have discussed are those that are likely to be most relevant to students of business and management. However, this relatively broad treatment has meant that each particular topic has been covered as simply and succinctly as possible, without going into too much detail. Hence, I highly recommend the additional readings suggested at the end of each chapter for those who intend to take a particular method or approach further.

The model of a qualitative research project that has been presented in the book is represented in Figure 19.1. This particular model focuses solely on the process of qualitative research, not substantive issues (topics, theoretical framework, and so forth). The model illustrates the tremendous variety of qualitative research designs, although many other possible research designs exist.

One distinctive feature of this book has been its positive and unapologetic tone. I fail to see why qualitative researchers in business and management should continue to be defensive about the use of qualitative research (as many previous works have tended to be). All qualitative research methods and approaches have their limitations, but so do all quantitative research methods and approaches. No research method is perfect. A key feature of the book is that it has summarized the advantages and disadvantages of various qualitative research methods and approaches.

To emphasize the excellent quality of many qualitative research studies in business and management, I have chosen almost all of my examples of

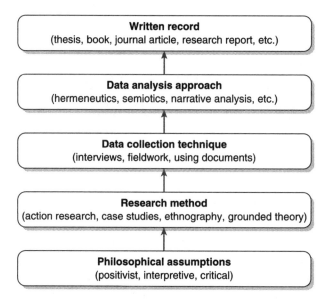

Figure 19.1 A model qualitative research design

qualitative research from first-tier academic journals in all of the business disciplines. There are more than two-dozen examples given in the book.

In conclusion, I hope you find the book useful and interesting. Make sure that you do not follow the guidelines and recommendations in this book in a mechanical or slavish manner. Rather, treat this book as a resource, and make sure that you enjoy your own qualitative research project.

GLOSSARY

Action research   A qualitative research method that aims to solve practical problems while contributing to research in a particular academic discipline.

Analytic induction   An approach to qualitative data analysis that tries to develop causal explanations of a phenomenon.

Appropriation   A concept in hermeneutics suggesting that we must appropriate the meaning of a text for ourselves if we are to properly understand it.

Autonomization   A concept in hermeneutics referring to a text taking on an autonomous, objective existence.

CAQDAS   Computer-Assisted Qualitative Data Analysis Software.

Case study research   A qualitative research method that aims to explore or explain contemporary real-life situations; in business and management the focus is normally on one organization.

Coding   Attaching keywords or tags to segments of text to permit later retrieval.

Content analysis   A systematic approach to qualitative data analysis that looks for structures and patterned regularities in the text.

Conversation analysis   An approach to qualitative data analysis that looks at language use by people as a type of action.

Critical incidents   An approach to qualitative data analysis that focuses on crucially important events.

Critical research   Assumes that reality is socially constructed but focuses on social critique of current conditions.

Culture   A common set of values, beliefs, and behaviours, many of which are taken for granted.

Diagnosing   The first phase of action research where the primary problems to be addressed are identified.

Discourse analysis An approach to qualitative data analysis that focuses on the way that texts are socially constructed.

Distanciation A concept in hermeneutics referring to the distance in space and time between the text and its original author.

Documents In qualitative research, documents are a source of qualitative data.

Empirical Based on evidence from the senses, such as data from a case study or experiment.

Engagement A concept in hermeneutics that suggests that meaning emerges from the engagement of the reader with the text.

Ethics The moral principles governing or influencing conduct.

Ethnography A qualitative research method that relies on participant observation and fieldwork in order to provide a deep understanding of people within their social and cultural context.

Explanatory research An approach to research where the primary motivation is to test, explain, or compare phenomena.

Exploratory research An approach to qualitative research where the primary motivation is to discover and explore new phenomena.

Field The physical and social setting where ethnographic research takes place.

Field notes Your own record of and commentary on your experiences in the field.

Fieldwork In qualitative research a data gathering technique where the researcher participates in and observes people in their natural setting; similar to participant observation.

Focus groups In qualitative research a data gathering technique where the researcher interviews a group of people to get collective views on a defined topic.

Gatekeeper Someone who has the power to grant or refuse access to a person or research site.

Generalizability The extent to which the research findings can be applied to other settings.

Genres A concept in narrative analysis referring to the idea that narratives can be written in different styles.

Grounded theory   A qualitative research method that seeks to develop theory that is grounded in data systematically gathered and analysed.

Hermeneutic circle   Refers to the dialectic between the understanding of a text as a whole and the interpretation of its parts, in which descriptions are guided by anticipated explanations.

Hermeneutics   Provides the philosophical grounding for interpretivism; also can be used as a qualitative approach to the analysis of texts, focusing on meaning and human understanding.

Historicity   A concept in hermeneutics that suggests that people are who they are because of their own history.

Hypothesis   A testable proposition that purports to explain a phenomenon.

Icon   A concept in semiotics referring to a sign that signifies its meaning by qualities of its own.

Index   A concept in semiotics that refers to an indexical sign that points to or indicates something else.

Inductive   Where the construct or theory emerges from the data.

Informed consent   An ethical principle suggesting that the subjects of research should be given the choice of whether they want to participate in a research project.

Interpretant   A concept in semiotics referring to the office of an interpreter (usually a person).

Interpretive research   Assumes that reality is socially constructed.

Interviews   In qualitative research a data gathering technique that involves questioning a subject (the informant or interviewee).

Memos   Your own commentary on the research process.

Metaphorical analysis   An approach to qualitative data analysis that looks at the systematic use of metaphors in a text.

Narrative analysis   A qualitative approach to the interpretation and analysis of data involving a story with a plot.

Observation   In qualitative research a data gathering technique where the researcher watches people from the outside with little if any interaction.

Paradigmatic analysis A concept in semiotics referring to the study of the surface structure of a text.

Participant observation In qualitative research a data gathering technique where the researcher participates in and observes people in their natural setting; similar to fieldwork.

Peer review The process in academia of research work being evaluated by one's peers (other qualified researchers).

Plagiarism The deliberate copying of someone else's work and presenting it as one's own.

Polysemy A concept in semiotics referring to the fact that texts and signs can have multiple meanings.

Positivist research Is the natural science model of social research and assumes that reality is objectively given.

Prejudice A concept in hermeneutics that suggests that prior knowledge or pre-judgement plays an important part in our understanding.

QDA Qualitative Data Analysis.

Qualitative research Is used to study social and cultural phenomena in depth, with a focus on text.

Quantitative research Is used to study general trends across a population, with a focus on numbers.

Research design A plan for a research project.

Research method A strategy of enquiry, a way of finding empirical data about the world.

Semiotics An approach to qualitative data analysis that focuses on signs and symbols and their meaning.

Series of events An approach to qualitative data analysis that focuses on the relationships between events, normally organized in chronological order.

Signified A concept in semiotics; what the sign or symbol represents.

Signifier A concept in semiotics; a sign or symbol that can stand for something else.

Symbol   A concept in semiotics referring to something that stands for or is symbolic of something else; more generally symbols are an important subject in social and cultural research.

Syntagmatic analysis   A concept in semiotics referring to the analysis of the structure of a text and the relationship between its parts.

Triangulation   Refers to the comparison of different kinds of data, whether qualitative and quantitative data, or qualitative data obtained from different sources (e.g. triangulating data from multiple interviewees).

Variables   Specific factors that are considered to be of interest to the researcher; often used in positivist and quantitative research.

REFERENCES

Academy of Management. (2008). Revised Code of Ethics. Retrieved 31 January 2008 from http://www.aomonline.org

Agar, M. (1986). *Speaking of Ethnography.* Beverly Hills, CA: Sage.

Ahuvia, A. C. (2005). Beyond the extended self: loved objects and consumers' identity narratives. *Journal of Consumer Research, 32*(1), 171–84.

Altheide, D. L. (1996). *Qualitative Media Analysis.* Thousand Oaks, CA: Sage.

Alvesson, M., & Deetz, S. (2000). *Doing Critical Management Research.* London: Sage.

Alvesson, M., & Willmott, H. (1992). On the idea of emancipation in management and organization studies. *Academy of Management Review, 17*(3), 432–64.

Annells, M. P. (1996). Grounded theory method: philosophical perspectives, paradigm of inquiry, and postmodernism. *Qualitative Health Research, 6*(3), 379–93.

Argyris, C., & Schön, D. A. (1991). Participatory action research and action science compared: a commentary. In W. F. Whyte (Ed.), *Participatory Action Research* (pp. 85–98). Newbury Park, CA: Sage.

Arnold, S. J., & Fischer, E. (1994). Hermeneutics and consumer research. *Journal of Consumer Research, 21*(1), 55–70.

Arnold, S. J., Kozinets, R. V., & Handelman, J. M. (2001). Hometown ideology and retailer legitimation: the institutional semiotics of Wal–Mart flyers. *Journal of Retailing, 77*(2), 243–71.

Atkinson, P. (1990). *The Ethnographic Imagination: Textual Constructions of Reality.* London: Routledge.

Avison, D. E., Baskerville, R., & Myers, M. D. (2001). Controlling action research projects. *Information Technology & People, 14*(1), 28–45.

Avison, D. E., & Wood-Harper, T. (1990). *Multiview: An Exploration in Information Systems Development.* Maidenhead: McGraw-Hill.

Baburoglu, O. N., & Ravn, I. (1992). Normative action research. *Organization Studies, 13*(1), 19–34.

Ball, M. S., & Smith, G. W. H. (1992). *Analyzing Visual Data.* Newbury Park, CA: Sage.

Barley, S. R. (1983). Semiotics and the study of occupational and organizational cultures. *Administrative Science Quarterly, 28*(3), 393–413.

Barratt, E. (2002). Foucault, Foucauldianism and human resource management. *Personnel Review, 31*(2), 189–204.

Barry, C. A. (1998). Choosing qualitative data analysis software: Atlas/ti and Nudist compared. *Sociological Research Online, 3*(3), http://www.socresonline.org.uk/

Barry, D., & Elmes, M. (1997). Strategy retold: toward a narrative view of strategic discourse. *Academy of Management Review, 22*(2), 429–52.

Barthes, R. (1985). Rhetoric of the image. In R. E. Innis (Ed.), *Semiotics: An Introductory Anthology* (pp. 192–205). Bloomington, IN: Indiana University Press.

Baskerville, R., & Myers, M. D. (2004). Special issue on action research in information systems: making IS research relevant to practice – Foreword. *MIS Quarterly, 28*(3), 329–35.

Baskerville, R. L., & Wood-Harper, A. T. (1996). A critical perspective on action Research as a method for information systems research. *Journal of Information Technology, 11*, 235–46.

Benbasat, I., Goldstein, D. K., & Mead, M. (1987). The case research strategy in studies of information systems. *MIS Quarterly, 11*(3), 369–86.

Bennis, W. G., & O'Toole, J. (2005). How business schools lost their way. *Harvard Business Review, 83*(5), 96–104.

Bentley, R., Hughes, J. A., Randall, D., Rodden, T., Sawyer, P., Shapiro, D., et al. (1992). Ethnographically-informed systems design for air traffic control. Paper presented at the ACM 1992 Conference on Computer-Supported Cooperative Work: Sharing Perspectives, New York.

Bernstein, R. J. (1983). *Beyond Objectivism and Relativism.* Pittsburgh: University of Pennsylvania Press.

Bleicher, J. (1980). *Contemporary Hermeneutics: Hermeneutics as Method, Philosophy and Critique.* London: Routledge & Kegan Paul.

Bleicher, J. (1982). *The Hermeneutic Imagination.* London: Routledge & Kegan Paul.

Bohm, A. (2004). Theoretical coding: text analysis in grounded theory. In U. Flick, E. v. Kardorff, & I. Steinke (Eds), *A Companion to Qualitative Research* (pp. 270–75). London: Sage.

Boje, D. M. (2001). *Narrative Methods for Organizational and Communication Research.* London: Sage.

Boland, R. J. (1991). Information system use as hermeneutic process. In H.-E. Nissen, H. K. Klein, & R. A. Hirschheim (Eds), *Information Systems Research: Contemporary Approaches and Emergent Traditions* (pp. 439–64). Amsterdam: North-Holland.

Boland, R. J., & Day, W. F. (1989). The experience of system design: a hermeneutic of organizational action. *Scandinavian Journal of Management, 5*(2), 87–104.

Bourdieu, P. (1977). *Outline of a Theory of Practice* (R. Nice, Trans.). Cambridge: Cambridge University Press.

Bourdieu, P. (1990). *The Logic of Practice* (R. Nice, Trans.). Stanford, CA: Stanford University Press.

Bouty, I. (2000). Interpersonal and interaction influences on informal resource exchanges between R&D researchers across organisational boundaries. *Academy of Management Journal, 43*(1), 50–65.

Braa, J., Monteiro, E., & Sahay, S. (2004). Networks of action: sustainable health information systems across developing countries. *MIS Quarterly, 28*(3), 337–62.

Brooke, C. (2002). Editorial: Critical research in information systems: issue 1. *Journal of Information Technology, 17*(2), 45–7.

Brown, R. (2003, 1 October). God defend the All Black brand. *Unlimited, 54.*

Bryman, A. (1989). *Research Methods and Organization Studies.* London: Unwin Hyman.

Buchanan, D., Boddy, D., & McCalman, J. (1988). Getting in, getting on, getting out, and getting back. In A. Bryman (Ed.), *Doing Research in Organizations.* (pp. 53–67) London: Routledge.

Burgess, R. G. (2005). Approaches to field research. In C. Pole (Ed.), *Fieldwork* (Vol. I, pp. 13–32). London: Sage.

Burrell, G., & Morgan, G. (1979). *Sociological Paradigms and Organizational Analysis.* London: Heinemann.

Buxey, G. (2005). Globalisation and manufacturing strategy in the TCF industry. *International Journal of Operations & Production Management, 25*(2), 100–13.

Carr, W., & Kemmis, S. (1986). *Becoming Critical: Education, Knowledge and Action Research.* London: Falmer Press.

Chandler, D. (2008). Semiotics for beginners. Retrieved 2 January 2008 from http://www.aber.ac.uk/media/Documents/S4B/sem01.html

Chase, S. E. (2005). Narrative inquiry: multiple lenses, approaches, voices. In N. K. Denzin & Y. S. Lincoln (Eds), *The Sage Handbook of Qualitative Research* (3rd edn, pp. 651–79). Thousand Oaks, CA: Sage.

Checkland, P. (1991). From framework through experience to learning: the essential nature of action research. In H.-E. Nissen, H. K. Klein, & R. A. Hirschheim (Eds), *Information Systems Research: Contemporary Approaches and Emergent Traditions* (pp. 397–403). Amsterdam: North-Holland.

Checkland, P., & Holwell, S. (1998). *Information, Systems and Information Systems: Making Sense of the Field.* Chichester: Wiley.

Checkland, P., & Scholes, J. (1990). *Soft Systems Methodology in Action.* Chichester: Wiley.

Chrzanowska, J. (2002). *Interviewing Groups and Individuals in Qualitative Market Research.* London: Sage.

Chua, W. F. (1986). Radical developments in accounting thought. *The Accounting Review, 61*(4), 601–32.

Ciborra, C. U., Patriotta, G., & Erlicher, L. (1996). Disassembling frames on the assembly line: the theory and practice of the new division of learning in advanced manufacturing. In W. J. Orlikowski, G. Walsham, M. R. Jones, & J. I. DeGross (Eds), *Information Technology and Changes in Organizational Work* (pp. 397–418). London: Chapman & Hall.

Clark, P. A. (1972). *Action Research and Organizational Change.* London: Harper & Row.

Clifford, J., & Marcus, G. E. (1986). *Writing Culture: The Poetics and Politics of Ethnography.* Berkeley, CA: University of California Press.

Collis, J., & Hussey, R. (2003). *Business Research: A Practical Guide for Undergraduate and Postgraduate Students* (2nd edn). Basingstoke: Palgrave Macmillan.

Connerton, P. (Ed.). (1976). *Critical Sociology, Selected Readings.* Harmondsworth: Penguin Books.

Cooper, C. (2002). Critical accounting in Scotland. *Critical Perspectives on Accounting, 13*(4), 451–62.

Corley, K. G., & Gioia, D. A. (2004). Identity ambiguity and change in the wake of a corporate spin-off. *Administrative Science Quarterly, 49*, 173–208.

Czarniawska, B. (1998). *A Narrative Approach to Organization Studies.* Thousand Oaks, CA: Sage.

Danis, W. M., & Parkhe, A. (2002). Hungarian-Western partnerships: a grounded theoretical model of integration processes and outcomes. *Journal of International Business Studies, 33*(3), 423–55.

Darnell, R. (1974). *Readings in the History of Anthropology.* New York: Harper & Row.

Davidson, E. J. (1997). Examining project history narratives: an analytic approach. In A. S. Lee, J. Liebenau, & J. I. DeGross (Eds), *Information Systems and Qualitative Research* (pp. 123–48). London: Chapman and Hall.

Davie, S. S. K. (2005). The politics of accounting, race and ethnicity: a story of a chiefly-based preferencing. *Critical Perspectives on Accounting, 16*, 551–77.

deMarrais, K. (2004). Qualitative interview studies: learning through experience. In K. deMarrais, & S. D. Lapan (Eds), *Foundations for Research: Methods of Inquiry in Education and the Social Sciences* (pp. 51–68). Mahwah, NJ: Lawrence Erlbaum.

Denzin, N. K. (2004). Reading film: using films and videos as empirical social science material. In U. Flick, E. v. Kardorff, & I. Steinke (Eds), *A Companion to Qualitative Research* (pp. 237–42). London: Sage.

Denzin, N. K., & Lincoln, Y. S. (Eds). (2005). *The Sage Handbook of Qualitative Research* (3rd edn). Thousand Oaks, CA: Sage.

Desai, P. (2002). *Methods Beyond Interviewing in Qualitative Market Research*. London: Sage.

Dey, I. (1993). *Qualitative Data Analysis*. London: Routledge.

Dey, I. (1999). *Grounding Grounded Theory: Guidelines for Qualitative Inquiry*. San Diego, CA: Academic Press.

Diesing, P. (1991). *How Does Social Science Work? Reflections on Practice*. Pittsburgh: University of Pittsburgh Press.

Dubé, L., & Paré, G. (2003). Rigor in information systems positivist case research: current practices, trends, and recommendations. *MIS Quarterly, 27*(4), 597–636.

Dutta, S., Zbaracki, M. J., & Bergen, M. (2003). Pricing process as a capability: a resource-based perspective. *Strategic Management Journal, 24*, 615–30.

Eco, U. (1976). *A Theory of Semiotics*. Bloomington, IN: Indiana University Press.

Eco, U. (1984). *Semiotics and the Philosophy of Language*. Bloomington, IN: Indiana University Press.

Elden, M., & Chisholm, R. F. (1993). Emerging varieties of action research: introduction to the special issue. *Human Relations, 46*(2), 121–42.

Ellen, R. F. (Ed.). (1984). *Ethnographic Research: A Guide to General Conduct*. London: Academic Press.

Ereaut, G. (2002). *Analysis and Interpretation in Qualitative Market Research*. London: Sage.

Esterberg, K. G. (2002). *Qualitative Methods in Social Research*. Boston, MA: McGraw-Hill.

Evans-Pritchard, E. E. (1950). *Witchcraft, Oracles and Magic among the Azande*. Oxford: Clarendon Press.

Fetterman, D. M. (1998). *Ethnography* (2nd edn). Thousand Oaks, CA: Sage.

Fiol, C. M. (1989). A semiotic analysis of corporate language: organizational B. *Administrative Science Quarterly, 34*(2), 277–303.

Firth, R. W. (1983). *We, the Tikopia: A Sociological Study of Kinship in Primitive Polynesia*. Stanford, CA: Stanford University Press.

Flint, D. J., Woodruff, R. B., & Gardial, S. F. (2002). Exploring the phenomenon of customers' desired value change in a business-to-business context. *Journal of Marketing, 66*(4), 102–17.

Floch, J.-M. (1988). The contribution of structural semiotics to the design of a hypermarket. *International Journal of Research in Marketing, 4*(3), 233–52.

Fontana, A., & Frey, J. H. (2000). The interview: from structured questions to negotiated text. In N. K. Denzin & Y. S. Lincoln (Eds), *Handbook of Qualitative Research* (2nd edn, pp. 645–72). Thousand Oaks, CA: Sage.

Fontana, A., & Frey, J. H. (2005). The interview: from neutral stance to political involvement. In N. K. Denzin & Y. S. Lincoln (Eds), *The Sage Handbook of Qualitative Research* (3rd edn, pp. 695–727). Thousand Oaks, CA: Sage.

Forester, J. (1992). Critical ethnography: on field work in an Habermasian way. In M. Alvesson & H. Willmott (Eds), *Critical Management Studies* (pp. 46–65). London: Sage.

Foucault, M. (1970). *The Order of Things*. London: Tavistock.

Foucault, M. (1972). *The Archaeology of Knowledge*. London: Tavistock.

Fournier, S. (1998). Consumers and their brands: developing relationship theory in consumer research. *Journal of Consumer Research, 24*(4), 343–73.

Frazer, J. G. (1980). *The Golden Bough*. London: Macmillan.

Frost, P. J., Moore, L. F., Louis, M. R., Lundberg, C. C., & Martin, J. (Eds). (1985). *Organizational Culture*. Beverly Hills, CA: Sage.

Gadamer, H.-G. (1975). *Truth and Method*. New York: Seasbury Press.

Gadamer, H.-G. (1976a). The historicity of understanding. In P. Connerton (Ed.), *Critical Sociology, Selected Readings* (pp. 117–33). Harmondsworth: Penguin Books.

Gadamer, H.-G. (1976b). *Philosophical Hermeneutics*. Berkeley, CA: University of California Press.

Geertz, C. (1973). *The Interpretation of Cultures*. New York: Basic Books.

Geertz, C. (1988). *Works and Lives: The Anthropologist as Author*. Cambridge: Polity Press.

Giddens, A. (1976). *New Rules of Sociological Method*. London: Hutchinson.

Gill, R. (2000). Discourse analysis. In M. W. Bauer & G. Gaskell (Eds), *Qualitative Researching with Text, Image and Sound: A Practical Handbook* (pp. 172–90). London: Sage.

Glaser, B. G. (1978). *Theoretical Sensitivity: Advances in the Methodology of Grounded Theory*. Mill Valley, CA: Sociology Press.

Glaser, B. G. (1992). *Emergence vs. Forcing: Basics of Grounded Theory Analysis*. Mill Valley, CA: Sociology Press.

Glaser, B. G., & Strauss, A. L. (1967). *The Discovery of Grounded Theory: Strategies for Qualitative Research*. Chicago: Aldine.

Gottschalk, L. (2006). The historian and the historical documents. In J. Scott (Ed.), *Documentary Research* (Vol. I, pp. 43–82). London: Sage.

Graebner, M. E., & Eisenhardt, K. M. (2004). The seller's side of the story: acquisition as courtship and governance as syndicate in entrepreneurial firms. *Administrative Science Quarterly, 49*, 366–403.

Grayson, K., & Shulman, D. (2000). Indexicality and the verification function of irreplaceable possessions: a semiotic analysis. *Journal of Consumer Research, 27*(1), 17–30.

Greenwood, D. J., Whyte, W. W., & Harkavy, I. (1993). Participatory action research as a process and as a goal. *Human Relations, 46*(2), 175–92.

Grills, S. (1998a). An invitation to the field: fieldwork and the pragmatists' lesson. In S. Grills (Ed.), *Doing Ethnographic Research: Fieldwork Settings* (pp. 3–18). Thousands Oaks, CA: Sage.

Grills, S. (Ed.). (1998b). *Doing Ethnographic Research: Fieldwork Settings*. Thousand Oaks, CA: Sage.

Guba, E. G., & Lincoln, Y. S. (1994). Competing paradigms in qualitative research. In N. K. Denzin & Y. S. Lincoln (Eds), *Handbook of Qualitative Research* (pp. 105–17). Thousand Oaks: Sage.

Gubrium, J. F., & Holstein, J. A. (2002). From the individual interview to the interview society. In J. F. Gubrium & J. A. Holstein (Eds), *Handbook of Interview Research* (pp. 3–32). London: Sage.

Habermas, J. (1984). *The Theory of Communicative Action* (Vol. 1). Boston: Beacon Press.

Hackley, C. (2003). *Doing Research Projects in Marketing, Management and Consumer Research*. London: Routledge.

Hammersley, M., & Atkinson, P. (1983). *Ethnography: Principles in Practice*. London: Routledge.

Harper, D. (2004). Photography as social science data. In U. Flick, E. v. Kardorff, & I. Steinke (Eds), *A Companion to Qualitative Research* (pp. 230–36). London: Sage.

Harvey, L. (1997). A discourse on ethnography. In A. S. Lee, J. Liebenau, & J. I. DeGross (Eds), *Information Systems and Qualitative Research* (pp. 207–24). London: Chapman and Hall.

Harvey, L., & Myers, M. D. (1995). Scholarship and practice: the contribution of ethnographic research methods to bridging the gap. *Information Technology & People, 8*(3), 13–27.

Henson, K. T. (1999). *Writing for Professional Publication: Keys to Academic and Business Success*. Boston: Allyn and Bacon.

Hermanns, H. (2004). Interviewing as an activity. In U. Flick, E. von Kardorff, & I. Steinke (Eds), *A Companion to Qualitative Research* (pp. 209–13). London: Sage.

Hesse-Biber, S. N., & Leavy, P. (2006). *The Practice of Qualitative Research*. Thousand Oaks, CA: Sage.

Hill, M. R. (1993). *Archival Strategies and Techniques*. Newbury Park, CA: Sage.

Hirschheim, R. (1992). Information systems epistemology: an historical perspective. In R. Galliers (Ed.), *Information Systems Research: Issues, Methods and Practical Guidelines* (pp. 28–60). Oxford: Blackwell Scientific.

Holliday, A. (2002). *Doing and Writing Qualitative Research*. London: Sage.

Holmqvist, B., Andersen, P. B., Klein, H., & Posner, R. (Eds). (1996). *Signs of Work: Semiosis and Information Processing in Organisations*. Berlin: Walter de Gruyter.

Holstein, J. A., & Gubrium, J. F. (1995). *The Active Interview*. London: Sage.

Hughes, E. C. (2005). Introduction: the place of field work in social science. In C. Pole (Ed.), *Fieldwork* (Vol. I, pp. 3–12). London: Sage.

Hughes, J. A., Randall, D., & Shapiro, D. (1992). Faltering from ethnography to design. Paper presented at the ACM 1992 Conference on Computer-Supported Cooperative Work: Sharing Perspectives, New York.

Hult, M., & Lennung, S.-A. (1980). Towards a definition of action research: a note and bibliography. *Journal of Management Studies, 17*(2), 241–50.

Huxham, C., & Vangen, S. (2000). Leadership in the shaping and implementation of collaboration agendas: how things happen in a (not quite) joined-up world. *Academy of Management Journal, 43*(6), 1159–75.

Iversen, J. H., Mathiassen, L., & Nielsen, P. A. (2004). Managing risk in software process improvement: an action research approach. *MIS Quarterly, 28*(3), 395–433.

Jackson, B. (1987). *Fieldwork*. Urbana and Chicago: University of Illinois Press.

Johnstone, B. (2002). *Discourse Analysis*. Oxford: Blackwell.

Kain, D. L. (2004). Owning significance: the critical incident technique in research. In K. deMarrais & S. D. Lapan (Eds), *Foundations for Research: Methods of Inquiry in Education and the Social Sciences* (pp. 69–85). Mahwah, NJ: Lawrence Erlbaum.

Kajuter, P., & Kulmala, H. I. (2005). Open-book accounting in networks: potential achievements and reasons for failures. *Management Accounting Research, 16,* 179–204.

Kaplan, B., & Maxwell, J. A. (1994). Qualitative research methods for evaluating computer information systems. In J. G. Anderson, C. E. Aydin, & S. J. Jay (Eds), *Evaluating Health Care Information Systems: Methods and Applications* (pp. 45–68). Thousand Oaks, CA: Sage.

Kaplan, R. S. (1998). Innovation action research: creating new management theory and practice. *Journal of Management Accounting Research, 10,* 89–118.

Kendall, J. (1999). Axial coding and the grounded theory controversy. *Western Journal of Nursing Research, 21*(6), 743–57.

Kleiber, P. B. (2004). Focus groups: more than a method of qualitative inquiry. In K. deMarrais & S. D. Lapan (Eds), *Foundations for Research: Methods of Inquiry in Education and the Social Sciences* (pp. 87–102). Mahwah, NJ: Lawrence Erlbaum.

Klein, H. K., & Myers, M. D. (1999). A set of principles for conducting and evaluating interpretive field studies in information systems. *MIS Quarterly, 23*(1), 67–93.

Klein, H. K., & Truex III, D. P. (1995). Discourse analysis: a semiotic approach to the investigation of organizational emergence. In P. B. Andersen & B. Holmqvist (Eds), *The Semiotics of the Workplace.* Berlin: Walter De Gruyter.

Kogler, H. H. (1996). *The Power of Dialogue: Critical Hermeneutics after Gadamer and Foucault.* Cambridge, MA: MIT Press.

Kohli, R., & Kettinger, W. J. (2004). Informating the clan: controlling physicians' costs and outcomes. *MIS Quarterly, 28*(3), 363–94.

Koller, V. (2004). *Metaphor and Gender in Business Media Discourse.* Basingstoke: Palgrave Macmillan.

Kozinets, R. V. (1997). 'I want to believe': a netnography of the X-philes' subculture of consumption. *Advances in Consumer Research, 24*(1), 470–75.

Kozinets, R. V. (1998). On netnography: initial reflections on consumer research investigations of cyberculture. *Advances in Consumer Research, 25*(1), 366–71.

Kozinets, R. V. (2001). Utopian enterprise: articulating the meanings of star Trek's culture of consumption. *Journal of Consumer Research, 28*(1), 67–88.

Krajewski, L., Wei, J. C., & Tang, L.-L. (2005). Responding to schedule changes in build-to-order supply chains. *Journal of Operations Management, 23,* 452–69.

Krippendorff, K. (1980). *Content analysis: An introduction to its methodology.* Beverly Hills, CA: Sage.

Kuhn, T. (1996). *The Structure of Scientific Revolutions* (3rd edn). Chicago: University of Chicago Press.

Kuper, A. (1973). *Anthropologists and Anthropology.* New York: Pica Press.

Kvale, S. (1996). *Interviews: An Introduction to Qualitative Research Interviewing.* Thousand Oaks, CA: Sage.

Kvasny, L., & Richardson, H. (2006). Critical research in information systems: looking forward, looking back. *Information Technology & People, 19*(3), 196–202.

Larsen, M., & Myers, M. D. (1999). When success turns into failure: a package-driven business process re-engineering project in the financial services industry. *Journal of Strategic Information Systems, 8*(4), 395–417.

Lee, A. S. (1989). Case studies as natural experiments. *Human Relations, 42*(2), 117–37.

Lee, A. S. (1991). Integrating positivist and interpretive approaches to organizational research. *Organization Science, 2*(4), 342–65.

Lee, A. S. (1994). Electronic mail as a medium for rich communication: an empirical investigation using hermeneutic interpretation. *MIS Quarterly, 18*(2), 143–57.

Lee, A. S., & Baskerville, R. L. (2003). Generalizing generalizability in information systems research. *Information Systems Research, 14*(3), 221–43.

Lee, J. C., & Myers, M. D. (2004). Dominant actors, political agendas, and strategic shifts over time: a critical ethnography of an enterprise systems implementation. *Journal of Strategic Information Systems, 13*(4), 355–74.

Lévi-Strauss, C. (1996). *The Savage Mind [La Pensée Sauvage]*. Oxford: Oxford University Press.

Levine, H. G., & Rossmore, D. (1993). Diagnosing the human threats to information technology implementation: a missing factor in systems analysis illustrated in a case study. *Journal of Management Information Systems, 10*(2), 55–73.

Lewin, K. (1946). Frontiers in group dynamics: II. channels of group life; social planning and action research. *Human Relations, 1*(2), 143–53.

Lewis, I. M. (1985). *Social Anthropology in Perspective*. Cambridge: Cambridge University Press.

Liebenau, J., & Backhouse, J. (1990). *Understanding Information: An Introduction*. Basingstoke: Macmillan.

Lincoln, Y. S. (2005). Institutional review boards and methodological conservatism. In N. K. Denzin & Y. S. Lincoln (Eds), *The Sage Handbook of Qualitative Research* (3rd edn, pp. 165–81). Thousand Oaks, CA: Sage.

Lincoln, Y. S., & Guba, E. G. (1985). *Naturalistic Inquiry*. Beverly Hills, CA: Sage.

Lindgren, R., Henfridsson, O., & Schultze, U. (2004). Design principles for competence management systems: a synthesis of an action research study. *MIS Quarterly, 28*(3), 435–72.

London, T., & Hart, S. L. (2004). Reinventing strategies for emerging markets: beyond the transnational model. *Journal of International Business Studies, 35*, 350–70.

Luthans, F., & Davis, T. R. V. (1982). An idiographic approach to organizational behavior research: the use of single case experimental designs and direct measures. *Academy of Management Review, 7*(3), 380–91.

Macey, D. (2000). *The Penguin Dictionary of Critical Theory*. London: Penguin Books.

Madison, G. B. (1990). *The Hermeneutics of Postmodernity*. Bloomington and Indianapolis: Indiana University Press.

Major, M., & Hopper, T. (2005). Managers divided: implementing ABC in a Portuguese telecommunications company. *Management Accounting Research, 16*, 205–29.

Manning, P. (1992). *Erving Goffman and Modern Sociology*. Cambridge: Polity Press.

Manning, P. K. (1987). *Semiotics and Fieldwork*. Newbury Park, CA: Sage.

Markus, M. L. (1983). Power, politics and MIS implementation. *Communications of the ACM, 26*(6), 430–44.

Markus, M. L. (1994a). Electronic mail as the medium of managerial choice. *Organization Science, 5*(4), 502–27.

Markus, M. L. (1994b). Finding a happy medium: explaining the negative effects of electronic communication on social life at work. *ACM Transactions on Information Systems, 12*(2), 119–49.

Marshall, C., & Rossman, G. B. (1989). *Designing Qualitative Research*. Newbury Park, CA: Sage.

Mårtensson, P., & Lee, A. S. (2004). Dialogical action research at Omega Corporation. *MIS Quarterly, 28*(3), 507–36.

Martin, P. Y., & Turner, B. A. (1986). Grounded theory and organizational research. *The Journal of Applied Behavioral Science, 22*(2), 141–57.

Maylor, H., & Blackmon, K. (2005). *Researching Business and Management*. Basingstoke: Palgrave Macmillan.

McKenna, S. (2007). Deconstructing a personal 'academic'/'practitioner' narrative through self-reflexivity. *Qualitative Research in Organizations and Management: An International Journal, 2*(2), 144–60.

McNabb, D. E. (2002). *Research Methods in Public Administration and Nonprofit Management: Quantitative and Qualitative Approaches*. Armonk, NY: M. E. Sharpe.

Mick, D. G. (1986). Consumer research and semiotics: exploring the morphology of signs, symbols, and significance. *Journal of Consumer Research, 13*(2), 196–213.

Miles, M. B., & Huberman, A. M. (1994). *Qualitative Data Analysis: An Expanded Sourcebook* (2nd edn). Newbury Park, CA: Sage.

Miller, J. M. (2006). Covert participant observation: reconsidering the least used method. In J. M. Miller & R. Tewksbury (Eds), *Research Methods: A Qualitative Reader* (pp. 12–19). Upper Saddle River, NJ: Prentice Hall.

Mingers, J. (2001). Combining IS research methods: towards a pluralist methodology. *Information Systems Research, 12*(3), 240–59.

Monteiro, E., & Hanseth, O. (1996). Social shaping of information infrastructure: on being specific about the technology. In W. J. Orlikowski, G. Walsham, M. R. Jones, & J. I. DeGross (Eds), *Information Technology and Changes in Organizational Work* (pp. 325–43). London: Chapman and Hall.

Morey, N. C., & Luthans, F. (1984). An emic perspective and ethnoscience methods for organizational research. *Academy of Management Review, 9*(1), 27–36.

Morris, C. (1985). Signs and the act. In R. E. Innis (Ed.), *Semiotics: An Introductory Anthology* (pp. 178–89). Bloomington, IN: Indiana University Press.

Mueller-Vollmer, K. (Ed.). (1988). *The Hermeneutic Reader*. New York: Continuum Publishing.

Myers, M. D. (1994). A disaster for everyone to see: an interpretive analysis of a failed IS project. *Accounting, Management and Information Technologies, 4*(4), 185–201.

Myers, M. D. (1995). Dialectical hermeneutics: a theoretical framework for the implementation of information systems. *Information Systems Journal, 5*(1), 51–70.

Myers, M. D. (1997a). Critical ethnography in information systems. In A. S. Lee, J. Liebenau, & J. I. DeGross (Eds), *Information Systems and Qualitative Research* (pp. 276–300). London: Chapman and Hall.

Myers, M. D. (1997b). Interpretive research methods in information systems. In J. Mingers & F. Stowell (Eds), *Information Systems: An Emerging Discipline* (pp. 239–66). London: McGraw-Hill.

Myers, M. D. (1997c). Qualitative research in information systems. *MIS Quarterly, 21*(2), 241–42, http://www.qual.auckland.ac.nz

Myers, M. D. (1999). Investigating information systems with ethnographic research. *Communications of the AIS, 2*(23), 1–20.

Myers, M. D. (2004). Hermeneutics in information systems research. In J. Mingers & L. P. Willcocks (Eds), *Social Theory and Philosophy for Information Systems* (pp. 103–28). Chichester: Wiley.

Myers, M. D., & Avison, D. E. (Eds). (2002). *Qualitative Research in Information Systems: A Reader*. London: Sage.

Myers, M. D., & Newman, M. (2007). The qualitative interview in IS research: examining the craft. *Information and Organization, 17*(1), 2–26.

Myers, M. D., & Young, L. W. (1997). Hidden agendas, power, and managerial assumptions in information systems development: an ethnographic study. *Information Technology & People, 10*(3), 224–40.

Nardulli, P. F. (1978). *The Courtroom Elite: An Organizational Perspective on Criminal Justice*. Cambridge, MA: Ballinger Press.

Ngwenyama, O. K., & Lee, A. S. (1997). Communication richness in electronic mail: critical social theory and the contextuality of meaning. *MIS Quarterly, 21*(2), 145–67.

Noblit, G. W. (2004). Reinscribing critique in educational ethnography: critical and post-critical ethnography. In K. deMarrais & S. D. Lapan (Eds), *Foundations for Research: Methods of Inquiry in Education and the Social Sciences* (pp. 181–201). Mahwah, NJ: Lawrence Erlbaum.

Nöth, W. (1990). *Handbook of Semiotics*. Bloomington, IN: Indiana University Press.

Oates, B. J. (2006). *Researching Information Systems and Computing*. London: Sage.

O'Leary, C., Rao, S., & Perry, C. (2004). Improving customer relationship management through database/Internet marketing: a theory-building action research project. *European Journal of Marketing, 38*(3/4), 338–54.

Orlikowski, W. J. (1991). Integrated information environment or matrix of control? the contradictory implications of information technology. *Accounting, Management and Information Technologies, 1*(1), 9–42.

Orlikowski, W. J. (1993). CASE tools as organizational change: investigating incremental and radical changes in systems development. *MIS Quarterly, 17*(3), 309–40.

Orlikowski, W. J., & Baroudi, J. J. (1991). Studying information technology in organizations: research approaches and assumptions. *Information Systems Research, 2*(1), 1–28.

Otnes, C., Lowrey, T. M., & Shrum, L. J. (1997). Toward an understanding of consumer ambivalence. *Journal of Consumer Research, 24*(1), 80–93.

Palmer, R. (1969). *Hermeneutics: Interpretation Theory in Schleiermacher, Dilthey, Heidegger, and Gadamer*. Evanston, IL: Northwestern University Press.

Patton, M. Q. (1990). *Qualitative Research and Evaluation Methods*. Newbury Park, CA: Sage.

Payne, G., & Payne, J. (2004). *Key Concepts in Social Research*. London: Sage.

Perlow, L. A., Okhuysen, G. A., & Repenning, N. P. (2002). The speed trap: exploring the relationship between decision making and temporal context. *Academy of Management Journal, 45*(5), 931–55.

Platt, J. (2005). Evidence and proof in documentary research: 1. Some specific problems of documentary research. In C. Pole (Ed.), *Fieldwork* (Vol. II, pp. 215–32). London: Sage.

Polkinghorne, D. E. (1988). *Narrative Knowing and the Human Sciences*. New York: SUNY Press.

Prasad, P. (1997). Systems of meaning: ethnography as a methodology for the study of information technologies. In A. S. Lee, J. Liebenau, & J. I. DeGross (Eds), *Information Systems and Qualitative Research* (pp. 101–18). London: Chapman and Hall.

Preissle, J., & Grant, L. (2004). Fieldwork traditions: ethnography and participant observation. In K. deMarrais & S. D. Lapan (Eds), *Foundations for Research: Methods of*

Inquiry in Education and the Social Sciences (pp. 161–80). Mahwah, NJ: Lawrence Erlbaum.

Prior, L. (2003). *Using Documents in Social Research*. London: Sage.

Punch, K. (2000). *Developing Effective Research Proposals*. London: Sage.

Punch, M. (1986). *The Politics and Ethics of Fieldwork*. Beverly Hills, CA: Sage.

Quinn, B., & Doherty, A. M. (2000). Power and control in international retail franchising: evidence from theory and practice. *International Marketing Review, 17*(4/5), 354–72.

Radcliffe, V. S. (1999). Knowing efficiency: the enactment of efficiency in efficiency auditing. *Accounting, Organisations and Society, 24*, 333–62.

Radnitzky, G. (1970). *Contemporary Schools of Metascience*. Goteborg: Scandinavian University Books.

Rapoport, R. N. (1970). Three dilemmas in action research. *Human Relations, 23*(4), 499–513.

Ricoeur, P. (1974). *The Conflict of Interpretations: Essays in Hermeneutics*. Evanston, IL: Northwestern University Press.

Ricoeur, P. (1976). *Interpretation Theory, Discourse and the Surplus of Meaning*. Forth Worth, TX: Texas Christian University Press.

Ricoeur, P. (1981). *Hermeneutics and the Human Sciences*. Cambridge: Cambridge University Press.

Ricoeur, P. (1991). *From Text to Action: Essays in Hermeneutics, II* (K. Blamey & J. B. Thompson, Trans.). Evanston, IL: Northwestern University Press.

Riessman, C. K. (1993). *Narrative Analysis*. Newbury Park, CA: Sage.

Ritson, M., & Elliott, R. (1999). The social uses of advertising: an ethnographic study of adolescent advertising audiences. *Journal of Consumer Research, 26*, 260–77.

Royer, I., & Zarlowski, P. (1999). Research design. In R.-A. Thiétart (Ed.), *Doing Management Research: A Comprehensive Guide* (pp. 111–31). London: Sage.

Rubin, H. J., & Rubin, I. S. (2005). *Qualitative Interviewing: The Art of Hearing Data* (2nd edn). Thousand Oaks, CA: Sage.

Ryan, G. W., & Bernard, H. R. (2000). Data management and analysis methods. In N. K. Denzin & Y. S. Lincoln (Eds), *Handbook of Qualitative Research* (2nd edn). Thousand Oaks, CA: Sage.

Sanday, P. R. (1979). The ethnographic paradigm(s). *Administrative Science Quarterly, 24*(4), 527–38.

Schmitt, R. (2005). Systematic metaphor analysis as a method of qualitative research. *The Qualitative Report, 10*(2), 358–94.

Scholes, R. (1982). *Semiotics and Interpretation*. New Haven, CT: Yale University Press.

Schultze, U. (2000). A confessional account of an ethnography about knowledge work. *MIS Quarterly, 24*(1), 3–41.

Scott, J. (1990). *A Matter of Record: Documentary Sources in Social Research*. Cambridge: Polity Press.

Scott, L. M. (1994). The bridge from text to mind: adapting reader-response theory to consumer research. *Journal of Consumer Research, 21*(3), 461–80.

Seal, W., Cullen, J., Dunlop, A., Berry, T., & Ahmed, M. (1999). Enacting a European supply chain: a case study on the role of management accounting. *Management Accounting Research, 10*, 303–22.

Sebeok, T. A. (1994). *An Introduction to Semiotics*. London: Pinter.

Silverman, D. (2005). *Doing Qualitative Research* (2nd edn). London: Sage.

Slagmulder, R. (1997). Using management control systems to achieve alignment between strategic investment decisions and strategy. *Management Accounting Research, 8*(1), 103–39.

Soanes, C., & Stevenson, A. (Eds). (2004). *Concise Oxford English Dictionary* (11th edn). Oxford: Oxford University Press.

Spradley, J. P. (1980). *Participant Observation.* Orlando, FL: Harcourt Brace Jovanovich.

Straub, D., Gefen, D., & Boudreau, M.-C. (2004). The ISWorld Quantitative, Positivist Research Methods Website, from http://dstraub.cis.gsu.edu:88/quant/

Strauss, A. (Ed.). (1987). *Qualitative Analysis for Social Scientists.* Cambridge: Cambridge University Press.

Strauss, A., & Corbin, J. (1990). *Basics of Qualitative Research: Grounded Theory Procedures and Techniques.* Newbury Park, CA: Sage.

Strauss, A., & Corbin, J. (1998). *Basics of Qualitative Research: Grounded Theory Procedures and Techniques* (2nd edn). Newbury Park, CA: Sage.

Street, C. T., & Meister, D. B. (2004). Small business growth and internal transparency: the role of information systems. *MIS Quarterly, 28*(3), 473–506.

Susman, G. I., & Evered, R. D. (1978). An assessment of the scientific merits of action research. *Administrative Science Quarterly, 23*(4), 582–603.

Taylor, C. (1976). Hermeneutics and politics. In P. Connerton (Ed.), *Critical Sociology: Selected Readings* (pp. 153–93). Harmondsworth: Penguin Books.

Tertiary Education Commission. (2005). *Performance-Based Research Fund Guidelines 2006.* Wellington, New Zealand.

Thomas, J. (1993). *Doing Critical Ethnography.* Newbury Park, CA: Sage.

Thompson, J. B. (1981). *Critical hermeneutics: A study in the thought of Paul Ricoeur and Jurgen Habermas.* Cambridge: Cambridge University Press.

Trauth, E. M. (1997). Achieving the research goal with qualitative methods: lessons learned along the way. In A. S. Lee, J. Liebenau, & J. I. DeGross (Eds), *Information Systems and Qualitative Research* (pp. 225–45). London: Chapman and Hall.

Truex, D., & Howcroft, D. (2001). Critical analyses of ERP systems: the macro level (1). *The Database for Advances in Information Systems, 32*(4), 13–18.

Urquhart, C. (1997). Exploring analyst-client communication: using grounded theory techniques to investigate interaction in informal requirements gathering. In A. S. Lee, J. Liebenau, & J. I. DeGross (Eds), *Information Systems and Qualitative Research* (pp. 149–81). London: Chapman and Hall.

Urquhart, C. (2001). An encounter with grounded theory: tackling the practical and philosophical issues. In E. Trauth (Ed.), *Qualitative Research in IS: Issues and Trends* (pp. 104–40). Hershey, PA: Idea Group Publishing.

Urquhart, C., Lehmann, H., & Myers, M. D. (2006). Putting the 'theory' back into grounded theory: a framework for grounded theory studies in information systems. Unpublished Working Paper. Department of ISOM Working Paper Series, University of Auckland.

Van Maanen, J. (1988). *Tales of the Field: On Writing Ethnography.* Chicago: University of Chicago Press.

Wachterhauser, B. R. (1986). *Hermeneutics and Modern Philosophy.* Albany, NY: SUNY Press.

Walsham, G. (1993). *Interpreting Information Systems in Organizations*. Chichester: Wiley.

Walsham, G. (1995). Interpretive case studies in IS research: nature and method. *European Journal of Information Systems, 4*(2), 74–81.

Walsham, G., & Waema, T. (1994). Information systems strategy and implementation: a case study of a building society. *ACM Transactions on Information Systems, 12*(2), 150–73.

Weitzman, E. A., & Miles, M. B. (1995). *Computer Programs for Qualitative Data Analysis*. Thousand Oaks, CA: Sage.

Westmarland, L. (2005). Blowing the whistle on police violence: gender, ethnography and ethics. In C. Pole (Ed.), *Fieldwork* (Vol. III, pp. 275–88). London: Sage.

Whitley, R. (1984). *The Intellectual and Social Organization of the Sciences*. Oxford: Clarendon Press.

Whyte, W. F. (Ed.). (1991). *Participatory Action Research*. Newbury Park, CA: Sage.

Wolcott, H. (1990). *Writing Up Qualitative Research*. Thousands Oaks, CA: Sage.

Wolcott, H. F. (2005a). Fieldwork vs. (just) being in the field. In C. Pole (Ed.), *Fieldwork* (Vol. I, pp. 43–58). London: Sage.

Wolcott, H. F. (2005b). Fieldwork: the basic arts. In C. Pole (Ed.), *Fieldwork* (Vol. II, pp. 102–29). London: Sage.

Wong, P. L.-K., & Ellis, P. (2002). Social ties and partner identification in Sino-Hong Kong international joint ventures. *Journal of International Business Studies, 33*(2), 267–89.

Wynn, E. H., Whitley, E. A., Myers, M. D., & De Gross, J. I. (Eds). (2002). *Global and Organizational Discourse about Information Technology*. Boston, MA: Kluwer Academic.

Yin, R. K. (2002). *Applications of Case Study Research* (2nd edn). Newbury Park, CA: Sage.

Yin, R. K. (2003). *Case Study Research: Design and Methods* (3rd edn). Newbury Park, CA: Sage.

Zuboff, S. (1988). *In the Age of the Smart Machine*. New York: Basic Books.

INDEX

Please note that page numbers relating to Figures and Tables will be in *italic* print; titles of publications beginning with 'A' or 'The' will be filed under the first significant word.

Avison, D. E. 60
axial coding, grounded theory 110

balanced scorecard, action research 56
Ball, M. S. 156
Barley, S. R. 207–8
Baroudi, J. J. 36, 37
Barry, C. A. 177
Barry, D. 218–19
Barthes, R. 205
Baskerville, R. 57, 63
Benbasat, I. 37, 77
Bennis, W. G. 14
Bernard, H. R. 167, 168
Bernstein, R. J. 39
Berry, T. 64–5
bibliographic database and reference
    management software 235
bibliographies 160
Blackmon, K. 46, 49
Bleicher, J. 190
Bohm, A. 110
Boje, D. M. 174, 215–17, 221
Bourdieu, Pierre 43
Bouty, I. 114–15
British anthropological tradition 147–8
BTO (build-to-order) supply chains 89, 90
Burke 217
business management 12–13, 14
business schools 14, 99, 239
Buxey, G. 76

canonical action research 68
capital 43
CAQDAS (Computer-Assisted Qualitative
    Data Analysis Software) 177, 257
Carr, W. 61
case study research
    and action research 73
    advantages and disadvantages 80–2
    approaches to 77–80
    critique 80–5
    cross-case analysis 88, 89, 90
    definitions 74–7, 257
    and ethnographic research 95
    evaluation 82–5
    examples 85, 87–90
    Harvard studies 174
    interpretive case studies 78
    interviews 79
    in management 72
    mergers and acquisitions 87–9
    operations management 89–90
    positivist case studies 78

case study research *cont.*
    practical suggestions 78–80
    principles 84–5
    qualitative research 8
    scope of study 75
    teaching, case studies used in 70–1
    theory building, case studies in
        management 72
    within-case analysis 88–9, 90
causality analysis 217
CDVC (customers' desired value
    change) 115–16
Chandler, D. 171, 199, 203–4
change-based data, action research 59
Chase, S. E. 212, 215, 217
Checkland, Peter 60
Chicago sociological tradition 148
Chisholm, R. F. 59, 60–1
Chrzanowska, J. 133
Chua, W. F. 36
Clark, P. A. 56, 60
codebooks, building 167
coding
    axial 110
    'bottom-up' approach to 112
    definitions 257
    ethical codes 50–1
    grounded theory 109, 110–11, 112
    open 110
    qualitative research data 167
    selective 110
    theoretical 110–11
collaboration, and action research 55, 56, 57, 61
Collis, J. 21
compromising 220
concentration camps 191
conditional matrix, grounded theory 109
confessional writing style 231
confidence intervals 83
confidential reports 155–6
Connerton, P. 42–3
constructivism 36, 214
consumer research
    identity narratives 219–20
    in marketing 150–1, 206
    special possessions, value of 208–9
contemporary records 155
content analysis 172, 173, 257
contextualization, principle of 86
contingency theory, management accounting 87
conversation analysis 172–3, 257
Corbin, J. 108, 109, 110, 111
Corley, K. G. 78
corporate language 209

Gioria, D. A. 78
Glaser, Barney 107, 109, 113
golden rule, ethical principle 46
The Golden Bough (Frazer) 94
Goldstein, D. K. 37, 77
Gottschalk, L. 155–6
government documents 156
Graebner, M. E. 87
grand narratives 213, 216
Grayson, K. 208
Greenwood, D. J. 61
Grills, S. 98, 225–6
grounded theory 106–16
  advantages and disadvantages 111–12
  approaches to 109–11
  critique 111–13
  customers' desired value change 115–16
  definitions 106, 107–9, 259
  evaluation of research studies 112–13
  examples 113–16
  informal resource exchanges, R&D
      researchers 114–15
  in international business 32
  interpretive, in marketing 32
  mechanism of action 110–11
  qualitative research 8
group-think 63
Guba, E. G. 36, 155

Habermas, Jurgen 42, 43, 61, 85, 190
Hackley, C. 199, 206
Hammersley, M. 97
Harkavy, I. 61
Hart, S. L. 37
Harvard Business School 70
hermeneutic circle *86*, 185–6, 259
hermeneutics
  appropriation 189, 257
  autonomization 188–9, 257
  concepts 184–9
  critical 190–1
  critique 194
  definitions 181, 182–4, 259
  depth 191
  distanciation 188–9, 258
  double hermeneutic 39, 190
  engagement 189, 258
  example 192–4
  historicity 184–5, 259
  philosophy 182
  post-modern 190
  prejudice 186–8, 260
  pure 190
  purpose 182

hermeneutics *cont.*
  qualitative data analysis 170–1
  types 190–1
Hesse-Biber, S. N. 156–7
Hill, M. R. 160
historical documents 155–6
historicity 184–5, 259
holistic school, ethnographic research 96
honesty, ethical principle of 47
Hopper, T. 81
Huberman, A. M. 133, 167
Hughes, E. C. 137
Hughes, J. A. 98
Hult, M. 49
Human Relations (Elden and Chisholm) 59
Hussey, R. 21
Huxham, C. 67
hypothesis/hypothetico-deductive logic 40, 75, 259

ICIS (International Conference on Information
      Systems) 32
icons 202, 259
ICVs (international cooperative ventures) 32
IFIP (International Federation of Information
      Processing) 31–2
impressionist writing style 231–2
index 202, 259
infiltration, fieldwork 149
information technology
  see also Internet
  action research in information systems 67–8
  and control of work 151
  critical ethnography in information
      systems 32–3
  email messages, using and reusing 161–2
  information systems development
      projects 220–1
  Internet 47, 50, 66–7
  use of 93
informed consent 48, 259
interaction, principle of *86*
interaction theory 74
international business, grounded theory in 32
International Conference on Information
      Systems (ICIS) 32
international cooperative ventures (ICVs) 32
International Federation of Information
      Processing (IFIP) 31–2
Internet
  see also information technology
  and customer relationship management 66–7
  documentation 158
  online ethics 50
  and plagiarism 47